Ben Groundwater is an Australian travel writer, blogger, journalist and anything else someone will pay him to be. A professional writer for 10 years, Ben began his career in Brisbane before deciding to see the world, taking off to write freelance travel features for newspapers like the *Sydney Morning Herald* and the *Courier-Mail*, as well as various travel magazines. He now lives in Sydney, and writes Fairfax Media's hugely popular travel blog The Backpacker, upon which this, his first book, is based. Ben's parents would really appreciate it if he'd find a proper job and settle down.

5 WAYS TO CARRY A GOAT

a blogger's world tour

Ben Groundwater

UQP

First published 2010 by University of Queensland Press
PO Box 6042, St Lucia, Queensland 4067 Australia

www.uqp.com.au
www.bengroundwater.com

Typeset in Janson Text 11/15pt by Post Pre-press Group, Brisbane
Map on pp. viii and ix by MAPgraphics Pty Ltd
Printed in Australia by McPherson's Printing Group

National Library of Australia Cataloguing-in-Publication Data
Groundwater, Ben.
Five ways to carry a goat: a blogger's world tour.
    9780702237775 (pbk)
    9780702237997 (pdf)
    Groundwater, Ben – Blogs.
    Groundwater, Ben – Travel.
    Blogs – Social aspects.
    Voyages and travel.
910.92

This book is a work of non-fiction; however, some names have been
changed for privacy reasons.

For Mum, Dad, Tim . . . and the Lawyer

Contents

Introduction   1

Another Bloody Temple – Seoul and Gyeongju, Korea   9

Lab Rats – Shanghai, China   31

The Real Thailand – Ubon Ratchathani and Ban Khum, Thailand   53

Rats, Roaches and Roadkill – Chittagong, Bangladesh   74

5 Ways to Carry a Goat – Addis Ababa and Lalibela, Ethiopia   99

Back to School – Nice and Paris, France   129

Raving Mad – Munich, Germany   153

Here Comes the Bride – Litomysl and Sudislav, Czech Republic   175

Girls, Girls, Girls – Warsaw, Poland   197

Cycling Killed the Radio Star – The Hague and Amsterdam,
        the Netherlands   223

The Dull Life – South-east London, United Kingdom   244

Getting a Brazilian – Sao Paulo and Ilheus, Brazil   256

Stars and Stripes – New York, United States   288

A Dose of Reality – Toronto, Canada   299

And the Emmy Goes to . . . – Seattle and Los Angeles, United States   318

Epilogue   339

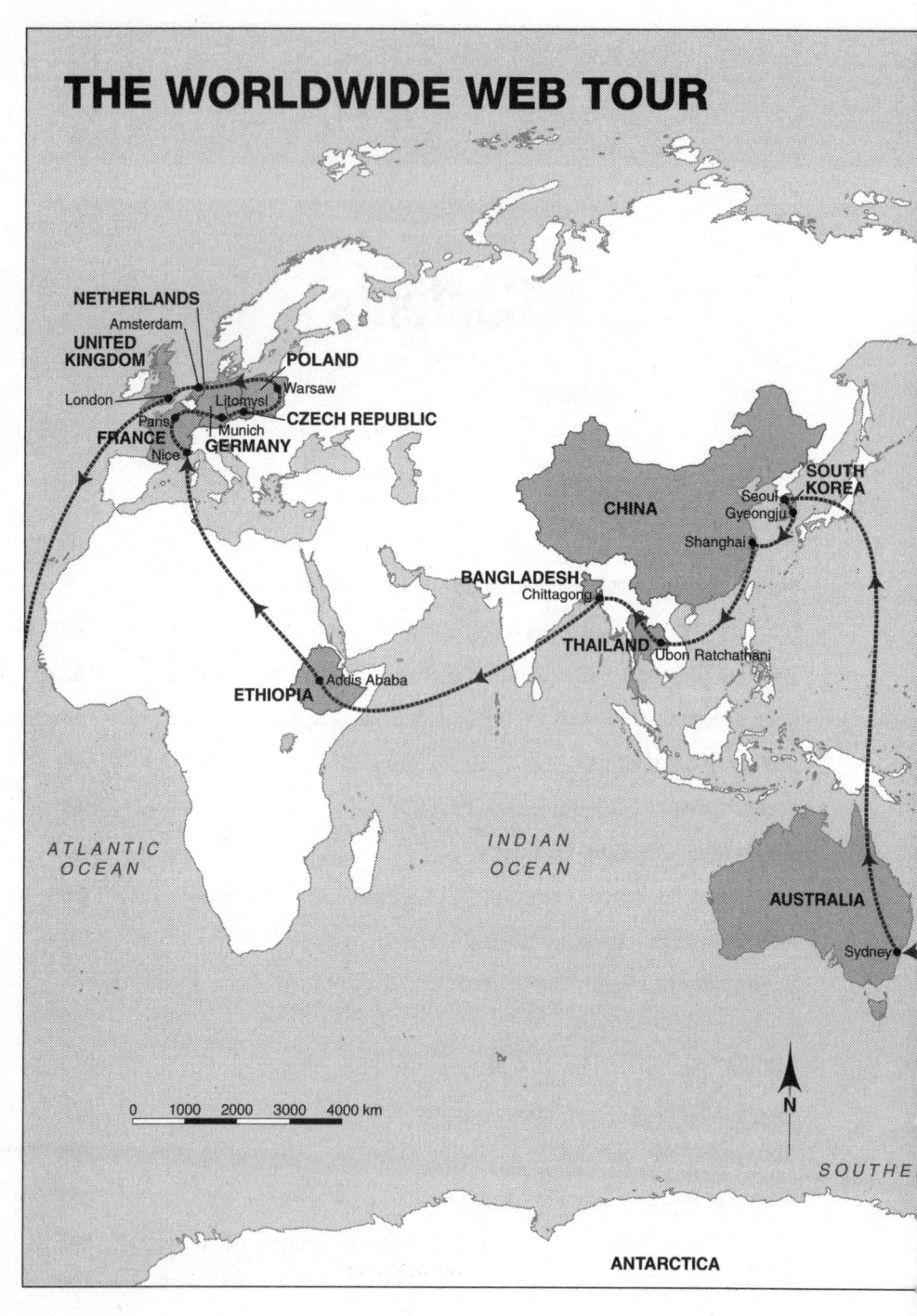

THE WORLDWIDE WEB TOUR

NETHERLANDS
Amsterdam
UNITED
KINGDOM
POLAND
London
Warsaw
Paris
Litomysl
CZECH REPUBLIC
FRANCE
Munich
Nice
GERMANY

CHINA
Seoul
SOUTH
KOREA
Gyeongju
Shanghai

BANGLADESH
Chittagong

THAILAND
Ubon Ratchathani

ETHIOPIA
Addis Ababa

ATLANTIC
OCEAN

INDIAN
OCEAN

AUSTRALIA
Sydney

0 1000 2000 3000 4000 km

N

SOUTHE

ANTARCTICA

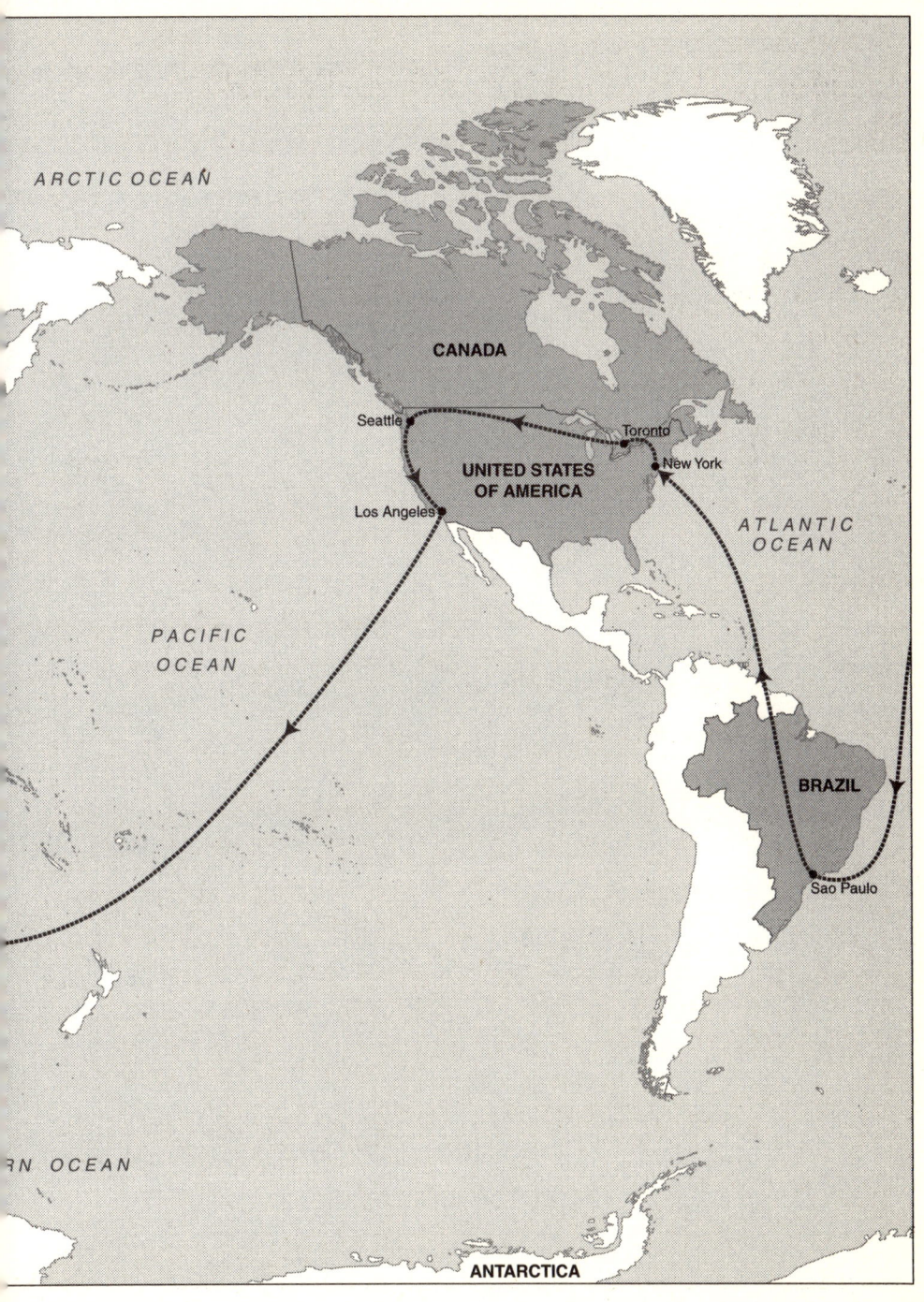

Introduction

You might not be aware of this, but there are a lot of dickheads on the internet.

Cracked.com, January 2009

Friends. I've got hundreds of them. Thousands, probably. They're out there, spread across the globe, tapping away on their keyboards to thousands of their friends too.

Trouble is, I've never met most of my 'friends'. They're just names on emails and comments on blog posts. We tweet each other on Twitter. We post pointless status updates on Facebook ('Ben is making a GIANT sandwich!'). But we never meet. For all I know, my friend 'Elin' from Stockholm could be a 100-kilogram transvestite from San Francisco. My mate 'Arnaldo' in Chile could actually sit next to me on the train to Town Hall Station every morning. Such is the way with web 2.0 – you can make friends from all over the world without ever having to buy them a beer, meet their parents or pat their dog.

If it seems like I've got more anonymous friends than most, it's because I'm a blogger. Sure, you're thinking, everyone's a blogger.

You can't throw a cyber rock these days without taking out at least a few amateur scribes – and you'd probably be doing the world a favour if you did. These days, most travellers have given up the boring group email in favour of posting their musings on a boring public blog in the hope people will follow their travels, send them the odd comment and get jealous. It's the ultimate form of travel wankery – and one I've wholeheartedly embraced.

For the past couple of years I've been writing a blog called The Backpacker for Fairfax Media, posting on the *Sydney Morning Herald* and *Age* websites. Unlike the 'Here's me and Baz at the Shepherd's Bush Walkie'–type of travel blog though, it's a weekly opinion piece about the issues travellers face – the countries with the best food, most beautiful people, or the worst toilets in the world (China, if you're wondering) – written by someone who, like a lot of travellers, is chained to a desk for most of the year. I post my opinions then everyone else posts theirs. And it's during the writing of these blogs that I've come to realise the inalienable truth that comedy website Cracked so succinctly acknowledged above: there are a lot of dickheads on the internet. And some of them read The Backpacker.

Blog readers are like drivers with road rage. For starters, they're angry – unreasonably so. And the anonymity provided by a few million bytes of cyberspace is like being in the capsule of a car: it inspires people to abuse without restraint; to rant, rave and write things they'd never dream of saying in public. In three glorious years I've been called a 'fuckwit' and 'the ultimate travel wanker', been told I'm 'not fit to write jokes on Christmas crackers', and been accused of sexism, racism and pretty much any other 'ism' you care to think of. It goes with the territory. You can't please everyone in the blogosphere, so you write what's on your mind, and get ready to roll with the punches. You can always comfort yourself with, 'Well, at least they're reading it . . .'

Being a blogger for a large website has meant that I've made thousands of cyber friends, and probably just as many cyber enemies. And thanks to the 'worldwideness' of the worldwide web, they're everywhere. It's a strange feeling to know that some bloke behind a computer in Delhi hates you – but that's cool, because you've always got fans in Bogota.

So, like any obsessive traveller with a passion for cheap accommodation, this got me thinking. Whether they like me or not, I know people all over the world. They live in idyllic places. They know their country better than any guidebook author could ever hope to. They sound like interesting people.

I should go stay with them.

About six months ago, I hatched a plan: do a full lap of the globe, touching every inhabited continent on earth, with the help of my blog readers. The ones who liked me would surely be happy to give up their couch for a few nights to exchange travel tales over a local brew. Those who didn't like me . . . Well, most of the time I seem to annoy people by bagging something in their home town, so I hoped they might at least want to set me straight if I'd done them wrong. Or just give me a light beating.

I was prepared to go anywhere. I'd sleep on couches, beds, floors, kennels . . . If someone was kind enough to put a roof over my head, I was game enough to visit their country and meet them. And I'd just pray they were who they said they were. After all, I reasoned, it was time I saw the world through someone else's eyes: I'd been to 55 countries over almost 30 years of travel, but I'd rarely had the chance to hang out with locals. Travellers can try all they like to discover the 'real' country, but in most cities they just end up following the tourist bunch, getting drunk in backpacker bars with other expats – you might fancy exploring Prague's outer suburbs to see the 'real' Czech Republic, but you'll inevitably end up in some dive bar yelling the words to 'Down Under' with Trevor from Newcastle.

It's not easy seeing a country from a local's point of view, but I figured I'd found a way. So for three weeks, I put out the call on the bottom of my blog entries:

EXPATS AND OVERSEAS READERS!
I need your help! I'm about to head off on a lap of the globe –
my Worldwide Web Tour. But here's the catch: I want to come
stay with you, and see the world through your eyes. Show me
the real sights of your city; show me how you live. I don't care
if you're in Toronto or Tbilisi, Bangkok or Buenos Aires – if
you're willing to let a friendly, mildly alcoholic travel writer
crash on your couch for a night or two, hit me on Facebook, or
email me. I leave in April – see you then.

I also set up an event on my Facebook profile, and invited
everyone on my friend list whose name I didn't automatically
recognise as one of my flesh-and-blood mates. Then I waited.

The first Wednesday the blog went live, I sat nervously at the
desk at a job I was still pretending to care about, and watched my
email account. Half an hour ticked by. This whole trip relies on the
kindness of people who've been proven to not particularly like me,
I thought – so what if I only get a couple of offers? What if they
sound like complete psychos? What if they're all in Port Moresby?
What if they all watch *Two and a Half Men*?

Suddenly: *ping*! My email lit up. I had a hit. I stifled a 'Woo
hoo!'

G'day Ben, I live in Phuket, Thailand, and while it's not really
on the backpacker's major wish list, it can be a fun place to be.
If you are heading through here let me know and my Thai wife
Aung and three-year-old son Maxi will be happy to put you up
for a few days. Cheers mate, Ian.

Success. From there, it took off. Watching my email light up
was like watching the globe slowly spin as people from around
the world got out of bed, fired up their computers and – for some
reason I'll never properly understand – invited me into their lives.
They started off in south-east Asia, from Vietnam to Cambodia to

Thailand. Then emails started coming in from Bangladesh, India and Nepal. Africa awoke a few hours later as invitations to stay in Kenya, Ethiopia and South Africa arrived. Europe was next, with generous offers from Germany, Hungary, Sweden and the UK. Brazil followed, then Argentina, Chile, the US and Canada. Some crazy bugger in Bondi even offered up a couch for me to start my trip from. It was happening.

Over the next three weeks more than 400 complete strangers contacted me to offer a place to stay. They also offered to be my tour guides, chauffeurs, travel agents and drinking buddies. Their enthusiasm was ridiculous. All were willing to down tools and spend a few days with an errant travel writer on a mission to see someone else's world. I was stoked. My friends and family, not so much.

'Um . . . How do you know these people are even who they say they are?' my friend Mike asked over a beer one night. 'What if they turn out to be an axe murderer? Or a Mac banker? What if you turn up and they're not even there?'

Others were similarly unconvinced. 'What kind of person would offer a complete stranger a bed?' Jim asked. 'I mean, if you were reading a blog, and you saw that request, would you email that person?'

He had a point.

'What background checks have you done on these people?' my lawyer friend Alice added.

'Well . . . none, really,' I replied. 'I'm friends with a few people on Facebook, so I looked up their profiles. Does that count for anything?'

'No Ben, it doesn't. What if they really hate you?'

In truth, that unpredictability was going to be part of the fun. Alice was right, I really didn't know much about the people whose lives I was going to invade. Some had emailed me a couple of pages of details about themselves and their city. Others had just sent a single line. Andrew, for example, wrote:

Hey mate, I realise Ethiopia is a wee bit random, but let me know if you're keen.

Good enough for me. After all, I reasoned, if these people didn't turn out to be who they said they were, or *where* they said they were, all the better. I'm trying to write a book here – if I wanted safety I'd go on a Trafalgar tour. Bring on the nutters.

My original worry, of course, was that I wouldn't get enough invitations to get me around the globe, and to every continent. As it turned out, I had the opposite problem: I had hundreds of invitations, but only three months to travel. I was going to have to pare things back and decide where I wanted to go, and who I wanted to visit; quite a luxury considering I could have ended up moving from flat to flat in Shepherd's Bush for three months. There were a few invitations I could weed out straight away. Like:

Hey Ben, I'm more than willing to put you up here for a few nights: Street 16, House 15/1, Area 226, Al Tasheera District, Baghdad, Iraq. Let me know what time you get into BIAP and I'll have the boys swing by and pick you up! No need to bring your own body armour – we'll shout you a set. Cheers, Pete

Actually, I will admit I was pretty interested in that one. But after a few minutes of googling I couldn't find any mention of an 'Al Tasheera' district in Baghdad, so I put it down to a piss-take. In fact, I'd expected a lot more piss-takery than I got. I thought there'd be invites to S&M parties in Azerbaijan, offers to wrestle tigers in Tamil Nadu . . . maybe even an offer to go to Tasmania. Damn you people, I need material!

Of the real invitations, there were a few more that went straight into the 'probably not' folder on my desk.

Hi Ben. I live in Tokyo. I'm a 38-year-old Mac banker, and . . .

Hmm . . . Probably not. Then there was Jan from Lodeve in France:

Ben, I might be a boring old fart, but . . .

Ah, that'll do you, Jan. Thanks. Anyone else?

Ben, If you can stand being woken up by a two-year-old and a new-born baby, you're most welcome to stay at my dingy flat in Barcelona . . .

Ahem. Thanks, James, but no thanks.

Then there was the bombardment of overly enthusiastic Americans to sort through. One of the blogs I wrote in those three weeks of promoting this trip was picked up by gigantic American internet provider AOL, who linked to it from their homepage. So a blog that would usually attract about 150 comments from Australians and expats instead ended up with about 600 comments, mostly from irate Seppos mad that I'd slagged off Times Square, and that I kept spelling 'realise' with an 's'. But if you've ever been to the US of A, you'll know that, while Americans might be fiercely defensive of their own country, they're also insanely hospitable and friendly, which explains why I was inundated with offers for 'y'all to come check out our place'. There were readers in Albuquerque, South Bend Indiana (spruiking a seven-foot couch), Cincinnati, Seattle . . . Even some guy in west Texas who offered to teach me how to shoot a gun (although he didn't specify at what). I couldn't visit them all, much as I wanted to. I'd only have about a week in each country, and the US is a big country.

And then there were a few offers that were just too good to turn down – most notably, the seemingly crazy invitation by a Hungarian man to his daughter's wedding in the Czech Republic. Add a shirt and tie to the backpack then.

Ultimately, I went with a scattering of the big cities, and a few out-of-the-way places – some I'd visited before, some I'd always wanted to see, and others I would never have dreamed of going to if someone hadn't invited me.

There were a few comforts of home I was going to have to give up for this trip. First, there was my job, which, as a writer, is not the easiest thing to give away, because, like leaving your wallet on a street corner, you can be pretty sure that it will be gone by the time you get back. And it won't be easy to replace. Especially as I'd been writing for *FHM*, a men's magazine which afforded me the opportunity to sit around in an office listening to music and discussing how much extra boob the Photoshop guys should add to our cover models. I'd applied for three months' leave without pay, and had been given an answer to the effect of 'you're kidding yourself'. So I quit.

The other thing I was leaving behind, which, once again, may not be there when I got back, was my girlfriend of two years, the Lawyer, who'd inexplicably agreed to my going away for three or four months to stay with complete strangers. The only concession was that I had to give her power of veto over my invitees, so every now and then she'd go through the piles of invitations I'd printed out yelling out things like, 'No, she sounds hot' or 'No way, she sounds like a slut', while screwing the printouts into balls and throwing them over her shoulder. I'd sneak around behind her picking them up, straightening them out and surreptitiously slipping them into the 'maybe' folder. Still, I think we came to general agreement over who I was going to visit.

In fact, six weeks after putting out the call asking the world to let me stay at their place, I had my itinerary set and my flights booked. Armed with a backpack, a laptop, and a cover story in case of emergency, I kissed my lovely girlfriend goodbye, and jumped on a flight to Seoul, South Korea.

It was time to start putting faces to the made-up names. It was time to go meet my 'friends'.

Another Bloody Temple

'I'm not supposed to shower while I've got this thing on, so if you smell something bad, that's me.'

It was dark and cold in Seoul. I was standing on what I thought was the right street corner in front of what I thought was the right train station, having taken a bus from the airport to the middle of the city, and I was waiting for Steve to arrive. How would I know him, I thought. How would he know me? I wonder what he's like. Will he be old? Really young? Live in a nice place or scratch out a living and doss in a slum? Was he planning to rob me? Shoot me? Buy me a beer?

I had no idea. This wasn't like one of those CouchSurfing things, where you could check up on someone by reading their profile, or even read a review of what their couch was like. I knew absolutely nothing about this bloke. If he even *was* a bloke.

I would come to know this feeling well. In fact, it would almost seem normal after a few months. For now though, I was worried.

The email hadn't given much away.

'Hi Ben, I'm a longtime reader and fan of your blog,' Steve had written.

> I currently live in Seoul, Korea and you'd be very welcome to crash in my spare room whilst on your tour. Seoul is definitely not the most beautiful or exciting tourist destination, but it has its attractions and fun when you know where to look . . .

Rereading that now, I'm not sure why I even chose Korea. I doubt they use phrases like 'not the most beautiful or exciting' in the tourist brochures. In fact, I'd always wanted to go to Japan, and was sweating on a few good offers coming in from the land of the rising sun. Sadly, they never materialised – except for my man the Mac banker – so I was left with a choice: skip that part of the world altogether, or fly straight over the top of Japan and head to Korea. I'd had a few offers in Korea as well as Steve's, so I decided to take a punt. I didn't know much about the country, only that the food was tasty and there was a lunatic running the country to its immediate north. So it was kind of like the Mexico of east Asia as far as I was concerned.

The country also fitted my 'off the beaten track' mantra. Given an open itinerary, there's no way I would have chosen to visit Korea. I'd have gone to 'find myself' in a trendy destination like Vietnam or Laos, or disappeared into a drug-fuelled haze in southern Thailand for a few months (except I'd already done that with my brother a few years ago). I wanted something new. Plus, most tourists don't go to Korea, which seemed reason enough for me to include it on this trip.

Landing at Seoul's Incheon Airport, I immediately realised that there are two kinds of Asia. The Asia that most Australians, including me, know is the south-east version – the kind that's a manic crush of yelling touts and tuk-tuk drivers and food vendors selling the kind of stuff you'd probably avoid hitting with your car, let alone put in your mouth. Incheon was different. I walked into the arrivals hall, tensed up for the inevitable rush, but it never came. I stood, alone, on the polished stone floor for a few minutes, before I was finally approached by one polite man with white gloves on who said softly, 'Tassi?'

I'd been told not to bother with the taxis. Steve had instructed me to walk outside and take a bus to 'Seoul Station', but from what I could make out from the signs, there were four or five different Seoul stations. So my first contact with my first contact was a semi-panicked phone call to get some clarification.

'G'day mate, how are ya?' Steve managed to steer me in the right direction, and I finally boarded a bus into town, where I found Seoul Station and the street corner where I was fidgeting nervously while I waited to meet up with my first host. A few Westerners shuffled past me in the darkness, and I looked at them hopefully, trying to make eye contact and give them my best 'Are you Steve?' look. Most continued past without a glance; others gave me their best 'God, no' look back. Finally, I felt a tap on my shoulder, and spun around to what could have been a slightly different version of me grinning back.

'You're Ben, right?'

'Yup. Steve?'

'Sure am. Welcome to Seoul, mate. Let's grab a cab, eh?'

I was relieved. Steve looked about my age – in his late 20s – and had a friendly, I'm-probably-not-going-to-shoot-you smile. He was also around my height and build, and was the proud owner of four strands of hair on his head. Just like me. About the only difference was that he had one arm strapped to his chest in a sling, plus a few large scratches criss-crossing his face.

'So what happened to the arm?' I asked as we slid into the back of a taxi and Steve gave directions in halting Korean.

'Oh, came off my bike the other day. I've been training for a triathlon. I was riding along with a group, and this piece of metal flew up and lodged itself in my spokes. Threw me over the top of the bike, totally fucked my shoulder. Fortunately, the Korean medical system is pretty good. I'm not supposed to shower while I've got this thing on though, so if you smell something bad, that's me.'

After 15 minutes or so, the cab dropped us outside a steep alley. 'This is us,' Steve said, grabbing hold of my day pack and jumping out of the cab, leading me into a three-storey apartment block framed by typically Asian tiled walls. We headed up to the top floor flat.

'Better slip your shoes off mate,' Steve said, winking. 'It's a Korean thing; better to just go with it.'

Steve's place was great – a little flat with wood panelling everywhere, like a 70s ski chalet. 'This is your room,' he said, pointing at a doorway to the left of the kitchen. 'It might be a bit of a squash.'

He wasn't kidding. Technically, it was a room, with a bed, so therefore much more luxurious than the couch I'd been expecting. Thing is, the room was only just big enough for a single mattress on the floor – you had to lift the end of the mattress up to close the door. I could lie on the bed, spread my arms out and touch both of the walls. If I pointed my toes, I could almost brush the door as well. The room was also home to Steve's wardrobe, meaning I'd have to go through the bed lifting, door opening ritual every morning before he went to work.

'Okay, let's get some food,' Steve said, poking his head in the door and thus reducing the space in my room by about half. 'I suppose you probably want something Korean, don't you?' I nodded. 'Okay, there's a place about 15 minutes away we can check out.'

When Steve said there was a place 15 minutes away, he didn't mean there was a place he liked 15 minutes away. He meant the nearest Korean restaurant was 15 minutes away. As we walked down the street, I realised Steve's neighbourhood, Yongsan Gu, was kind of like 'Americatown' – a den of Western culture nestled within an Asian city. The street was lined with Western-style bars advertising pizza and burgers, with crowds of boozing expats spilling out onto the pavements. In fact, you were hard-pressed to find a Korean walking around.

'I always say I need my "white time",' Steve explained. 'I spend all day doing Korean stuff – I work with Koreans, I teach Koreans, I eat the Korean food at the school I work at . . . So when I get home I want to do white stuff. Hang out with white people, eat white food, do white things.'

Steve was an English teacher at one of the local schools. Unlike a lot of expats who teach English overseas, Steve was actually qualified. At the restaurant, as we took our seats at a stainless steel table with a small pot of burning coals sunk into the middle of it, he explained that he hadn't really wanted to come to Korea. He'd had his eyes on a job in Hong Kong, but had been too late in applying.

'The Koreans were looking for teachers, so I thought I'd check it out,' he said with a shrug. 'I've been here two-and-a-half years now.'

The restaurant was a traditional Korean barbecue joint, a small place that looked like a dream job for a lazy chef – the cooks do the slicing, and the customers do the cooking. Steve yelled something in Korean at one of the waiters and a whole pile of accompaniments started arriving on our table. We had slices of onion, chunks of garlic, lettuce leaves, a red bean paste, a bowl of rice, and a plate of thin slices of raw beef. Oh, and *kimchee*.

Of all the things you see a lot of in Korea – apartment blocks, temples, Koreans – none has anything on the ubiquity of kimchee. It's not so much a foodstuff as a way of life: nothing in Korea seems to be served without it. I'd be surprised if you could get a coffee without being offered some kimchee to dip into it.

Kimchee at its very basic form is just pickled vegetables – bits of radish or cucumber or cabbage that have spent a few months buried underground. Every Korean family has their own special recipe. In the south, they add things like fish heads and guts to the mix. Others just stick with plain old cabbage. Add to that plenty of chilli, garlic and onion, plus some sort of fermented fish sauce, stuff it into a terracotta pot, bury it in the ground for a few months, and you've got kimchee. (It doesn't even have to be underground – with the massive push towards urbanisation in Korea, some companies have even released special kimchee fridges to store the terracotta pots.)

The way to eat a Korean barbecue, Steve explained, is pretty simple: you pick up a slice of meat with the thin metal chopsticks the Koreans use (and which must be the least ergonomically appropriate utensils I've ever seen), put it on the grill over hot coals, and wait for it to cook. Once that's done, you do your best to pick the little bugger up without doing yourself a wrist injury, then lay it on a leaf of lettuce, upon which you pile the onion, garlic, bean paste, rice and kimchee. Then you ditch the chopsticks, use your hands to fold up the whole thing into an almost fist-sized bundle, and shove it all into your mouth.

'That's the whole thing,' Steve reminded me, manoeuvring a wad of food towards his mouth, managing to perform the whole operation with one arm strapped to his chest. 'No cheating and taking little bites.'

Even with the use of both hands, I still managed to smoosh most of my little parcels across my face before they got anywhere near my mouth, and even then I almost choked on the massive amounts of food you're expected to chew your way through in one go.

In between performing the Heimlich manoeuvre on me after each bundle, Steve told me a bit about himself. He was a Sydney lad, and had studied teaching at uni before ditching it for a career in sales, which he later ditched for a career as a personal trainer, which he later ditched to get back into teaching. During his time in Seoul, he'd worked his way up to now control about 80 English teachers in the area. He still taught his regular classes, though.

'There's, like, this stereotype of Asian students being really hardworking and studious, but that's not strictly true,' Steve explained. 'That's probably just the ones that we see in Australia. Here, you still get the little bastard 15-year-olds who'll just sit there and glare at you when you ask them a question. They're just like, "Nup."'

Outside of work, Steve spent most of his 'white time' playing sport, and talking to his Canadian girlfriend on Skype. Glancing at his watch, he announced that that was what he was heading home to do right then. Slightly jetlagged and relieved to be heading to bed, I followed.

*

Steve had left a note on the dining room table the next morning: 'Hey mate, gone to work. Not sure what you want to do today, but you should find some ideas here. Good luck!'

'Here' was the Korean Lonely Planet guidebook sitting under the note, which was not quite what I'd been hoping for when I set out to see the world through the eyes of the locals. Suddenly, I realised the folly of my decision to not do any research for this trip under the pretence that I didn't want to colour my view of the destination. What I'd really done was just take the easy option. Don't bother researching; let other people tell me what to do. I'd already hit a snag – Steve was telling me to read the Lonely Planet.

I sat down and flipped through the book. It looked like there were a few temples around, a few palaces and, for the really keen, a few more temples. I picked a destination at random (the one with the cheapest entry), and decided to make my way over there.

It appeared every other Western tourist in Seoul was also checking out Changdeokgung, an imperial palace built during the 1400s. The highlight, for me, was King Taejong's 'secret garden', a walled-off area behind the main palace built for the king to study and read in. Or, as our guide put it: 'To spend time away from wife.' Basically, it was like the ancient Korean version of the backyard shed.

The other highlight, as I strolled around this beautiful 600-year-old palace, was the sight of a chipmunk scurrying along the top of a wall. A real chipmunk! I could feel the ridicule of the northern-hemisphere-dwelling tourists as I trotted down the path, happily snapping off photos of the first chipmunk I'd ever seen not in Looney Tunes form. To those other tourists: whatever. I refuse to be embarrassed about taking photos of a chipmunk.

That excitement over, I ducked into a local restaurant for some lunch. Now, I like to think I'm pretty skilled at picking restaurants when I'm overseas. There are certain things I keep an eye out for: any signage out the front should be in the local language; there should be plenty of people sitting at the tables; the place should be a bit dirty and look a bit dodgy. In this case, I found a restaurant that fit the criteria just near the palace – bare tables with a few sauce bottles on them, and little wooden boxes filled with thin metal chopsticks and long, metal spoons. The menu was entirely in Korean, only with small photos of each dish accompanying it.

A waitress came over, and I pointed at what I thought looked like a noodle and dumpling soup. I was spot on. Of course, this steaming bowl of goodness was served with kimchee. The other accompaniment was the stares of 20 or so Korean diners, probably wondering what a foreigner was doing in their restaurant.

I spent the rest of the day doing what I do best: wandering aimlessly. I found some interesting places; I found some incredibly boring places. I found a crowded main street filled with hastily erected stalls selling everything. Everything. There were people selling flowers, cacti, tree roots, trowels, spades, weird white balls whose use I couldn't figure out, rubber thimbles, Q-tips, corn, fruit, soap, handbags, belts, sunglasses, wallets and watches. One lady seemed to be selling just thimbles and Q-tips.

With the three o'clock bell gone, Steve was out of school, so we met up to climb Namsan, the tower-topped mountain that splits Seoul in half.

'It's so great that you're here during cherry blossom season,' Steve said as we trudged up the wooden boardwalk towards the top.

'Really? Is that a big deal?'

'Well, yeah man. They only come out for about two weeks a year. It's a pretty special time to be here.'

I was sceptical – big tough travel writers don't like things like flowers – but Steve was right. The white blossoms pretty much covered the mountain, making it look like the whole thing had been doused in icing sugar, and even I got sucked into taking one of the cliched 'arty, extreme close-up of a flower' photos like everyone else.

Up top of the mountain, surrounding the N Seoul Tower, we found a fence studded with thousands and thousands of padlocks, affixed, apparently, in gestures of love. Most had scribbled inscriptions on them like 'RS 4 BH' or the Korean equivalent. There was also a game of one-upmanship going on with the locks. While some had confirmed their love with a mere padlock, others had latched on giant industrial locks about the size of your arm, while some had even gone with bike locks. The proprietors obviously weren't getting too carried away with the romance though, as there were signs all over the place advising people to 'Make sure you don't lose your key'.

Steve didn't have a lock of his own up there. Unlike most of the Westerners in town, he'd barely even dated any of the Korean girls.

'I did, but only for a few months,' he said as we sat down on a bench to watch the sun set between the trees. 'It was hard, you know, because you can't really communicate well. I mean, she had lived in Australia before, but we still couldn't really have a proper conversation.'

Korean girls are gorgeous. It took one trip on the subway for me to realise that. And for some inexplicable reason, they're attracted to Western guys. Really average-looking Western guys.

I lost count of the number of aesthetically challenged Western guys I saw walking down the street, or hanging out in bars, with absolutely gorgeous Korean girls on their arms.

Still, Koreans are quite traditional, and most fathers want their daughter to end up with a nice Korean gent. Steve's friend Rob was dating a Korean girl, who'd taken him home to meet her parents after six months of dating, and things had gone reasonably well.

'Or so I thought,' Rob told me. 'I then found out a week later that her dad had gone and set her up on a blind date with some Korean guy!'

These relationships don't seem to go both ways though. For all the hot-Korean-girl, average-Western-bloke couples I saw around, I didn't see a single Western girl with a Korean guy. It just doesn't happen, apparently, and no one I talked to was quite sure why.

For dinner that night, we had a traditional Korean . . . Ah, actually, we went over to Steve's friend Rachel's house for a home-cooked meal of chicken and pasta salad, washed down with a few plastic two-litre bottles of Cass. This was a typical night in expat Korea, apparently. Dinner at someone's house, a few cheap beers, then, as all the TV is in Korean, you play a few rounds of 'YouTube VJ' – taking turns picking songs to play on YouTube.

*

I'm not one of those people who enjoyed school. I made a few friends in the last couple of years, but the rest of the time it was hell. I grew up in small-town Central Queensland, a place where pasty-skinned, liberal-minded kids whose parents take them on regular overseas holidays aren't the most popular. Tough guys bullied me, girls rejected me, and every spring, a magpie would swoop and attempt to peck my ears off while I tried to manoeuvre my 10-speed past its gum tree on my way to class.

My main problem, I think, was that I decided early on in my life that I was a pacifist – which, in playground speak, is a wuss. I didn't want to fight anyone; something the tough guys quickly picked up on. If you wanted to boost your ego or your social standing at my school, all you had to do was announce you wanted to fight me, and wait for me to back down. I wasn't smart enough to figure out that if I'd just put aside this pacifism for five minutes or so and taken a few air swings at some dickhead, my life would probably have been a lot more peaceful. But I had my principles. And one of those principles was that I really, really didn't want to get beaten up.

So, strangely enough, I've never felt any compulsion to go back to school. Any school. Even the sound of bells ringing makes me tense up like a Vietnam War vet hearing fireworks.

But here I was on a cold morning in Seoul, Korea, waiting with Steve to catch the bus to school. Walking into the school grounds was like walking into any schoolyard in the world, only the soccer pitch out the front was dirt, and all the writing on the front of the school block was in Korean. I could feel the old nervousness return as we paced the lino-floored halls, past the rows of lockers and staring kids. These kids, though, were staring because their white, balding teacher seemed to have brought along a white, balding friend.

Once we were up in Steve's empty classroom, he walked over to a locker, kicked off his trainers, and slid his feet into some plastic slippers. 'They're my inside shoes,' he explained. 'In Korea, you have inside shoes and outside shoes. All the kids have them too; you just change when you come in.'

I raised an eyebrow.

'Look, Ben, if they're going to pay me to work in slippers, I'm not going to complain.'

The classroom, like the rest of the school, was the same as any other in the world. There were groups of little wooden desks with graffiti scratched into them and artwork done by the kids all over the walls. I had to chuckle at one of the collages hanging from the roof, which said in neat, deliberate script: 'I hate math. I hate learning Chinese. I hate bananas. I hate heresy.'

Who doesn't?

'What are the other teachers here like?' I asked as Steve shuffled through some notes at his little teaching lectern.

'They're okay.'

'Do they socialise much?'

'Yeah, but I don't go with them anymore.'

'How come?'

'They just get fucking wankered. Seriously. It's a very polite tradition in Korea that if someone pours you a drink, you have to drink it. And because I'm the Westerner, they all want to drink with me. So someone will come up and pour a shot of *soju*, the rice wine, and they'll want to drink it with you. Then someone else will come up, and someone else, and within half an hour you're absolutely wrecked. But they just don't stop, and they won't let you leave. It's insane.'

Eventually, the kids all poured into the classroom, and after I'd wedged my knees under a little desk, the lesson began. I sat there praying the teacher wouldn't ask me any questions (I've never been much good with that grammar stuff – I know which words to use, I just don't know why). After an hour and a half, the bell rang, the kids piled out, and Steve and I were left alone again.

'So that's it mate,' he said. 'In half an hour, a new lot comes in, and I do it all again. Pretty exciting, huh?'

'Ah, sure.'

I was done with English lessons for the day though, so I set out to tackle Seoul on my own again. I went for a largely uneventful bicycle ride down the Han River, amusing myself by trying to take photos while pedalling along at high speed, almost taking out a few joggers in the process. Soon after that, as I again consulted Steve's Lonely Planet, I realised that there really isn't that much to do in Seoul. Sure, it's a nice enough city, all modern tall buildings and bright lights, and there are a few temples and palaces of note. But beyond that, there ain't a whole lot to look at. As someone would later tell me while I was in Gyeongju, Korea's trailing miles behind its big rival Japan in the 'bling' stakes. Japan has Mount Fuji, plus amazing temples, and huge cities, while Korea is a slightly smaller, less impressive version of all of that. It's a great place to live, but not the most exciting place to visit.

I was getting worried. I'm supposed to be writing a book here, and so far, nothing interesting had really happened. I'd decided to throw myself in the deep end on this trip, to meet crazy people and do crazy things, and here I was crashing with a nice Aussie school teacher who spent most of his evenings eating burgers at the local expat bar and going home to play YouTube VJ. Sure, it was good from the 'I'm not getting shot' point of view. But from the point of view of writing a hilarious book, things weren't going swimmingly. There was only one thing for it: go to a bathhouse.

Bathhouses, in my experience, are ripe for the mining of comedy, mainly because they're perfect places for me to make a dick of myself. I'd visited a couple of them when I was in Russia a few years ago, and it had all gone wrong. I'd hit myself with a birch branch without wetting it first (painful), and sat in a sauna for half an hour thinking I was a tough guy before some Russian bloke came in and actually turned it on (painful after that).

So it didn't seem like too much of a stretch to assume that Korean bathhouses would be just as crazy. Only, they weren't. Maybe it was because I'd had some experience, but the biggest faux pas I committed was not taking my shoes off on entry. Everything else I dealt with admirably. I wasn't even that surprised by the sight of the miniature barber's shop set up inside the change room. It was all disappointingly relaxing, and I walked out feeling fresh, revived, and without any usable material.

*

In Europe, it's known as ABC: Another Bloody Cathedral. You've seen one, you've seen them all. Notre Dame was amazing, St Paul's Basilica was great, St Peter's was nice enough . . . and that'll do. Anything else is just Another Bloody Cathedral. It might be 1000 years old, hand-painted by blind nuns, but that's hardly as interesting as the inside of a pub, is it?

In Asia, travellers get the similar-but-not-quite-as-catchy ABT syndrome: Another Bloody Temple. You take about 100 photos of the first temple you see, maybe 10 photos of the following one, and by the next one, you couldn't care less.

In Gyeongju, I had a serious case of ABT. If I didn't see another temple in my life, it would be time well spent. This is probably something I should have thought about before committing to visiting the city, a small place in the south-east of Korea that's the historical capital of the ancient Silla Empire. Don't worry, I had no idea what that meant either.

'Hey Ben,' someone called Maria had written.

If you're heading to South Korea, you can always crash at my place in Gyeongju (historical capital of the Silla kingdom, world heritage listed blah blah blah). I work at one of the universities here.

As you can see, my Korean contacts weren't the most verbose. But still, Maria's invitation sounded good. I was going to visit Korea anyway, and I was keen to see something other than just the big city, so a few nights in the ancient capital of whatsahoosit would suit me fine.

Going along with my rule about not doing any research before I arrived, I knew nothing about Gyeongju except for those brief words in Maria's email. I figured it'd be old, there'd be some temples, probably a few ruins, and that was it.

The first thing I saw as my bus pulled into the station was old, but not what I'd been expecting. On each street corner on the main intersection next to the station, groups of blue-and-white-clad senior citizens were standing in lines, dancing in odd synchronisation to music I soon realised was just one Korean pop song stuck on repeat, being blasted out of twin speakers strapped to a truck on one of the corners. As I stood on the street, waiting for Maria to meet me, the groups all stopped dancing, and started waving white-gloved hands at a man on a dais while the pop song cycled through its endless repeats.

I had even begun humming the tune to myself by the time Maria turned up, slightly out of breath.

'Oh, that,' she said, nodding at the dancing posses while smoothing down her sensible hiker's fleece. 'There's a local election on. The guy they're waving at is their candidate.' She shrugged. 'I guess it's a Korean thing. You should see it when they open a new store – they usually have dancing girls in fluffy boots and miniskirts out the front.'

'I see. They're not opening any new stores today are they?'

'We'll have a look. Do you want to get some lunch or something first?'

We wandered down the street a few blocks, me enjoying the relative smallness of Gyeongju. It's a city of a few hundred thousand, but after having been in Seoul, which feels like a city of a few hundred million, Gyeongju was a sleepy little haven. There were no skyscrapers and no highways – just old one- and two-storey houses with terracotta-tiled roofs and whitewashed walls. Even the restaurant Maria took me to was small – there was barely enough room for the two of us, plus my day pack.

Maria was 37, born in India, raised in Australia, and had lived and worked in Mexico, San Salvador and Korea since leaving university. She'd been living in Gyeongju for three years and she knew it, she told me, as well as anyone. What she didn't know about, though, was me, or my blog. She explained that she'd only read the one entry in which I'd put out my call for couches, and that was enough. 'Is it still going?' she asked.

Over a *bibimbap* for lunch – a dish of rice, vegetables, meat, egg and, of course, kimchee, all mixed up together – Maria outlined her plans for me for the next few days. There was no Lonely Planet in sight; this tour was pure Maria. She whipped out a large map of the city from a zipped pocket in her cargo pants, and began pointing out the sights and walks we'd have to tick off before I left town.

'Now, you've been invited to two barbecues already on Saturday,' she finished, 'and there's the soju and *ddok* festival on that day as well, so you definitely have to stay at least until then.'

'Ah, that's a pity,' I said. 'I'll have to miss it unfortunately. I'm flying out of Seoul on Sunday, so I'll have to be back the day before.'

Maria squinted into the distance for a second. 'Sunday? Nope, that's fine, we'll just throw you on a bus straight to Incheon Airport from here on Sunday morning. You'll get there in plenty of time.'

'Oh . . . But I have to get my backpack from Steve's house. He's the guy in Seoul.'

Maria paused again. 'Okay, that's fine, we'll get him to bring the bag out to the airport and give it to you.'

'Well, I don't really want to have to ask him to do that.'

'Hmmm . . .' Maria sighed. 'I'm starting to not like this Steve. I know, we can get him to courier your pack down for you!'

This would be the start of a two-day-long tug-of-war between Maria and me, as she attempted to get me to stay for the barbecues with her friends on Saturday, and I attempted to get myself back to Seoul to hang out with Steve and his friends for one more night. Maria, I was to find, could be bizarrely persuasive, and she wasn't taking no for an answer.

After lunch we headed to Maria's house. Winding through tiny alleys, we eventually found her apartment, a top-floor one-bedder in a fairly old area of the city. She'd warned me that the house would be untidy, which people always do regardless of the fact that their place is spotless, but in Maria's case, she wasn't kidding. Her two cats immediately bolted upon seeing me walk through the door, and didn't return the entire time I stayed there. They'd occasionally poke their heads up from below the windowsill to confirm I was still around, and scamper off again. As Maria showed me around the place I soon realised she was going to give me her bed while she slept on the floor in her study. I felt incredibly bad about it, but, as with most things, I couldn't talk her out of the decision.

Her house, I soon noticed, was a bit like Ned Flanders's holiday home in *The Simpsons*, in that it was covered with Post-It notes explaining everything about the place. If the cats had been there, they'd have probably had notes stuck to their chins telling people how to feed them. It was a little bizarre, although I later found out Maria had a housesitter coming in the next few weeks, and wanted to make sure they knew how everything worked.

The first box to tick on Maria's Grand Tour was to do a hike through the surrounding mountains, where, gloriously, we'd also find a Buddhist temple. So we set off on our mountain stroll, passing hordes of tracksuited Korean hikers (or rather, being passed *by* hordes of tracksuited Korean hikers). The attention to detail in the leisurewear department is all part of the culture, Maria explained, as is a fairly rigid set of old-fashioned gender roles.

'Girls here live to have boyfriends,' she said as we pushed our way up through the pine trees. 'That's all they want in life. If they get to 23 and they don't have a boyfriend, people start to wonder why. If they get to 27, they almost become outcasts.

'Some girls start dating foreigners, which makes them damaged goods in many Koreans' eyes. Some of the girls just go a bit crazy. I've seen on two occasions girls go out with the intention of getting so drunk that they'll be able to do what they really want, to touch boys the way they want to.

'But the men are no angels. Prostitution is everywhere, for starters. It's very much acceptable for men to go away on a business trip and hire a bunch of hookers. And have you seen the coffee girls?'

I shook my head.

'Right, keep an eye out for them. They're the attractive girls riding around on scooters with no helmet on. Basically, men can call them up, order a coffee, and then they bring it over to their house. Then they also give them a blowjob. Seriously. My girlfriends and I didn't believe it was true, so we decided to test it out. We were all at my house one day, and we called up and ordered a coffee. So this poor girl knocks on the door, it opens up and she sees three girls looking at her. She almost fainted! She was saying, "No, no, I can't do this!"'

After the walk (yeah, yeah, the temple was lovely), we had some time to kill, as Maria wanted to take me to the city's ancient kings' tombs after the sun had gone down. It was still early afternoon, so we decided to go to a 'DVD *bang*', which translates literally as 'DVD room', which I could have just said in the first place, but wouldn't have sounded as exotic. A DVD bang is just like one of those Asian karaoke places you find in Australian cities now, with a whole bunch of private rooms for people to rent out – only in these, rather than massacre 'New York, New York', you sit back on the comfy couch and watch a DVD on the room's big screen. I thought it was a great idea until I watched the attendant make a big show out of spraying the couch with disinfectant and wiping it down, and realised what most young Koreans probably use the rooms for.

Still, it was too late to turn back, as Maria had already picked a Korean film for us called *Old Boy*. So we grabbed a few supposedly clean blankets from the cupboard in the room, and settled back sipping our juices from the front bar. Maria had warned me that Korean films often dealt with slightly different topics to Hollywood flicks, and this one was a prime example – *Old Boy* was about incest.

It was dark by the time we stumbled out, meaning it was time for the tombs, which are in a national park close to the city. The builders of the tombs, back in the fifth, sixth and seventh centuries, kind of had the same idea as the Egyptians, only with less technical nous. Rather than build huge stone pyramids on top of their kings, they built huge mounds of dirt, which are now covered in grass, making Gyeongju look like it has a whole lot of green boobs.

They were interesting enough, but already I was starting to get templed – and tombed – out.

Maria, however, was having the time of her life, babbling away about the history of the sites and being generally enthusiastic. After three years in the city, she really considered it her own, to the point that she snapped like a mad woman when she discovered a plastic bottle that had been thrown into one of the ponds near the temple.

'What fucking arseholes live here?' she screamed into the empty night. 'I can't fucking believe this!' She then threw aside her bag and phone, lay down on a nearby rock, and furiously fished the bottle out of the pond.

*

There are certain phrases that set off alarm bells for seasoned travellers. 'Special massage' is one of them. 'Family restaurant' is another. So I wasn't exactly excited when Maria announced the next day that we were going for lunch with her friend Yolanta to a Korean family restaurant. The place was a giant buffet – like a Korean Sizzler – which at least gave me the chance to try a few different types of kimchee. Midway through the meal, Maria started having what sounded like an argument with the old Korean couple at the table next to us. She looked over at me and laughed.

'I'm getting in trouble here,' she chuckled. 'She thinks you're my boyfriend, and they can't believe I'm making you get up to get your own food. She said I would know better which foods to get, and should be looking after you better.'

I eyed my plate of miscellaneous kimchee. 'Well, off you go then . . .'

With lunch over, it was time for . . . more temples. This time, however, Maria had organised something to spice things up a little bit: Yolanta. Or, to be more precise, Yolanta's driving. Yolanta, like Maria, was an English teacher from the local university, a middle-aged Canadian divorcee who joyfully admitted within the first five minutes of my meeting her that she was 'probably born with dementia'. She was also, without doubt, the worst driver I have ever seen. Asian drivers might have a bad reputation, but I'd drive around Baghdad with a blindfolded Mongolian before getting in a car with Yolanta at the wheel again.

Jumping into the back of our mad Canadian's beaten-up old Daewoo, I started off with no seatbelt, but quickly buckled up when I looked up and noticed her careening between lanes without indicating, and at one point attempting to stick herself between two buses, before eventually conceding defeat and swerving away. In the four hours I spent in her car, she almost hit a taxi, was sideswiped by a bus, and screamed to a halt in the middle of a busy street so that she could get a better look at some magnolias by the side of the road.

('Yes, I forgot to tell you about that,' Maria told me later. 'I had actually promised myself I'd never go in a car with Yolanta again.')

'How long are you planning on staying in Gyeongju, Ben?' Yolanta asked.

'Well . . .'

'We've been invited to some barbecues,' Maria jumped in, 'so we'll go to those, and then I was thinking we could get Ben on a night bus, get him back to Seoul by early Sunday morning.'

I groaned. 'Um, Maria, I don't think I want to wake Steve up that early to let . . .'

'Oh, this Steve! All right, what does he do?'

'Maria, I'm going back to Seoul tomorrow morning.'

Maria looked at me for a second, and slowly, finally, conceded defeat. 'All right, but we can squeeze in a few more things on Saturday morning before you leave. I think the soju festival starts at nine, so there's plenty of time for that. The guys at the barbecue are going to be very disappointed though.'

As Yolanta's Wild Ride continued, I realised I had developed a serious case of ABT. She drove us to Seokguram, a statue of the Buddha in a beautiful hilly grotto, then to Bulguksa, a huge temple in the flower-dotted hills, and then to a stone carving of the Buddha in the middle of a forest. At each one Yolanta made whatever signs of obeisance Buddhists make at their holy places, while Maria snapped off photos with her giant SLR camera, and I tried to make the appropriate noises of polite interest.

Maria was a weapon of mass tourism – and her excess enthusiasm for her city, I decided, could be a product of her aversion to alcohol. The stuff tends to dull enthusiasm to an acceptable level, but Maria was a teetotaller, something I found out when we went to a bar with some friends of hers that night. As I'd written on my original plea for places to stay, I am certainly not a teetotaller. So by 3am, I was steaming drunk, and a sober Maria had fallen asleep on someone's shoulder. I decided it was time for us to leave.

'Don't forget about the temples in the morning,' Maria mumbled. 'If we leave early there's still time . . .'

I patted her on the shoulder. 'Okay, we'll see, hey?'

*

Oh, we saw all right.

There was a weird banging noise coming from my bedroom door. There it went again. And again. I groaned, and flicked open my phone. 6.30am. I'd been in bed three hours.

'Ben? You awake? We're leaving in 15 minutes.'

It was Maria. I lay in bed and considered my options. One: stay in bed and figure out a way to explain to Maria that I wasn't coming to look at any more temples. Two: get up, sober up, and battle through the next three-and-a-half hours before I could get on that bus back to Seoul and sleep the sleep of the dead. Of the two options, the latter seemed far easier to achieve, so I dragged myself out of bed, slapped my cheeks a few times, and opened the bedroom door.

'Hi there,' Maria said, swishing through the kitchen, her long dark hair tied in a neat plait, sensible hiking shoes already laced up. 'Don't worry about breakfast – I've made us some ham sandwiches to eat at the temple. Are you ready to go?'

'Maria, it's 6.30 in the morning.'

'I know, we're making good time. Come on, get your shoes on.'

I'd like to tell you about the next three hours, but I don't really remember much of it. I know we went to Manbulsa, a place called 'The temple of 10,000 Buddhas', and I know Maria must have taken a photo of every single one of them while I sat on the grass and tried to cram my eyeballs back into their sockets, but that's about all I've got from there. I know we went to the soju and ddok festival (dedicated to rice wine and rice flour dumplings), and I drank shots of soju while Maria laughed and took photos of me, but even that's a blur. I know that I finally, gloriously, bid Maria goodbye, hopped on that bus, and fell instantly asleep. But that's all.

*

A bus ride, a train ride, a taxi ride, and a medium McChicken meal later, I was lacing up my boots to play for one of Steve's soccer teams (actually, they were Steve's boots). We played a group of Malaysian expats on a small Astroturf pitch, and won 9–5.

'Since I scored a hat-trick, will I get to go in the book?' asked some guy whose name I can't remember.

I shook my head. 'No chance.'

After the game, we all headed back to Steve's expat district, and went to Phillies, the pub that sponsors the team. There, me, Steve and his English soccer-playing buddies drank free jugs of beer, ate hamburgers, watched IPL cricket on the big screen, and talked about how well we'd played in the game. In other words, pretty much exactly what I would do on a Sunday afternoon in Sydney.

Pretty crazy trip, I know.

Lab Rats

'Fuck man, look at this place. There's wires hanging overhead, who knows what they're for. They use bamboo scaffolding everywhere. Bamboo! The whole city's an OH&S claim waiting to happen.'

I recognised Pete immediately. Not because of the photo he'd emailed through but because of the sign he was holding across his chest when I walked into the arrivals hall at Pudong Airport. Printed in big black type, it read: 'Mr Ben Groundwater.'

I grinned. 'Pete, right?'

'How'd ya guess?'

Pete had dived on a proverbial grenade for me. I hadn't expected to stay with him for long. There was a chance, in my mind at least, that I wouldn't get around to meeting up with him at all. But things had changed a lot in the last few days, and I'd had to come grovelling. A one-night stay, he'd been fine with – but five?

Originally, the invites from China had come pouring in. There'd been Richard, a former triple j newsreader now based in the western city of Chengdu, who wanted me to come and check out the pandas. Done. Joey in Shanghai also sounded good. 'I live about as central as you can get,' he wrote.

I have a very comfy couch available in a nice, modern and secure apartment in an old building. My fellow residents raise pigeons and carp and wander around our compound in their pyjamas until late at night gossiping, gambling and playing mah-jong with their neighbours. My stairwell smells of frying garlic and peanuts. I've been down-and-out and comfortable in Shanghai, so my restaurant and bar knowledge runs from cool funky dives to the swankiest riverside establishments. Let me know . . .

Done. There was also Ruth, a teacher who lived on the outskirts of Shanghai, and then Pete, who'd written:

I work for a mechanical and architectural consultancy, stationed in Shanghai. I, and a group of other expats, work predominantly for multinational pharmaceutical companies designing their new facilities in China. I think we could accommodate something for your tour – it might actually give us an excuse for yet another party.

I'd planned to spread myself around throughout the group. Midway through my Korean adventure though, things started falling apart. Ruth wasn't answering emails. That wasn't a problem though; I had a few other Shanghai contacts. The bigger problem was that Richard had announced he'd decided to go back to Australia for a wedding, and was happy to leave a key out for me, but wouldn't be around to show me the place. Not ideal. Plus, I'd just figured out it would take me a good couple of days on the train to get from Shanghai to Chengdu, and I didn't have a good couple of days.

The biggest problem, however, was Joey, who sent me a short email a few days before I was due to arrive:

Mate, really sorry about this, but I'm going to have to opt out of your stay. Long story, but I've got visa issues, and have to get out of the country. I was going to just jet over to Hong Kong for a day, but then I just found really cheap flights to Paris, so I'm going to head over there for a few weeks. Hope that doesn't cause any problems.

Suddenly, my exciting, multi-faceted Chinese trip had turned very one-dimensional. I had five nights to play with, all of which I was now going to spend crashing with Pete. We'd better get on well.

*

'The train's running a bit slow today,' Pete said as we pushed through the turnstiles at the airport. 'On the way out here it only got up to 300 kilometres an hour. Can you believe that?'

I raised my eyebrows, not quite sure if he was joking or not. The last train I'd taken in China had been lucky to give 30km/h a nudge, so I wasn't expecting much from this one. This, however, was my first trip to Shanghai, where things are done a little differently. There's not much room for history in Shanghai – it's all about bigger, brighter, newer and faster. The train I was on was the new maglev, the airport shuttle that usually hits 430km/h as it zips passengers to and from the city. Today, however, just as Pete had predicted, the speedo in the carriage topped out at 300km/h.

'Seven minutes into the city,' Pete said as Shanghai's outskirts flashed past behind his head in a smog-laden blur. 'Not bad for a communist backwater, eh?'

Pete's interest was more than just amateur curiosity. He was a mechanical engineer, he explained, and had a passion for all things technical. 'What do you do here?' I asked.

'I'm working on air-conditioning units at the moment,' he said. 'You know, for pharmaceutical labs in big office blocks? It's pretty awesome work. I do a lot of animal housing, which adds a whole different layer to what you're doing.'

'Animal housing? What's that?'

'Oh, like, I dunno, animal testing labs, I guess you'd call them. The air in there has to be strictly filtered, you don't want any crap getting in there and messing up the experiments. So you've got these multi-staged units in there which . . .'

Okay, I admit, I stopped listening around then. Pete, it turned out, had a habit of talking in the sort of technical jargon that might as well have been Mandarin for all I knew. Most of it went over my head. He also had two major passions which seemed to drive his life: gadgets and sailing. If they were gadgets designed for sailing, then all the better. Pete could quite happily talk about these two passions with no more encouragement from me than the odd grunt every now and then to signify the fact that I was still awake.

From the end of the maglev line, we jumped on an underground train and headed to Pete's neighbourhood, in the north of the city. It had started raining by the time we emerged onto the street, in a shiny new suburb filled with skyscrapers and modern shops. Pete lived in one of those apartment complexes that seem to go on forever. It took up an entire city block, with about 10 identical 40-storey buildings sprouting up from the earth. How anyone knew which one they lived in was beyond me.

'Hardly anyone seems to live here though,' Pete said, nodding at the security guard on the gate. 'They build these massive apartment blocks, and there's no one who can afford to move into them. They're pretty shoddy, too. It looks all nice, but scratch the surface, and these places are rubbish. I'm only here for a year though, so who cares, right?'

Pete's 10th-floor flat was a standard modern apartment, with one bedroom and a small balcony overlooking the street. For the first time on this trip though, I was going to be sleeping on an actual couch – although the white pleather three-seater looked pretty comfy to me.

'So here are the choices,' Pete said, absently flicking his laptop on. 'It's pissing with rain, so there's not much point doing anything outside. So we can stay here, and get stuck into one of those bottles of Bundy in the kitchen, or I know this good expat bar we can go down to, to watch the Shanghai Grand Prix. Whaddaya reckon?'

'Oh well, if the Grand Prix's on, we might as well watch it.'

'Cool. Okay, I'm just gonna check my position before we go.' He stared at the laptop screen for a second. 'Oh, I'm gaining! Some of these blokes have got no idea.'

'What are you doing?'

'It's this Volvo Ocean Race game you can play on the net. It goes for months. You race yachts around the world. There's like 100,000 people playing. I'm about 32,000th at the moment, but I haven't really been trying. My mate's a few hours ahead of me, so I just have to catch him. Might just adjust my heading actually.'

Once again, I tried to nod knowingly. Pete remained glued to the game in most of his downtime for the next five days, and I just settled for feigning interest, smiling and nodding.

With Pete's heading altered, we headed out into the rain, and over to Bamboo Bar, an expat haven in a nearby neighbourhood. The place was filled with miserable-looking Westerners, most nursing pints on their own at the bar, staring into space or absently watching the cars zooming around on the big screen. Pete and I got a table, and I ordered my first meal in China (spaghetti bolognaise, I'm ashamed to say). I sighed inwardly. Seeing the city through my hosts' eyes, I reminded myself, doing what they do . . . And even I had to admit, it was a pretty darn good spag bol.

Pete, I soon realised, was the biggest fan of my blog so far. Steve had said he'd been reading it for a long time, but never mentioned it in conversation, while Maria freely admitted that she'd read it once, and that'd been enough for her. Pete, on the other hand, could quote things that I'd written back to me: 'So, remember that one you did about making lists,' he asked in between mouthfuls of pasta. 'That true? Or just bullshit? Did you make a list for this trip? C'mon, you can tell me.'

I finally got my hit of Chinese food that night, when we joined two of Pete's work friends and their partners for a meal just near Pete's apartment block. David and Graham, fellow expats and mechanical engineers working for the same company, lived in the same apartment complex, only in one of the other identical towers. The company must have got a bulk discount on rental properties, and living so close together meant the three – plus Michelle, another staffer on site – could share a chauffeur-driven ride to work each morning. Put on by the company, of course.

'Have I told you about Chinese roulette?' Pete asked, flipping through a menu at the restaurant. I shook my head. 'We do it all the time. You walk around, pick a restaurant with no English menus, then go in, and just point at a few things on the menu. We haven't got a bad meal yet.'

This restaurant, however, did have English menus, so we were able to order what we thought would be a pretty good meal. There was a goose curry, some fried prawns, steamed broccoli, and a seafood soup. It was all pretty tasty, but after a few big nights in a row in Korea (plus some early temple viewings), I was fading fast.

'What do you reckon mate, should we go check out the red light district tonight?' Pete asked, grinning.

'Ah . . . What about tomorrow night?'

'Okay, tomorrow it is. The girls will have to wait.'

*

I hate Starbucks. Not because it's a multinational corporation of evil – I'm no Naomi Klein. I eat McDonald's sometimes, and I've been to Disneys Land and World. The reason I hate Starbucks is their coffee tastes like bath water. I once saw a bumper sticker in San Francisco that said: 'Friends don't let friends go to Starbucks.' I second that.

Still, Starbucks is one of those places that make Westerners feel comfortable when they're travelling. It might be bath water, but you know exactly what sort of bath water you're getting, plus, there's usually a selection of stale cakes and pastries – again, a far more familiar breakfast option than the bowl of mystery meat and noodles that everyone else seems to be eating.

We'd come to Pete's office building in Pudong, an area of Shanghai that until about a decade ago was nothing more than a patch of swampland, but is now home to a dizzying array of high-rise monstrosities housing all sorts of people whose professions I probably don't understand. We'd woken up in time to catch a lift with the company driver, as Pete had to send a few emails before taking the rest of the day off to show me around the city. Even from the air-conditioned seclusion of our chauffeur-driven ride, rush hour in Shanghai was manic, a crazed crush of cars and pedestrians fighting for space.

Pete's office tower was bang in the middle of the business district, and I could look out over most of the skyscrapers as I sipped a venti-soy-mocha-latte-frappe-cino (or whatever it was), chewed my cardboard croissant and waited for Pete to fire off his correspondence. (He'd checked his progress in the Volvo Ocean Race from home – he was now somewhere in the high 31,000s. And he'd changed his heading.)

The office looked mind-numbingly boring, with rows and rows of identical desks staffed by Chinese and expat workers tapping away at their keyboards in silence. David caught my eye, and sidled over to where I was standing staring out the window.

'If anyone asks,' he said, 'you were never here, and you're not a journalist.' I nodded. 'Gotta look after our clients' privacy, you know?'

That warning may have made David feel better, but it just made me want to know what the hell they were all up to. Plotting world domination? Or just the torture of a few bunny rabbits?

I never did find out. Pete had finished on the computer and we were off out the door, joining the lemmings on the street shuffling their way to work. Pete had only been in the city for four months, but he had a few highlights in mind for our tour. First port of call was the Oriental Pearl, a 468-metre-high futuristic tower that dominates the Pudong skyline. It was also about a block away from Pete's office. At the top, we enjoyed the uninterrupted view of Shanghai's smog while about 50,000 Chinese school kids did their best to be everywhere we wanted to be. Back on the ground floor, we had a quick walk through the museum charting Shanghai's history from tiny village through to the British invasion, the annexing of the concessions (the 'infestations of foreigners'), ending with the booming present.

Seeing pictures of old Shanghai made me realise what I'd been missing. China might be one of the oldest countries in the world, with a fascinating culture stretching back thousands of years, but you'll be lucky to find any evidence of it in Shanghai. It's a thoroughly modern city – something its older residents must be thoroughly worried about. See, in the spot where every high-rise now stretches its metallic finger into Shanghai's polluted sky, there was once someone's home. Throughout the city, you can watch the systematic destruction of the old to make space for the new.

Like Beijing, Shanghai has its older areas, the clusters of rickety little buildings where the city's poorer residents live. Unlike Beijing though, these clusters are gradually being wiped out. During my stay I saw plenty of houses whose residents could peer out of their dirty windows and watch their neighbour's house being flattened and a high-rise block of apartments put in its place.

Shanghai's the financial capital of the world's fastest growing economy, and, to put it mildly, the place is going nuts. Its population has topped 20 million. The number of cars on the road rose by 180 per cent in the late 90s. It's home to the world's busiest cargo port, and has enjoyed double-digit economic growth for the past 15 years (actually, I'm only assuming they enjoyed it). What that equates to is a heaving city big on development, but small on character. There might be some pretty funky-looking skyscrapers around, but if you're looking for quaint little restaurants in old, run-down areas – good luck.

The other downside of all this construction is the dust. On rainy days like the one I arrived on, it's not a problem. But on dry days, when the wind gets up, you spend all day inhaling giant lungfuls of construction site grit. That, coupled with your normal workaday smog, makes you feel like you've got fur balls. Walking through the city, Pete wasn't happy with the average Chinese construction worker's conditions, either.

'Fuck man, look at this place,' he said at one point, waving his arm around. 'There's wires hanging overhead, who knows what they're for. They use bamboo scaffolding everywhere. Bamboo! The whole city's an OH&S claim waiting to happen.'

The obsession with modernity also leaves room for a healthy interest in Western culture, which probably explains the many neighbourhoods bulging with modern cafes and bars.

'You're like, "What city are we in?"' Pete said as we walked through one of the city's newer areas, a pedestrian mall filled with all the comforts of home. 'You could be anywhere. This is where expats come when they want to pretend they never left home.'

About the only semi-cultural thing we managed to fit in on Pete's tour (aside from some Chinese girls in lederhosen at the local German pub), was a walk down Dongtai Lu, Shanghai's 'antique street'. You have to question the antiqueness of the products, though, when every stall seems to be selling exactly the same thing, and about four or five of each product. There must be a few factories around town doing a good trade in manufacturing Mao Zedong 'antiques' on a production line, going by the amount of statues, watches and other bric-a-brac for sale on the street.

Pete, however, was a keen customer. After a short and half-hearted haggle ('I could have got her down further, but what's the point?'), Pete became the proud owner of a Mao watch – one of those ones with a picture of the former chairman on it, waving his little metal hand as each second goes by. Pete had paid about five dollars for it, and was convinced it was a real antique.

I didn't have the heart to tell him I'd bought an exact replica of his timepiece for the Lawyer when I'd been in Hong Kong a few years ago. Anyway, there would have been little point. Pete wore his watch to dinner that night, and snapped the pin on it almost immediately. Then we noticed that Mao's little waving hand had fallen off. 'I'll just get it fixed in Australia,' Pete said with a shrug. 'See, I told you it was old.'

We rounded off Pete's tour with the ultimate in expat wankery: cocktails at Glamour Bar in the flashy Bund area, down by the river. The place was ridiculous, a trendy enclave with soft mood lighting, views over the bright lights of Pudong, waiters who only spoke English, and a full menu of cocktails that cost $18 a pop. Most people in the old town only a few streets away probably wouldn't earn that in a month.

Sipping on our fluorescent beverages, I then made the error of asking Pete about sailing. A Sydneysider and budding ocean racer, Pete had done two Sydney-to-Hobart runs, as well as a few races to Norfolk Island. He'd worked just about every job there is on a cruising yacht, and been to pretty much every competition you could travel to.

As someone who frequently bores his friends into catatonia with stories that start with, 'This one time, when I was in . . .', I knew just what to do about Pete's stories: sit back and pretend to listen.

'I've done a few European championships, and some worlds as well,' he was saying, leaning forward in his seat as he warmed to the subject. 'We did a Euro in Switzerland, and it was a nightmare getting stuff over there. You're allowed seven sails, so that has to include your mainsail and your spinnaker, so you've also got to think about your foresails and . . .'

It was about this time that I tuned out. Instead, I just stared out of the window for a while, watching the traffic on the river. Sorry, Pete.

*

'Oh, what? No!'

I opened an eye, peering out from my spot on the couch. Pete, dressed somewhat frighteningly in a skimpy bath towel, a few gingery hairs across his pale chest, had his laptop open on the dining room table.

'That's fucked.'

'What's that?'

'Oh, the race. My mate's bloody rocketed up! He's like, 20,000th or something. I'm gonna have to start putting some more work into this. Actually start trying.'

'Where are you now?'

'Um . . . 31,428th. Just off the coast of Brazil. There's still, like, a few thousand nautical miles to go, so I'll catch him.'

I nodded. Unbelievably, I was actually starting to take an interest in Pete's ocean racing game. His enthusiasm was rubbing off on me. I was silently wondering to myself if it was too late to enter my own little cyber boat. My dad's a mariner – it runs in the blood, surely?

With Pete going to work for the day, I was soon left on my own, although Pete had been good enough to leave me his indispensable travelling companion: a copy of the Shanghai Lonely Planet. This was getting ridiculous. I'd hoped for inside knowledge from my contacts but I was getting Tony Wheeler's greatest hits.

Ditching the guidebook, I decided I'd follow my stomach. Another problem I was finding on this trip was that I wasn't having the culinary tour de force I'd been expecting. I'd figured that, staying with locals, I'd get the best food each city had to offer. Unfortunately, neither Steve, Maria nor Pete had any real interest in the food scene, so I'd just been getting Western food, or the local stuff I'd found myself. I'd even introduced Pete to a few new foods the day before, including *xiao long bao*, the soup-filled dumplings Shanghai is famous for.

So on my first day flying solo, I figured I'd trudge the streets of Shanghai in search of culinary nirvana. The first thing I realised on this amazing quest was that I may have made an error in judgement in my choice of wardrobe. Seeing as it was pretty humid outside, I'd opted for shorts, but ever since I'd left the house they'd been attracting an unreasonable amount of attention. I'd even seen people nudging their friends and pointing at my bare legs. One woman almost disappeared under the wheels of a taxi as she strained to get a better look at my white legs flashing by.

I told Pete about it later that day, and he had a chuckle. 'It's your legs,' he said, clapping me on the shoulder, 'look how hairy they are! Have you seen a Chinese guy's legs? Barely a hair on them. You're a freak, basically.'

Plenty of Shanghainese got to catch sight of my hairy Antipodean pins that day as I walked and walked, inhaling clouds of dirt, in search of my perfect meal. I found dumpling places, noodle soup places, stir-fry places, and more dumpling places. I was struggling with the ordering process. At one place, I ordered six dumplings and a seafood soup. Simple enough, you'd think. Except the waitresses were actually giggling as they struggled over to the table with my soup, a family-sized portion in a bowl the size of a motorbike helmet, which could easily have fed most of the people in the restaurant.

I was also struggling with pronunciations. I'd tried to order tea ('*cha*') a few times, and got blank looks in return. I later discovered that there are three possible intonations you can use for the word 'cha', all of which completely change its meaning. One of those intonations makes it mean 'bad'. So it's no wonder I got a few strange looks as I ran around the city trying to order a cup of bad.

The tea, I'd hoped, would settle my stomach. Much as I love foreign food, my body has a bit of a problem with it. In fact,

my body has a bit of a problem with most food. I suffer fr[...]
charmingly named affliction called Irritable Bowel Syndrome,
which, you'd have to agree, isn't ideal for the world traveller. My
body sometimes just decides to reject food of its own volition,
making it pretty important for me to get to a toilet as soon as
possible. This presents certain problems when you're travelling,
to the point where I'm constantly trying to weigh up what sort
of mood my intestines are in, trying to figure out if I should be
making my way towards some amenities in the next . . . 10 seconds
or so.

Consequently, the state of a nation's toilets is a big issue for
me. I can compare the relative merits of a Mongolian squat to a
Ugandan outhouse like some people could compare their socio-
economic policies. I've also become an expert on knowing where to
look for public toilets. McDonald's is always a good bet, although
some, like in Prague, will make you buy something to use them.
Shopping malls are ideal – the toilets are always clean and free (I
might have IBS, but I'm still a tight-arse). Pubs and bars are also
a winner, as no one is likely to notice you sneaking in and heading
straight to the dunnies. If you're really desperate, train and bus
stations will also do, although you may want to pinch your nose.
And close your eyes.

So far, all had been going well in the guts department on
the Chinese leg of my journey. After each meal I could feel my
stomach sizing up the food I'd forced into it, and it had so far given
everything a pass mark. I was on my guard though. I hadn't had
an 'incident' since the time I *just* didn't make it to that Ugandan
outhouse, and I was determined to continue my incident-free run.

Dinner that night was a good test. Pete's friend from work
had suggested we eat at a Burmese restaurant famous for serving
food so spicy that as well as napkins, the waiters provide little paper
towels to wipe the sweat off your brow. They even served a vodka
cocktail flavoured with fresh chilli seeds.

Aside from the searing heat of the food, and the warning

rumbles in my stomach, dinner was largely uneventful. We were hanging out with 10 people from Pete's work – all short-term expat workers of various ages, drawn together in a foreign land with no more in common than the fact that they didn't know anyone else in the city, and probably never would. They'd all be home within a year, and just seemed to be making time pass.

I'd often wondered how expats lived, and this trip was giving me a perfect insight. I've never been an expat myself. I've spent six months living in Scotland, six months as a tour guide around Europe, but never been in one spot long enough to call myself a true local. But I've always wanted to do it. I mean, what could give you a better insight into a culture than actually living in it, becoming part of it? I've got a pretty cushy life in sunny Sydney, but I wanted to see how good I could have it if I took the plunge and moved overseas.

I'd liked Steve's life in Seoul – it looked comfortable and good fun. Maria's was okay, but I think I'd get bored in Gyeongju after a while. Pete? I was not jealous of Pete. He lived in a decent apartment, ate nice food, earnt plenty of money. But living and working with the same people for a whole year, then disappearing back to Australia wasn't my idea of expat utopia.

As I pondered this, the conversation at the table flowed around two main topics: crazy things they'd seen Chinese people doing or eating, and the bloody torture of cuddly animals. Okay, maybe I misheard the second one. Pretty much unable to contribute to either topic, I spent most of my time wiping sweat off my face, and trying to decide whether I needed to go to the toilet.

Pete, on the other hand, was having fun ribbing his work mates about various things I didn't quite catch.

'I'm a bit of a shit-stirrer really,' he confided to me. 'But look, that's just the way I am. Some of them are a bit pissed off that I got the office banned from using Facebook at work, but seriously, mate, the girls were wasting way too much time on it. When you're at work, you should be doing work, you know? Some of these blokes even went to the Shanghai Motor Show the other day in a work afternoon. I would've gone, but unfortunately my work ethic doesn't allow me to do that.'

I nodded, thinking that my work ethic allows me to do pretty much whatever I want. If Pete had a Protestant work ethic, mine must have been strictly atheist.

Hopping in a taxi after dinner, Pete attempted to exercise his Mandarin skills by directing the driver in the local tongue, which was met with a blank look.

Pete looked miffed. 'That usually works,' he said.

I shrugged. 'Maybe his Mandarin isn't as good as yours.'

*

It wasn't until I was completely naked that I started to question the wisdom of my decision. As I lay there in the softly lit room, a young Chinese masseuse straddling my bare buttocks, her hands drenched in warm massage oil, I began to realise that maybe – just maybe – this wasn't going to be the traditional foot rub I'd originally signed up for.

The signs had all been there. After another day of endless wanderings, I had my heart set on one of the true joys of travelling through China: a reflexology foot massage. I'd had one about a year ago in Beijing, and it had been amazing. A wiry little Chinese man had soaked my feet in rose-scented water, then poked, pressed, rubbed and ground my weary soles until I felt like a new man.

I'd heard you could get the same thing done in Shanghai, only even better. Here, they were supposed to be done by blind old women, schooled in the art of reflexology for years, working on touch alone to realign your *qi*. I wasn't sure how out of whack my qi was, but I definitely had sore feet, so I was on the lookout for a massage joint as I wandered through Pete's neighbourhood.

The first sign that something was amiss should have been, well, the sign, which said MASSAGE in giant pink, English letters.

There was also no trademark picture of a foot outside, which most reflexology places seemed to have. The next warning bell should have started jingling in my head when I walked down the steps into the basement parlour, and was greeted by a woman who couldn't have been more obvious if she had had a 'Brothel Madam' badge pinned to her chest. About 50, she was heavily made-up, had a big bouffant hairdo, and barked orders at her faultlessly pretty, young, female masseuses. Speaking lightly accented English, she seemed disappointed when I asked for just a foot massage.

'You don't want full body?'

'Um, no, just feet please.'

'You sure? Full body very good.'

'No no, just the feet is fine thanks.'

She sighed, wrote something down on a piece of paper, then yelled at one of her masseuses, who led me into the massage room, where, once again, I failed to pick up the rather obvious signs that this wasn't your average reflexology parlour. The place looked like a karaoke bar. There were the normal massage chairs there, but also a TV, large speakers, and a disco ball hanging from the ceiling. And, my masseuse was definitely not blind – or if she was, she'd memorised the room perfectly. She was also not old and crotchety, and probably didn't know a great deal about my qi. Still, it was a nice enough massage – but things were about to get odd.

'You want, um, whole body massage?' she said, smiling up at me mid foot-rub.

'I don't know,' I said, my conviction wavering. I was trying not to spend too much money, and a full body massage sounded out of my budget.

'I give you discount,' she said. 'Half-price with foot massage.'

Finally, I caved in. I was on holidays, after all. So my definitely-not-blind-or-old masseuse led me into a softly lit private room for the body massage. This is fine, I thought. Plenty of day spas in Australia go for this kind of mood lighting. I took off my trousers and shirt, and lay on the table. The rub started off as they usually do, before I felt the oily hands of my masseuse, whose English name was Joanne, start to tug on my boxer shorts. 'Okay?' she said. I nodded, figuring some masseuses prefer you to be naked, and, if I'm honest, starting to figure out that there was something else going on here, but interested to find out what.

It didn't take long. With my boxers now on the floor, I felt Joanne climb up onto the table, straddle my legs and start touching me in places only my girlfriend should touch. When her greased-up hand softly brushed a testicle, I finally shot up and wrapped a towel around myself. Joanne looked surprised.

'You want special massage?'

I blinked. 'Huh?'

'You know,' she said, and started making jerking motions with her hand, as if she was playing a rather vigorous game of scissors paper rock.

Now, there are some guys who are into the whole rub and tug scene, but I'm not one of them. Even if I didn't have a girlfriend, I don't really fancy the idea. For starters, I essentially just don't want to shell out the money. Like going to a car wash, or the dry-cleaners, why pay someone to do something you could just go home and take care of yourself? And there's the whole exploitation thing, which I'm not really comfortable with. It might be a thriving industry throughout the Asian business travel network, but that doesn't mean I want to support it.

Plus, there's that whole girlfriend thing. I haven't exactly been the best boyfriend to some of my exes, but with the Lawyer, I'd decided things were going to change. Each of those previous relationships had gone horribly wrong at some point, and it had taken me this long to figure out that maybe I might have had something to do with that. This time I was going to do it right, even if I was sitting in a massage parlour about 10,000 kilometres from where the Lawyer was tapping away at a keyboard in her office.

So I gave Joanne a polite 'no thanks', pulled on my clothes and made for the door, handing the bewildered manager a wad of notes as I made my way up the stairs and out into the cold light of day.

*

Seeking something slightly more cerebral after that encounter, I decided to do some proper touristy sightseeing. As Pete was no help, I decided to go against my modus operandi for this trip and consult the guidebook. My first choice was a hit – the Propaganda Art Centre, a tiny basement gallery hidden below a block of flats, which housed an incredible collection of original propaganda posters from China's communist past. The posters entreated the Chinese to 'Firmly embrace Mao Zedong Thought in the fight against imperialism', backed up with lots of pictures of strapping Chinese farmers beating up evil troll-looking things wearing US Army badges.

After that, I was privileged to visit what are possibly two of the worst tourist attractions on the entire planet. The first was the Bund Sightseeing Tunnel, a passageway under the Huang Po River that ferries tourists between Pudong and the Bund area. Inside, little cars chug through the tunnel, which is lined with neon lights and flashing signs, accompanied by voices that say things like, 'Meteor storm!' and 'Magma!' as the lights slowly change colour. It's craptacular. And it costs $10. A couple of Norwegians in my carriage were chuckling to themselves at the sheer crapness of the whole thing. 'I think I'm glad I saw this,' one of them said to me.

Next on my list was the Urban Planning Exhibit in the People's Park. Normally, the words 'urban' and 'planning' together sound about as exciting to me as 'eye' and 'gouging', but given Shanghai is going through some monumental changes, I thought it would be pretty interesting to check out. I was wrong. Not only were half of the exhibits 'closed for improvements', but the stuff that was open was mainly just written in Pinyin. Oh, and it was hellishly boring. I had to satisfy myself with trying to get a look at the scale model of

Shanghai while Chinese tour groups barged past me, most being led by guides screaming into megaphones at their groups.

After a few days in Shanghai though, I was starting to get used to the noise. It's always noisy in Shanghai. It might be car horns, cranes, bulldozers, sirens, screaming touts selling 'cheap, cheap Rolex', or, most annoying of all, the intersection attendants carefully patrolling every corner of the pavement. Armed with whistles and fancy white gloves, these attendants stand around at intersections and blow their whistle at pedestrians trying to jaywalk, and cyclists trying to run red lights. They seem to have an abiding passion for their little whistles. Take a step onto the road at the wrong time: '*Tweep tweep!*' Start to run a red light: '*Tweep tw-tweep!*' Shoelace untied: '*Tweeeeeeeep!*' After a while, it just blends into the Shanghai madness.

*

I hadn't learnt my lesson. On the other 'last nights' I'd had with Steve and Maria, I'd gone out drinking until the wee hours as a kind of last hurrah, woken up feeling as if death would be a welcome relief, then packed my bag to head out to the airport. For my last night in China, I was planning to do exactly the same thing. Pete had spent all week telling me what a booze hound he was, and on that last night he planned to prove it.

First though, we had stomachs to line, so we headed with Pete's friend Kyan to a traditional Sichuan place, where we ate duck tongues (kind of gross), bullfrog (very spicy), yabbies (not bad), beef shins (ugly, delicious) and chilli fried rice (pretty hard to mess up). The spice on the bullfrog was whole Sichuan peppers, which blasted a furnace-like heat into my mouth that only straight vodka would put out.

'Right, you ready for this mate?' Pete asked.

'Ready for what?'

'Time to hit Tongren. Remember I wanted to take you there

on the first night? The red light district? We're heading there. Doesn't get any seedier than that!'

The Tongren Lu area is like the Kings Cross of Shanghai, only without the influx of trendy bars. It's just sleaze, pure and simple – a favourite hang-out for business travellers far from home (and their wives).

'We've got pretty much three options here,' Pete said as we jumped out of the cab and started wandering the strip, ignoring the calls of 'Hi, how are you?' coming from the lingerie-clad girls in most of the doorways. 'There's straight-out strip clubs, then bars which are just full of hookers, or there's like a rock-type club which is a bit more relaxed.'

'Let's just check out the rock club for starters, eh?'

I saw straight away why Pete and Kyan liked hanging out at Tongren Lu. We'd barely sat down with beers when a couple of girls almost clambered over each other to get to our table and start talking to us. Well-dressed single white blokes equal money. We had to stop the chat, though, when a stripper came over and made use of the pole I hadn't noticed on our table. With her show over, and most of her clothes on the floor, the stripper then swung off the pole and, somewhat impressively, straight onto the spare seat next to me.

'You like to buy my drink?'

I sighed. I could barely afford my own drinks. 'Okay, what are you having?'

She stood up and yelled at the bar staff: 'Gin and tonic, now!'

The stripper, whose name was Kitty (hello Kitty, etc.), told me she ran her own pole-dancing studio during the day, and danced at night for extra cash.

'Have you ever travelled at all?' I asked.

She frowned, drawing her heavily made-up eyebrows together. 'I really want to, but last year I apply for my pass to travel, and they deny it. Government don't want young single girls to leave, because they don't think they'll come back.'

'Are they right?'

She shrugged. 'I guess so.'

With my wallet emptied on a couple of G&Ts, we headed to a bar called Muse, a swanky place where Shanghai's rich and famous hang out, and where Kyan decided to buy an entire bottle of Grey Goose vodka from the bar, just to fit in. Understandably, my memories of the rest of the night are patchy at best. We stumbled back to Pete's at some point, I threw up, then fell asleep until 1pm the next day.

*

Pete and I said our goodbyes that next afternoon as I prepared to head out to the airport (and Pete prepared to change his heading). I realised I'd been a bit impatient with Pete during my stay – trapped in a confined space with a stranger for five days can probably do that to you – but he was essentially a nice guy; we'd just spent far too much time together. He was probably just as glad to see the back of me.

Five nights, I figured, is much too long to spend with one person you don't really have a lot in common with. But Pete had been unfailingly good-natured about having a freeloading backpacker on his couch for the best part of a week, and extremely generous with his time. He'd even used a precious annual leave day to show me around. You can't ask much more than that.

We shook hands, and I made my way back out onto the mayhem of the Shanghai street, each beep and whistle sounding to my alcohol-rotted brain like the grinding of a chainsaw on corrugated iron. It made me think of the art exhibition I'd seen a few days before at 50 Moganshan Rd, a huge modern art space in the city's north. There, I'd read a sort of philosophical statement from one of the artists, Fang Min (who seemed to like painting giant laughing monks with insects on their faces), attempting to explain her take on Buddhism. She told the story of a man who couldn't stand the noise of his neighbours, so he moved to the country. There, the sound of insects drove him mad, so he moved to a cave. Fang then wrote, 'Peace and serenity depends on our own ability to receive the noise around us and not let it trouble us. All life has the right to exist!'

If you don't get that, I thought, you have no place in Shanghai.

The Real Thailand

'He wants to know if you fell into the squat toilet. I told him you were fine. You were fine, right?'

Thai roosters and I: we ain't no friends. I've had problems with Thai roosters before. Other countries' cocks seem to leave me in peace, but the Thais are pushy little bastards. And loud. The only other time I've been to Thailand, my brother and I had stayed in a hostel in Bangkok which, for some inexplicable reason, had a pet rooster. Every morning, rain, hail or hangover, this thing would wake us up like some sort of devil's alarm clock, screeching outside our bedroom as a ceiling fan slowly ticked above our heads. This trip, it took me all of three nights to get reacquainted.

I'd arrived in Bangkok on a late flight, and spent my first night at the Novotel by the airport, having booked an early flight to the country's north for the next day. Though I'm loath to admit it as a big tough backpacker, it was actually something of a relief to just relax by myself for the night, not having to worry about messing up someone's house, or having to lift my bed up whenever someone wanted to get changed. About my only worry was the fact my credit card had bounced while I was trying to check in.

The next morning I travelled all of 200 metres to the airport, and caught my flight to Ubon Ratchathani, which, to be honest, I still wasn't sure was even the right city, let alone whether anyone would be there to meet me once I arrived. I'd been in email correspondence with a guy called Andrew, who'd told me to fly to a place called Ubon something or other. As I soon found out when I logged on to the Air Asia website, there are two Thai cities that start with 'Ubon'. So I was hoping I'd picked the right one. A good sign was the fact I was the only *falang* – foreigner – on the plane, as from what I could understand from my brief glance at Google Maps one day, this Ubon place was in the middle of nowhere. Most of my fellow passengers seemed to be staring at me as if they couldn't figure out what I was doing on a flight to Ubon Ratchathani – and whether I'd made a mistake trying to board the flight to Phuket – and, in fairness, neither could I.

Touching down at the rickety little airport in Ubon Whatsitsname, I grabbed my bags and headed to the arrival hall, looking for what I assumed would be the only other foreigner in the building. I was right. Andrew's white skin stood out a mile. He stuck a hand out and grinned.

'You must be Ben, right?'

'That's me.'

'You're early! I heard the plane landing so I jumped in the truck to come get you.'

He heard the plane landing? Looked like this was going to be a smaller town than I thought. Andrew, dressed casually in an old T-shirt, board shorts and thongs, slung my day pack over his shoulder and set off towards the almost empty little car park, where he'd left his ute.

'Just throw it in the back, mate,' he said, jerking a thumb at my backpack. 'No need to worry about anyone nicking off with it here.' I slung my pack onto the tray, he gunned the engine, and we set off through Ubon's crumbling streets.

'Now, I dunno what you wanted to do today, but Ubon's not very exciting,' Andrew said, really getting my hopes up. 'The plan is, we're going to take the day off tomorrow, so we'll drive up to the village tonight, then stay there for tomorrow night as well, and head back here on Monday. Today, we're just going to be working on the shop, so you're going to be helping me.' He grinned. 'You like shopping centres, right?'

This section of the trip was going to be a little different to the others. There would be no famous tourist attractions here, no bright lights of the big city. In fact, there'd probably be no lights at all. Sitting in Thailand's north-east, Ubon Ratchathani is a few hours' drive from the Cambodian border to the south, and a few hours to the Laos border in the east. And it's different to your average Thai tourist destination. There'd be no beach trips here, no elephant rides, no full moon parties, no mushroom milkshakes, no buckets of whisky and coke, and no drunken hook-ups with slutty Canadian backpackers. I don't know if that made it any more 'real' than the Thailand I knew, but it was certainly going to be different.

The city itself has a few hundred thousand residents, but I wasn't staying in the city. Andrew was taking me into the wild. The subject line of his email was: 'Come and experience the real Thailand at my place.' I was hooked, particularly after I got around to reading the whole thing.

I live about 600kms north-east of Bangkok. I am the only Westerner in my small village, the only one for many villages actually, where I am seen as a curiosity by most of the adults, and a scary white ghost by all the kids! This place is really unique with many traditional practices since gone from other parts of the country still being carried out here every day.

There was a small problem: Andrew's email had come through late, by which time I'd decided on my itinerary. Time was already tight – how was I going to find an extra week to get to Thailand? Still, it was a no-brainer. The chance to hang out in a tiny Thai village? I couldn't pass that up. So I reworked a few things, carved a few days off Korea and China, and managed to make it happen. Village life, here I come.

Until we made the drive that night to the village, Ban Khum, though, there was work to be done. Since his original invitation, Andrew's circumstances had changed a bit. With his wife, Seerung, plus a Kiwi mate Ben and his Thai wife Nong, they'd bought into a cafe/bakery business in the big city. This would mean a move away from the village eventually, plus a whole lot of work to get the bakery into some sort of shape. The project wasn't Andrew's though, he assured me. It was Seerung's brainchild – he was just along for the ride.

'So what do you do here then?' I asked as we bumped our way towards the cafe.

'Here? Not that much,' Andrew laughed. 'Nah, I do a few things. My wife and I have the cafe in town. We're just setting that up now though. I've also got a plantation of agarwood trees in Laos, which is . . . Actually, I'll tell you more about that later. Then I also part-own a farm in South Australia, and a few properties with tenants too, back in Australia, so I have to manage that. Means it frees me up a fair bit when I'm here, so I can spend some time with the kids.'

'The kids' were Ariya and Marisah, who I would meet later. First though, we were heading to the cafe to see what needed to be done. I soon figured out why Andrew had heard my plane landing – his cafe basically sat at the end of the runway. The whole place shook whenever a plane landed, which, fortunately for their prospects of running a successful business, was only a couple of times a day.

Outside, the cafe looked like a regular European establishment, but inside, it was like a warzone. Tables and chairs were thrown all over the room, a large counter was about three-quarters of the way through being built (or one-quarter of the way through being torn down), and the floorboards were scuffed and dirty. In the small kitchen, four Thai women were working away, stirring, kneading and icing their way through a few different cakes. Seerung, Andrew's wife, smiled and waved a floury hand briefly before getting back to teaching her potential staff how to bake cakes, which seemed to be a trial and error process going by the amount of flour and sugar everywhere.

'Mate, when we got in here, this place was filthy,' Andrew explained. 'We had to pull everything out of the kitchen, and just scrub. We were going to do it ourselves but it was just getting too much, so we hired some local workers to come in and do it. For 100 *baht* an hour, why wouldn't you? There were friggin' rats in here! Huge! We caught one in a trap one night and it was so big that the trap didn't kill it. I had to bash it on the head with a screwdriver. I might be a farm boy, but I'm a bit squeamish with that sorta stuff.'

Andrew was 32, and had moved to Thailand from Kununurra, in northern Western Australia. He'd grown up on the family farm, and, he told me, he hadn't even considered travelling until he hit his 20s.

'My sister was living over in Thailand, so she'd been hassling me to come over for a while,' he said as we climbed back into the ute, shopping list in hand. 'To be honest, I had no interest in Asia at all really. But I decided to come over here and see her anyway.

'When I was eventually leaving after being here a few weeks, you should have seen my sister, it was weird. She was asking all these questions. She's like, "What did you think of the food? What about the traffic? Do you like Thai girls?" I was like, yeah, I like one Thai girl, that one who works downstairs at your hotel! Little did I know that my sister was actually quite good friends with her.

'So my sister goes back to the hotel and tells Seerung that I liked her. Turns out Seerung thought I was handsome or something like that, so my sister gave her my email address and we started emailing. We did that for about a year, and eventually I thought, bugger it, I might as well go and give this a try, see what happens. So I went and saw her, and about a year later we were engaged.

'I lived in Thailand for a while, then she came back to Australia, then we lived in New Zealand for a bit, and now we're living in Thailand. We were in the village for a while, but now we've got this business, so we'll be moving into Ubon I guess.'

Ubon itself was nothing to write home about. Power lines hung dangerously low over the cracking pavements, brightly painted tuk-tuks and little scooters ruled the streets, and no one seemed to be in any hurry to get anywhere or do anything. It was a pleasure to be out of the big city for a while. Andrew, chatting away, had missed a green light, and remained stopped at an intersection.

'Don't worry mate, no one's going to beep us here,' he said. 'I don't think I've ever heard any horns in Ubon. It's just too relaxed.'

We stopped, bizarrely, at a Tesco supermarket to buy a garbage bin and some nappies for Ariya, before calling in to another supermarket, and heading back to the cafe for lunch. Seerung, Ben and Nong were already tucking in by the time we pushed the tinted door open.

'Do you eat chillies, Ben?' a worried-looking Seerung asked in near-perfect English.

'Yeah, for sure, I eat hot stuff all the time.'

'Okay, well, I've made a not-spicy salad for you just in case.'

The Thais are obsessed with chillies, clearly, but they're also convinced that foreigners will never be able to handle them, so I was constantly being asked whether I minded a bit of heat before food was served. Seerung's lunch was typical of the area, apparently, in that it borrowed fairly heavily from Laotian cooking (the people in Seerung's village even spoke Lao). We had cold cuts of grilled chicken, an omelette, a green papaya salad, and sticky rice. The rice is a Laos staple – a gloopy mixture that's cooked by every family in the morning, and eaten with every meal throughout the day. It's stored in little bamboo baskets that you see people carrying everywhere, and it's not reheated, so it gets colder through the day.

Seerung's lunch was incredibly good, by far the best meal I'd had on the trip. I had a slight problem, though: even the 'not spicy' papaya salad was almost tearing a hole through the top of my mouth. Having announced that I was tough enough to take it, though, I had to suffer my pain in silence, sneakily wiping sweat off my brow as I pretended to be unaffected by the little red atom bombs being set off on my soft palate. At some stage, perhaps noticing my distress, one of the girls in the kitchen handed me a large green coconut with a straw sticking out of the top, and I sucked the cool coconut water down like I'd just stumbled in from the Sahara.

After the salads and rice, there was cake. Loads of cake. As Seerung had been trialling different recipes during the morning, we were forced to try them all. Still unable to feel the roof of my mouth, and not having the heart to tell Seerung that I don't really like cake, I had to struggle my way through a chocolate tart, a blueberry cheesecake, a coconut cream cake, a chocolate mud cake with a bizarre gelatinous icing, and some profiterole-type things. They were uniformly delicious, and exactly what I didn't need. It was all I could do to roll myself out of the cafe and back into Andrew's ute for more chores.

Andrew and I spent the rest of the day buzzing around Ubon, picking up supplies for the cafe, haggling at the market for some pork and squid to take back to the village, then going to pick up the kids for the two-hour drive.

I was a bit nervous about this bit. See, kids kind of frighten me. It's just that I don't really have any experience with them. My family's small, just limited to Mum, Dad and my younger brother Tim, so we've never had small kids around the house. None of my close friends had kids yet, meaning I hadn't had to deal with any of their offspring either. I even tend to avoid friends with kids, assuming that now they'd heard the pitter-patter of tiny feet, there would be no more socialising. All the things I enjoy doing can't really be done with a few toddlers running around.

So I was a little worried about accepting an invitation from someone with a wife and kids. It'd be all nappy changing and painful screaming, not beer drinking and chatting. And what are you supposed to say to kids? Or do I ignore them altogether? Am I allowed to pick them up, or play with them?

As you can see, I was a rank amateur, and I wasn't sure how this was all going to go down.

We pulled up outside the hotel where Andrew and Seerung were staying while they set up the cafe, and Andrew ran up to grab Ariya and Marisah, who were accompanied by their nanny, a Thai girl – and Seerung's cousin – called Joy. Joy, for a person so named, seemed to display an amazing lack of the stuff. As it turned out though, that was more a product of the shyness a lot of Thais display than any lack of personality. The closer we got to the village – also her home – the more joyful Joy seemed to get.

Stopping at a town called Det Udom for dinner, I got my first taste of the rock stardom that awaited in Ban Khum. As we sat down, a row of heads, cartoon-style, poked out from the kitchen door. Two waitresses scrambled to be the ones to serve us. Their attention, however, was as much on the two girls as Andrew and I. Having Western and Thai blood, the girls look Thai, but have much lighter skin than most of the locals – a prized trait. A waitress ran her hands through Marisah's curly hair as she took our order, and I noticed the Thai music playing in the background had immediately been replaced with what was probably the only Western CD they owned: Savage Garden. I'm sure it was a lovely gesture made in our honour, but I'd rather stick chillies in my ears than listen to Darren Hayes croon about lost love one more time.

Over dinner – steamed barramundi, fried rice, stir-fried vegetables – Seerung told me the story of Andrew going to meet her dad.

'In Thailand, you don't go to meet the dad until it is very serious,' she said. 'So I didn't introduce Andrew for a long time.'

'Which I was fine with,' he interjected.

'My sister had a foreign boyfriend as well, and my dad really didn't like this,' Seerung explained. 'He wouldn't even address him for a long time. He would come out to our village, and my dad wouldn't look at him when he was talking to him. I know for Western people, this is really annoying.

'But after Andrew asked me to marry him, I had to take him back to the village. Dad was much better with him, they got on almost straight away. But he had to meet the whole family on that trip, it was hard.'

About as hard as Seerung had had it in Australia, apparently. I asked Andrew later in the trip about the stigma of Western guys with Thai wives, and he admitted it hadn't been easy taking her to Kununurra.

'I had to set about half the town straight,' he laughed. 'Country town, mate, things get around pretty quickly. But you see why there's a stigma. Even around Ubon, there's definitely this element of dodgy old Western blokes with young Thai wives. You can spot 'em straight away. Blokes who were bad apples at home, who've come over here and married a prostitute or something.

'The Thais don't get it. They don't get the Westerners with the prostitutes. They're like "Why are they doing that?" I can see where they're coming from.

'So there were a few people in Kununurra that got the wrong end of the stick, but Seerung had the right idea: she just said, "Why do you care?" It's just this idea that people get in their head I guess.'

'Did Seerung have any problems like that in the village?'

'She doesn't care,' Andrew said. 'She's like, "They know I'm not a prostitute, so who cares?"'

Not every marriage between Westerners and Thais works out as well as Andrew and Seerung's. Foreigners aren't allowed to own land in Thailand, and Andrew told me there had been plenty of cases of Thais taking Western husbands, buying land – which has to be in the wife's name – and then doing a runner.

'The blokes haven't got a leg to stand on,' Andrew chuckled. 'I mean, if Seerung decided to, she could have our place to herself tomorrow. But some blokes are pretty dumb. It's like, you're 65 and nothing going for you, and this young Thai girl wants to marry you. What do you think's going on?'

From Det Udom, we motored on into the night. 'Hey, check this out,' Andrew said, pulling down the sun visor and showing me the 100 baht note wedged into the plastic pocket. 'Bribe money. Always a good idea to have that on you. The cops will just pull you over for no reason. Some of them are pretty good about it, but some want to have a go at the foreigner. You just offer them an "on-the-spot fine".'

As we drove on, the sealed bitumen road underneath us was gradually turning into potholed tarmac, which eventually gave way to a narrow dirt road, leading us further and further away from civilisation. Andrew turned to where Seerung was sitting in the back, and grinned. 'Geez, Ben's pretty trusting isn't he, Seerung?'

I laughed. 'Yeah, but so are you guys.'

Of more immediate concern than Andrew's turning nasty and knifing me in the middle of the Thai wilderness was his choice of music. He was an unashamed country music fan, and was treating us to the full gamut – from Garth Brooks, to Lee Kernaghan, to some bloke called Colin Buchanan, whom, Andrew explained, he'd once sat next to on a flight to Broome. It was a surreal experience driving through a foreign land, listening to Lee Kernaghan croon about his sick dog while the two little girls sang along happily in the back. I'll bet Kernaghan has no idea of the following he's established in north-eastern Thailand.

'Okay, tell me about this agarwood plantation,' I said to Andrew, as much to take my mind off the country twangs than anything.

'Ah, right. Okay. So there's this stuff called agarwood, right.

It's pretty easy to grow, but that's just the start. My brother and I have gone into business together, and we've got this plantation over in Laos, which we've had going for a few years now. Basically, if you can make the trees sick, they'll produce this black resin in the middle of the wood, as kind of a defence mechanism. And that resin is what you want. You can use it as incense. The rich Arabs go nuts for the stuff. It's really rare, really hard to produce, so it's literally worth more than its weight in gold. I don't really get it myself, but the Arabs love it, so I'm trying to give it to them.

'What happened was, I've met this Vietnamese bloke who reckons he's come up with a way of making the trees sick, so they produce this black stuff. We're just in the middle of trialling that now, seeing how much of the stuff the trees produce and whether it's going to be viable to farm them or not. Of course, the other problem is that the Lao workers we've got on the plantation keep stealing anything that's not bolted down, but that's another story.'

Andrew later burnt some of the resin for me to smell. It was okay, but much like any other incense to my untrained nose. I certainly wouldn't want to spend thousands of dollars of oil money on it.

Finally, after two-and-a-half hours of rattling through the bush, we arrived at the village, although it took a sharp eye to pick it. There were no lights on as we pulled into the single concreted street at 9pm, and no one about either.

'You don't see many young people here,' Seerung said from the back seat as Andrew pulled the car under a raised house. 'It's either young children or older people. When most people finish school, they move to Bangkok. They work there and send money home to their families. That's what I did. Except I was studying as well, so I couldn't really send money back very often. Maybe 1000 baht when I could. I never used to buy nice clothes or shoes or anything. I just couldn't bring myself to do it when I knew my family were still struggling in the village. That's just the way it is.'

Seerung seemed to be the rebel in her family, or at least the most free-thinking. While most of her relatives stayed in the village, she had moved to Bangkok, worked for two years to save money to go to university, then studied for two years while still working, took a year off to earn more money, then finished her studies. She was working in a hotel just after that when she met Andrew, and so had never put those studies into practice. The cafe was her chance to do that.

We lugged our gear upstairs, which was spartan to say the least. If Andrew was ever robbed, he'd lose a grand total of one TV and a stand, a dining room table, and a couple of pillows. I had my own bedroom, which had a small bookcase, and a thin mattress on the tiled floor.

'We only built the place a few months ago, so we haven't had time to really move in properly,' Andrew explained. 'The guys we got to build it, they'd never worked with concrete before. Just wood. They didn't tell us that of course, just gave it a red hot go. So the place isn't quite square. Look in the kitchen, you can see by the tiles that it's all a bit wonky.' He sighed. 'Oh well, as long as it stays up.'

*

Next morning, I heard my rooster. By 'morning', I don't mean it was light. It was about 4am when I heard the 'ERGH A ER A EEEEERRRRRGH!' I could have sworn it was that same Bangkok rooster, come back to pester me on my next visit to its country.

Just when I thought I was drifting back to sleep, the 6am town gossip kicked in. With no printing press for a newspaper – or computers for email – the only way for the town to get its news is for the village headman to get on the loudspeaker each morning and announce things of interest to the entire town. Things like council meetings, school issues, vaccination drives – anything important the headman decides everyone needs to hear about. It sounded like a fairly reasonable idea, although why it had to be done at 6am was beyond me – maybe the general population had been up for a few hours by the time the five minutes of badly amplified Lao was blasted around the village.

I stumbled out of bed bleary-eyed and wandered downstairs to the open area under the house, which is where most villagers spend their spare time. If a house is raised, it will always have the bottom open, and that's where most of the cooking and general living is done. It makes sense, given it's so damn hot. But there's a social side to it too – lives are lived out in the open here, and people wander from house to house all day, swapping gossip and sharing food. Seerung's brother Kum, a wiry Thai guy in a singlet and shorts, was already up doing chores when I wandered down, and, noticing the distressed falang stumbling down the stairs, pointed me in the direction of hot water and instant coffee. Kum, you're a lifesaver. Some morning rituals are truly global.

Kum was a farmer, working rice paddies and a small pig herd near town. He used to live in one of the wall-less shacks down the street, but moved into Andrew's house when it was built.

I made a quick cuppa, and walked out onto the street to have my first real look at the village. It didn't take long. Ban Khum was made up of one roughly concreted street with houses in varying states of disrepair clinging to the roadside. Andrew's was clearly the nicest, perched on its concrete stilts with the buzz of electricity and, well, walls. Some of the other houses were just a wooden floor and an iron roof. No walls. There was also mud everywhere thanks to the rain the night before, with a few mangy dogs and a brown cow snuffling through it by the side of the road. I found the bastard rooster, proudly strutting around flaring its feathers, still cock-a-doodle-dooing away, and chased him around, with *khao pad gai* – chicken fried rice – on my mind, but to no avail.

The human inhabitants were all up and about. There was a little market set up down the street, selling the sort of knick-knacks that we take for granted in the Western world, but which aren't easy to come by when you live in a tiny Thai village, like wash basins and scrubbing brushes.

Andrew, dressed in a Wallabies jersey, was just getting the kids up. 'Mornin', mate,' he smiled, a little slice of Aussie in a very foreign world. We had some breakfast – cornflakes for the foreigners, sticky rice and fish for the Thais – then took the girls for a walk around town. Actually, 'around' is the wrong word; more like up and back. People gaped and an entire family on a scooter almost ploughed into a tree as they swivelled to watch the two falang walking on the other side of the street.

'When I first arrived, I reckon I was probably only the second foreigner they'd ever seen here,' Andrew said. 'You just don't get tourists here. It's impossible for them to come. I mean, where would they stay? The nearest hotel is about an hour's drive away, and even that's pretty average. I've actually been considering getting something started here. I've even looked at a few properties. I'd want to make it real schmick, get the rich tourists from the States in here. It'd be all-inclusive. They'd stay for, say, five nights in a real nice place overlooking a rice paddy, and just soak up village life. We'd take them on excursions of the area, they could see how the farms work, see how people live, and it'd give some of the locals here work as well. I just need the right property. It has to look over a rice paddy, otherwise what are you doing here?'

I nodded, happy that some of the locals would probably benefit from a venture like that, but worried that this little piece of countryside could be spoiled by camera-toting Seppos running around in polo shirts and bum bags experiencing 'real' Thailand. (I'm the only camera-toting tourist allowed to spoil 'real' Thailand.)

Down the end of the street, Seerung's sister Bam and her husband Sibun ran a little shop from under their house. It wasn't much – fuel was sold by the litre in empty Coke bottles, cigarettes were sold singly, and you could get a shot of *lao khao*, the hideous Thai/Lao rice whisky, for 10 baht. As we sat on the raised bamboo platform at the front of the shop, a few locals pulled their scooters up, poured a shot of lao khao into the communal glass, necked it, wiped their chins and hopped back on their bikes. I was forced to try some of it later, and briefly considered swigging from the plastic bottles of petrol to wash the taste out of my mouth. Sibun almost toppled over laughing, then, once he'd composed himself, said something in Thai. Fortunately, Andrew could interpret.

'He wants to know if you like Thailand,' Andrew said.

'Tell him I love it.'

'He doesn't believe you. He says you should give him 10 baht to prove it.'

I looked over at Sibun and saw him chuckling with mirth, his legs tucked up underneath him on the bamboo platform.

'Now he wants to know if you have a girlfriend.'

I nodded, smiling.

'He wants to know why you aren't married.'

'Tell him to give me some time.'

Sibun looked shocked.

'He wants to know what she does, but I don't know the word for lawyer, so I've told him she works in a court. I think he now thinks she's a judge, and he's saying she'll put you in jail if you don't marry her.'

'Tell him he might be right,' I said, while Sibun went through a pantomime of putting handcuffs on me as he chuckled away.

It turned out Sibun and Bam had been to Australia, having worked on Andrew's dad's farm in Kununurra for six months a few years ago. Traditionally, Thai kids are expected to look after their parents in their old age. However, Sibun and Bam had been unable to have children, so they'd been worrying about their retirement until Andrew and Seerung came along. In six months on the farm they earned as much as they would in 10 years of running their shop in Ban Khum, and now have a handy nest egg for their later years.

'They were machines over there, wouldn't take a day off,' Andrew recalled. 'Can't blame 'em, I guess, when they're earning a week's wages every hour. Geez it was funny when we got to Bangkok Airport though. Neither of them had ever seen an escalator before.

Bam didn't want to even get on it, she walked up the stairs. Then we got to Darwin, and they're both shit-scared of the Aborigines. Never seen anyone so dark I guess. They got used to it all after a while.'

We left Sibun still cackling away, and headed to the ute. Andrew had been bitten by a dog a few months ago, and had to have regular rabies vaccinations at the local hospital.

'That bloody dog,' he said, shaking his head. 'It bit me, so Seerung went straight to the owners, and they were all sorry and everything, and paid for my shots. So then I told them we just had to keep an eye on the dog, and as long as it wasn't showing any signs of sickness after two weeks, I could stop getting the injections. So we go back two weeks later to see them, and they've already gotten rid of the dog! The hospital keep asking me what the dog's like, and I keep having to explain to them that it's gone. It's ridiculous.'

'So they killed the dog?'

'Nup, gave it to the bucket truck.'

'The what?'

'Bucket truck. It's this truck that comes through town, probably twice a week, and on the bottom there's a whole lot of dogs, and on top a whole lot of buckets. If you've got a dog you don't want, you just give it to them, and they give you a bucket as payment.'

'So where do the dogs go?'

'Vietnam. Trust me, I've seen it. The truck goes to the Laos border, and then they chuck the dogs on a different truck. I've seen that one going through Laos, just near the Vietnam border. So somehow they get them into Vietnam, and then into bellies. Crazy, huh?'

'Shit, yeah. Um, why do they give them buckets?'

'Don't know! Maybe some bloke had too many buckets, and that's how it got started.'

The town was a sleepy little place about half an hour's drive from Ban Khum. There was one central market selling fresh produce, with a few restaurants surrounding it. We grabbed lunch at a place Andrew knew, having khao pad gai – sans my rooster – plus a pork dish, and *pad see euw*. Those three, plus a couple of cokes, cost us 95 baht, or about four Australian dollars.

'She only wanted to charge us 85, but I managed to talk her up to 95,' Andrew explained. 'That's Thai hospitality for you.'

After getting the rabies shot, we headed back to the village and joined Kum on the bare lounge room floor to watch Muay Thai boxing. Kum, wiry and muscular, looked like he could have been a Muay Thai fighter, and spent the next hour laying bets on the fights with Andrew. It all looked pretty repetitive to me – two little guys wearing tassels enter the ring, spend about 10 minutes prancing around in a pre-fight ritual, then go three rounds of hugging and kneeing each other in the chest, then a winner is announced. Watching the fights with Thai commentary, I tried to pick the winner at the end of each bout, and failed miserably every time. Lucky I wasn't betting.

What sounded far more entertaining on Thai TV was the crime scene re-enactment shows. These are no ordinary re-enactments though, as they usually star both the actual perpetrator and actual victim of the crimes. I'm sure it's designed to embarrass the perp, but it doesn't sound much fun for the victim. And no one could give me a good answer on what they do for murders. Exhume the corpse and do it *Weekend At Bernie's*-style?

As evening fell we headed back with the family to Sibun's house, where we grilled some pork ribs over hot coals, and Seerung made up a salad of vermicelli noodles, pork, squid, mint, coriander, chilli, lime and fish sauce. There was a festival on down the road at the local Buddhist temple, so plenty of people were calling in for a fortifying lao khao and a gawk at the falang before heading up to pray. The food was amazing, and as we sat cross-legged on the bamboo platform under the house and gnawed on the pork bones, sipping Leo beers Thai-style (with ice in) as the sun went down, I had to admit, life in the village was pretty darn good. There would be times on this trip where

I would question the wisdom of my decision to ditch my job at *FHM* and follow my weird dream around the world. There would be times when I'd be stuck in some cramped apartment making chit-chat with someone I had nothing in common with, wishing I was interviewing a bikini model about her ideal cup size . . . But this was definitely not one of those times.

Sibun, meanwhile, was taking his chance to grill me again.

'He's asking what you've been eating,' Andrew translated. 'I told him only Thai food, and he's very impressed.'

This was turning out to be a common theme. Thais are obsessed with food. They seem to be constantly eating, planning the next feast as they're polishing off the last.

'We always talk about food,' Seerung confessed. 'We talk about what we've just eaten, we talk about what we're going to make the next day. There's even a saying: "Have you eaten rice yet?" It's what we say instead of, "How are you?"'

Feeling my stomach giving me warning signals, I ducked off to the toilet. This, again, fascinated Sibun.

'Haha! He wants to know if you fell into the squat,' Andrew said when I got back. 'I told him you were fine. You were fine, right?'

I nodded. Sibun beamed, and looked even more impressed. He would have been showing me a mouthful of teeth if he'd had any left.

*

With dinner over (and another shot of lao khao down my throat) Andrew and I took the kids up to the temple to check out the ceremony. It was there that the true rock stardom of being a falang in north-eastern Thailand kicked in. As the four of us walked into the packed temple grounds, the worshippers all briefly forgot about the giant gold Buddha they were supposed to be there to pray to, and began pointing and whispering. Ariya and Marisah were once again the main attractions though, all the worshippers breaking into huge grins and choruses of '*sawatdee-kaap*' (hello) when one of the girls waved to them.

While the Thais had all come down to pay their respects to the Buddha, Andrew had come down for a sneak peek at a deity of another kind. It turned out Thai pop singer Dai Orithai (don't worry, I'd never heard of her before, and nor have I since), was from Ban Khum's neighbouring village, and had dropped into town for the festival.

'She's basically like the Delta Goodrem of Thailand,' Andrew explained as we picked our way among the rows of white prayer strings dangling from the trees. 'She's all wholesome and family friendly – which explains what she's doing here – but she's also bloody hot. I've been asking for someone to introduce me, but it hasn't happened so far.'

We searched the temple grounds in vain for an hour or so, spending more time fending off Thais who wanted to touch Ariya and Marisah's hair than actually looking for our pop star, before giving up and jumping on the scooter to go back to the village, where it was almost time to put the girls to bed. Before that though, there was time for me to throw a ball for them to catch in the bare living room, while I talked to Seerung about her village.

'It's changed so much now,' she said, sitting at the table alone and sipping a coffee. 'Before, when I was a kid, it was much more friendly. I know to you it seems friendly now, but look at us here, upstairs watching TV. When I was young, even when my father was still alive a few months ago, it was different. If you had a buffalo and you worked your farm, you'd lend it to your friends the next day. Now, no one has buffalo, they have tractors, and you wouldn't lend one out, people have to pay for them.

'At night, people used to walk around the streets singing. Or people would come around just to talk to my dad. They'd all sit out the front there and just talk. At about 5 am, my father would get out of bed, stoke the fire, take his seat at the front, and it would start again. Now, everyone has TVs, so there's no need to talk. Everyone just stays in. It's very sad.'

Seerung might have been disappointed, but I was absolutely smitten with the place, and the people. Sibun, despite us sharing no more than three words of a common language, couldn't have been more welcoming, and I felt like I'd been taken in as the village's own. I could expect this sort of generosity from Andrew, who'd invited me, but here I was being taken in by a whole community. Everyone had been friendly, laughing and smiling with the dumb foreigner (or just pointing at me). They'd shared their food with me, drunk at the same table as me, and never asked for a thing in return, despite the fact it was painfully obvious I was from a far different, more privileged world.

As I threw the ball for Ariya and Marisah, who giggled hysterically before tossing the ball back in my direction, I heard Seerung say, 'Okay, last one, then Na Ben needs a break.'

I'd heard Kum referred to as 'Na Kum' earlier in the day, so I'd figured it was a kind of polite title you give to older people. 'What does "Na" mean?' I asked Andrew.

He gave me a smile. 'Uncle,' he said. 'Uncle Ben.'

I have to say, my little heart nearly broke.

*

We left the village early the next morning, as quietly as we'd come. It was 6am, but the news had already been read, the sticky rice already cooked and packed into bamboo baskets, and the residents had headed off to their farms to tend the crops. We drove back to Ubon Ratchathani – singing along to Lee Kernaghan, of course – for Seerung and Andrew to get back to setting up the cafe, and me to catch up on some emails and phone calls in town.

I had a phone full of messages from the Lawyer, convinced I'd been kidnapped by Thai bandits in the jungle. I called to reassure her that the most frightening thing I'd seen over the last couple of days had been Sibun's gap-toothed smile. I had time for a quick sampling of about 67 more of Seerung's cake creations, and then checked in to my flight back to Bangkok, where I almost had to declare my stomach as excess baggage.

After a few nights in the wilderness, Bangkok stunned me. I had a day to kill there before my flight to Bangladesh, and I felt a bit like Sibun and Bam must have the first time they were faced with an escalator at the airport. It was a different world, with bustling streets, trains running overhead, cars and tuk-tuks zipping by – and tourists. Actual tourists.

Plus, with the tourists came the people whose job it is to annoy the tourists. As I wandered around outside the walls of Bangkok's Grand Palace, trying to find the entrance, several Thais approached to tell me, 'Sorry, palace closed until 5pm.'

'That's okay,' I said. 'I'm just going for a walk around the outside.'

Sure enough, when I did actually find the entrance, it had been open all day, and was still open. A sign on the palace wall warned tourists to: 'Beware of wily strangers.' Wily strangers? Hadn't met any of those in the last few days.

So what is the 'real' Thailand, I wondered. The wily strangers of Bangkok? The wasted backpackers of Kho Pha-Ngan? Or the friendly locals of Ban Khum?

I still don't know the answer. But I know which one I'd prefer to visit.

Rats, Roaches and Roadkill

'I guess things are fairly stable. There hasn't been a suicide bombing here since 2007, so that's pretty good.'

What the hell was I doing in Bangladesh? It was a question more than a few of my friends had asked. It was a question my mum had asked, several times. It was a question even the Bangladeshi cab driver I had in Sydney before I began my trip had asked.

We'd jumped in his cab, and the Lawyer, liquored up and chatty, had started asking questions.

'So, where are you from, sir?'

The cabby glanced in his rear-view mirror. 'Me? I am from Bangladesh.'

'Oh, really? My friend here is going to your country soon.'

'You are going to Bangladesh?' he said, turning to me in the front seat. I nodded. 'What, for work?'

'No, for a holiday.'

He actually laughed out loud. 'No one goes to Bangladesh for a holiday.'

'Some must, surely. What's there to see?'

He shook his head slowly. 'Violence and corruption, my friend. Violence and corruption.'

Not quite the rap I'd been hoping to hear. But still, I was excited about Bangladesh. I had my reasons for visiting. For one, someone had offered me a place to stay. But it was more than that. Someone had also offered me a place in Kathmandu, which fit my itinerary just as well, but I'd decided to go with Bangers. Lyrian's email was simple:

> I just saw your plea and thought, hell yeah, what my couch needs is a slightly alcoholic writer on it for a night or two. The only catch is that you'll have to bring your own liquor since Bangladesh is a dry country. Anyway, the offer stands if you head this way. A few nights on a couch in Chittagong, Bangladesh is yours.

I'd really wanted to go to India, truth be known, but I hadn't received any invitations by the time Lyrian's email dropped into my inbox. Bangladesh, I thought. Well, the place is literally engulfed by India, so I'm sure it will be the next best thing. Then there was the fact Lyrian was in Chittagong, a port city my dad had often talked about visiting when he was working on ships in his 20s. I'd spent my childhood listening to his tales of roaming its dusty streets on cycle rickshaws, eating bizarre foods and meeting strange people.

Plus, I'd promised myself on this trip that I would visit at least a few countries that I would never normally think of travelling to, and Bangladesh fit the bill perfectly. I'd never even considered going there before this. Almost all I knew about it was that it would probably be like India, and that its residents would be into cricket. Oh, and that there had been a mutiny and subsequent massacre of 80 soldiers there a few weeks before I arrived.

That last bit was one of the reasons why I was soon sitting at the little wooden table in the kitchen of Lyrian's Chittagong flat, asking myself the very same question all my saner friends had been asking for months: What the hell was I doing in Bangladesh?

Lyrian, an Australian who worked for one of the local aid organisations, had cracked the bottle of gin I'd bought her in Bangkok duty free, poured a couple of drinks, and launched unbidden into a list of the ills I was likely to encounter in the country she called home.

'The UN, apparently, once described it as "one billion people's toilet",' she explained, probably enjoying the look on my face. 'You've basically got northern India, Pakistan, Nepal and bits of Afghanistan, and where do you think all the crap in their rivers flows into? The Bay of Bengal. Where we are. So that explains why it stinks a bit.'

I went to comment, but Lyrian wasn't done.

'How's your stomach? I'd be a bit careful if you can – the stomach bugs here are vicious, and a lot of Westerners get them. I've been here six months and have managed to stay out of hospital. You get pretty sick though. It's just part of life here. I reckon I'm probably healthy for about six days a month. All my friends have been in hospital. I thought I was going to have to go the other night, I was that close, but then I just started feeling better. You don't worry about it too much. It might bother you for a few hours in the morning, but after that it's fine. I just try not to eat out too much. I do pretty much all my own cooking here, so it's okay.'

I glanced doubtfully at the ratty kitchen we were sitting in.

'Oh yeah, cockroaches are a massive problem here. There's just no way to get rid of them. They're everywhere.'

As if on cue, a massive black roach scuttled across the kitchen floor. Lyrian barely glanced at it, but I followed its progress across the tiles closely. 'Um . . . Do you want me to kill that?'

Lyrian shrugged. 'You can, but there'll be more. You've just gotta get over it, there's no other way. I couldn't deal with the rat though.'

'The rat?'

'Yeah, there was a rat coming out of that drainpipe,' she said, pointing to a drain in the kitchen wall that had a two-litre bottle of water stuffed into it, which was in turn being held in place with an empty vodka bottle. 'I couldn't deal with that, man, so I came up with a little solution. Seems to be working so far.'

I gulped. Lyrian, however, was just hitting her stride.

'I'll give you some bug spray to take to bed with you, in case any cockroaches decide to attack. It's not a bad idea to give your room a spray anyway actually, 'cause it's dengue fever season with the mozzies at the moment. I know a couple of Westerners who've had it, and it knocks you around. There's malaria too, but that doesn't seem to be as prevalent. Have you had the rabies shots?'

I shook my head.

'Right, probably want to avoid the dogs then. Some of them can be pretty vicious, and people have died of rabies here. I wouldn't be too worried – just, like, cross the street if you see any stray dogs, that sort of thing.'

By now I had my head in my hands, staring glumly into the distance as Lyrian continued.

'Street crime's definitely on the up. You know it used to be under military rule here? Yep, but now we have a proper government, so the law and order isn't what it used to be. It's mainly opportunistic, people getting mugged at knifepoint, that kind of thing. I wouldn't go out on my own after 9pm, but that's more being a girl than anything else. Still, it's a good idea to be home by then.

'The mutiny seems to be over now though. I had to stay in the house for a couple of days, we were all ready to get shipped back home, but it worked out okay. It's going through the courts now, so we'll . . .'

She continued talking. By now though, I was making a little checklist of all the Bangladeshi nasties in my head: rabies, dengue fever, malaria, rats, cockroaches, street crime, general filthiness, vicious stomach bugs . . .

What the hell *was* I doing in Bangladesh?

*

I'd been in the country about 45 seconds before Bangladeshis began exerting their particular charms on me. The wheels were still moving on our plane when the man next to me leapt out of his seat and pulled his suitcase down from the overhead compartment, straight onto my head. 'Ooh, sorry, sorry,' he said. This, coupled with the fact there were several mobile phones ringing while we were still in the air, gave me a fair indication of what Bangladeshis thought of rules.

Outside the terminal in Dhaka, I accepted an offer from a chatty Bangladeshi with a mouthful of rotting gums to drive me to the bus station for 300 *taka*, or about three Aussie dollars. He spent the rest of the trip through Dhaka's nerve-shatteringly busy streets alternately watching where he was going and turning to talk to me to try to persuade me to stay in Dhaka for a few nights so he could be my guide.

'My friend is expecting me in Chittagong,' I told him, 'so I have to leave today.'

I then boarded the bus south to Chittagong, and began what would become The Scariest Bus Ride of My Entire Life. Now, I've had some pretty hair-raising experiences on roads, not least of which was the Vietnamese bus driver who steered with his knees while he smoked and talked on his mobile, while also overtaking other buses on blind corners as he swept through the Vietnamese mountains. But still, Bangladesh can mount the podium and receive its prize.

'Just a word of advice,' Lyrian had written in another email. 'If you're going to get a bus from Dhaka to Chittagong, don't sit at the front. It's better you don't see what's going on up there.' I had this in mind as I picked my way to the back of the bus, grabbed a window seat, and stared in jet-lagged confusion as a man with a huge video camera walked down the aisle, filming everyone on board. Am I starring in a promotional video, I wondered.

Lyrian's advice was good, except for one thing: my window seat was on the driver's side, placing me in the middle of the road, where I could still witness what I was certain would be my bloody, horrible death over and over again for the six hours it took to drive the 250 kilometres to Chittagong, Bangladesh's southern hub.

There are a few problems with the road linking Dhaka and Chittagong. The first is that it's just two lanes all the way. The second is that thanks to Bangladeshis' almost complete reliance on the bus networks, there are hundreds and hundreds of buses using the road at any one time, plus the usual network of trucks and regular cars. The third problem, which directly relates to the other two, is that in most places, the road hasn't been built big enough for two buses to pass each other safely, meaning at least one will be forced onto the verge at high speed whenever they pass. That'll be the verge that's constantly filled with pedestrians, rickshaws, markets, bits of debris . . . you name it.

Then there's the small problem of Bangladeshi bus drivers having absolutely no regard for their lives or anyone else's. Their attitude seems to be, 'If I have my hand on the horn, I have right of way', which would be fine, if everyone else didn't think the same thing. So you end up with buses travelling about 80km/h, horns blaring like mad, overtaking trucks directly into oncoming traffic, expecting that traffic to swerve out of the way. When you meet another bus coming the other way, there's a horrifying game of chicken until someone swerves back into the lane they're supposed to be in at the very last second, only to pull straight out again into the other lane to get past whatever's in the way. More than a few times I saw two buses, side by side, speeding headlong into two more buses, side by side. It was horrifying.

To keep my eyes off the oncoming traffic, I watched the

scene oustide the window. The first thing that struck me was that Bangladesh was poor – really poor. It's classed as a developing country, but I didn't see any development going on. The people tilling the fields and washing in the stagnant ponds by the side of the road were mostly dressed in rags, and looked to be on subsistence living at best.

At the rest stop – a must on a 250-kilometre journey, apparently – I also discovered that Bangladesh isn't exactly groaning under the weight of tourist dollars. You can usually tell how many tourists come to a country by how long the locals spend staring at you. Go to London or New York, and no one will give you a second glance. During our 20-minute stop, though, I think most passengers spent the entire time lingering out the front, staring at the *badeshi*. The attention I'd got in rural Thailand had nothing on this.

*

Six buttock-clenching hours later, at 8pm, I stumbled off the bus, probably still holding the two armrests I'd been clutching the entire trip, and spilled out into the seething mass of humanity that is Chittagong.

There are 4.5 million people in Chittagong, making it about the same size as Sydney, but the city has just the one set of traffic lights – which don't work. There are barely any cars either: just buses, auto-rickshaws (known as CNGs for the natural gas they run on) and cycle rickshaws, honking their horns and dinging their bells in mad attempts to cling to their little patch of dirt.

It was overwhelming, but I had a more immediate problem as I searched the dark night: how was I going to find Lyrian? All my meetings so far had gone quite smoothly. In Bangladesh, however, my mobile wasn't working. I had an address for Lyrian, but how was I going to get there? I hadn't been in contact with Lyrian for a week. Who knew what she was up to now? I decided to try to call her to get some directions, so I managed to find a little mobile phone shop down a dusty alley near where I'd been dropped off.

'I need to call my friend please,' I said, probably a little desperately, to the Bangladeshi behind the counter, who was coolly flicking a gigantic cockroach off his button-up shirt.

'You have a number?'

I passed it over, relieved he spoke English. 'Hmm . . . I don't think this is a right number,' he said, punching it into a mobile phone on the desk. He paused to listen. 'No, this is not a right number. You have another one?'

'That's all I've got.'

'Ah. Are you on your own?'

'Yes.'

'Ah. Show me this address.'

I passed it over. He held it out in front of him to study.

'Okay, this is a right address.'

There was a pause. He yelled something at one of the crowd of 20 or so people out the front of his shack watching the big white guy making a phone call. My phone guy paused again, thinking.

'So, maybe I can get a rickshaw to this place,' I said, hopefully.

'Yes, yes,' he replied, still hanging on to my address book.

'I will show the rickshaw wallah this address?'

'No, they are all illiterate. It is okay, I help you.'

Grabbing a spare piece of paper, he wrote out the address in Bangla (I assume), then led me through the crowd of rickshaw wallahs out the front of the shop. After a few minutes of talking to some very confused-looking people, he settled on a driver.

'He knows where to go?' I asked.

My man gave me a typically Indian wobble of the head, which can mean just about anything. 'No. But he will ask someone else when he gets close. Here, this is my phone number,' he said, passing me a slip of paper. 'Call me if you need any more help. I am Mohammad. I hope you enjoy Bangladesh.'

As Mohammad disappeared back into his cockroach-infested

shop, my rickshaw wallah leapt onto the bike, I clambered up onto the wooden seat and we set off. It was a tortuous journey through the crowded streets, during which the wallah regularly had to jump off and push the bike to get us up hills, and stop almost as frequently to ask for directions through the dark alleys. Finally, after three or four wrong turns and a lot of confused conversations with fellow locals, we pulled up outside a dark house at the end of an alley, and I rang the bell. After a long pause, I heard a click, and a white face appeared at the doorway.

'You must be Ben! Did you have any trouble getting here?'

Lyrian, dressed only in flimsy pyjamas, let me into the house past the gaping rickshaw wallah. She sat me down at her kitchen table to enjoy a stiff gin, while giving me the lowdown on the perils of living in Bangladesh. Lyrian worked in communications on NGO projects dealing with everything from basic nutrition to women's empowerment. I asked what her friends in Sydney had said when she announced she was moving to Bangladesh for a year.

Lyrian laughed. ' "What the hell are you doing in Bangladesh?" was the main one. My mum barely spoke to me for a few days. But they know this is me. Ever since I was probably 21, I'd always said I'd spend a year as a volunteer somewhere. So here I am. I applied for here, Laos and Cambodia, but I'm happy I ended up here.

'I mean, sometimes I sit here in the dark during another power cut, reading a book by candlelight and dying for a beer, and I think I miss my nice easy life back in Stanmore. But I adore this job. Adore it. I liked my job back home, but this is incredible. My only worry is, how am I going to go back to living in a first-world country after this?'

Pretty easily, I thought, as I looked around the house. It was a top-floor apartment annexed from a house owned by a Buddhist guy who was apparently one of the few land owners in town who could get his head around a bunch of single white girls all living together – in Bangladesh, girls either live with their parents, or their husbands. It was far from luxurious, although the girls, all aid workers, had given it their own touch, with labels on everything in Bangla, and an Ash Grunwald sticker on the fridge. (Obviously his hippy strummings were popular in this household.) The apartment had three bedrooms, but only one occupant at the time, since a few of Lyrian's fellow aid workers had just moved out, and would be returning in a few days to pick up their furniture. There were also three toilets – one a squat. Oh, and the rat.

While I was taking all this in, Lyrian had skilfully steered the conversation onto food. I was soon to find that among the volunteers and NGO workers in Bangladesh, one of the main topics of conversation is always food – namely, the stuff they can't get in Bangladesh. There are two supermarkets in Chittagong, but they don't sell much in the way of Western comforts. Luxuries like olives and capers are almost used as contraband among the volunteers, being sold and traded for other goods. If someone finds out another expat has been home recently, the first question is inevitably: 'What did you eat?' For Lyrian, a lactose-intolerant vegetarian, the situation was particularly dire.

'I've basically got two choices for Bangla food,' she explained. '*Subji*, which is vegetables fried to within an inch of their lives, or *bharta*, which is okay – it's like a whole lot of vegetables mashed together into balls. Then you get rice, and *daal*; but not the daal we know. If you can find a lentil in there, you've done well. And that's it. For six months.'

There was one more thing Bangladesh was missing: alcohol. With something like 92 per cent of its population being Muslim, Bangladesh is a dry country. Westerners are allowed to drink alcohol, but there's nowhere they can buy it or consume it – which is probably why Lyrian had asked me to buy her a bottle of duty free gin on my way out of Bangkok. There were other ways around the problem, too. The UN has a warehouse in Dhaka full of alcohol for its UN passport-holding workers to buy. There was also the odd party thrown by various organisations that you could attend in search of a drink.

'Oh man, the Australian High Commission put on a party in Dhaka last week,' Lyrian said, pouring another gin. 'They had free wine! I was just getting over a bout of gastro, but anyway, I got pants-shittingly drunk, didn't I? I literally couldn't move the next day.'

Lyrian's old flatmate had also had a magical UN passport, which was why I was able to drink a couple of cans of Foster's that first night. This place isn't so bad, I thought. There might be rats, cockroaches and stomach bugs, but at least you can get hold of a tin of Foster's.

*

I had a fitful sleep that night, tossing and turning underneath my mosquito net, convinced every scratch I heard was the rats come to carry me out of bed and up the drainpipe. By 6am there was no point trying to sleep anymore anyway, as it was already nudging 30 degrees and I was drenched in sweat.

While Lyrian went off to work that morning, I had a mission: to get to the train station and buy myself a ticket to get back to Dhaka. Because there was No. Freaking. Way. I was taking the bus back up there. In any other country, the buying of a train ticket would seem a pretty simple proposition – but not in Bangladesh. Lyrian had drawn me a little mud map of her area so I could find a taxi, had told me how much it should cost, and had even written down the Bangla words I'd have to say to secure my ticket. Simple, right?

After wandering in circles for half an hour or so, I eventually found a taxi (an actual car), whose driver had absolutely no idea where I was going. I'd been told the translation for 'train station' in Bangla was just that: 'train station'. Still, my cab driver was looking very confused as I slid into the back seat. Unperturbed, he gunned the engine, and took off. Where, we both had no idea. Eventually, he pulled over and waved down a well-dressed Bangladeshi who looked like he might be able to speak English. My driver pointed at me with a gnarled black finger, and said something to the man in Bangla.

The man looked at me. 'Where are you going?'

'The train station,' I said.

He looked at the cab driver: 'Trrrrrrrain a stashion.'

The cabbie's eyes lit up. 'Trrrrrrrain a stashion! Okay!'

We were off and, miraculously, had been heading in the right direction anyway. Down at the station, I found the right person to buy my ticket from, unravelled the crumpled piece of paper from my pocket, and launched into my spiel in Bangla.

'*Ami Dhaka jabo,*' I started. (I'm going to Dhaka.)

'*Shonibar naat.*' (Saturday night.)

'*Ekta ticket lagbe.*' (I need one ticket.)

I was so proud of myself. I'd nailed the language in seconds. I was a lingual genius. The guy at the window looked at me for a few seconds, then said in flawless English: 'We don't have any sleepers; will an air-con seat be okay?' The 20 or so Bangladeshis who'd crowded around to watch the transaction all gasped approvingly. It was a deal.

I then spent the next three hours trying to get home. My taxi had disappeared, so I tried to hail a CNG. In an hour only a few went past, none of which stopped or even seemed to glance at me. I found one parked by the side of the road, told the driver where I wanted to go, but he just dismissed me with a flick of his hand. How the hell does anyone get around in this city? I eventually managed to persuade a cycle-rickshaw to take me, and discovered why I'd had so much trouble: the CNG drivers were on strike. Not enough pay, and they were complaining that the job was too dangerous. It seemed the natural gas tanks on the rickshaws had the annoying tendency of blowing up whenever they were in a fender bender – not an uncommon occurrence on Chittagong's insane streets.

Bangladesh, I was starting to realise, was not as similar to India as I'd expected. For starters, there was none of the modernity that you find in the larger Indian cities. There's been no IT boom in Bangladesh; there was no Bollywood. So the associated wealth and change hadn't arrived in this tiny but jam-packed land. It seemed completely shut off from the Western world, and all that comes with it.

There certainly weren't any other tourists around. According to Lyrian, there were only seven Westerners living in the entire city, and she knew all of them. It's so untouched that Chittagong is regarded by NGOs as a 'remote posting' – a status normally reserved for tiny villages in the middle of jungles. In Dhaka, at least, there were a few comforts of home – the UN had its alcohol warehouse, and there's an Australian Club there that puts on barbecues every Thursday. In Chittagong, there's nothing.

It's also a deeply conservative place, and there didn't, to me, seem to be that overwhelming *joie de vivre* that you find throughout India. I asked Lyrian at one point whether she thought India had any plans to claim this little nation as its own. 'Are you kidding?' she answered. 'It's a shithole country, full of Muslims, and the whole place will be underwater in a few decades' time. Why would they want it?'

I spent that afternoon down at Lyrian's NGO offices meeting her Bangladeshi colleagues, who were apparently pretty excited about meeting another badeshi, but scandalised that I was a boy and would be staying at Lyrian's house. 'I may have to say we used to work together,' Lyrian said. 'Or even that we're married. I don't know yet. But just go with it. Trust me, there's no *way* I'm telling them you're a complete stranger that I met on the internet.'

The office was in the swanky part of Chittagong, if you can possibly describe any part of Chittagong as swanky; 'the North Shore end', as Lyrian described it. Still, that didn't mean there wasn't the usual pile of garbage and beggars lining the streets on the way in. When the NGOs wanted to begin their aid work each morning, all they needed to do was step out of the front gate.

A single fan chopped up the humid air in Lyrian's tiny office as I met a few of her work friends, and first encountered the odd question that most Bangladeshis will ask at some point: 'How are your feelings in Bangladesh?'

How are my feelings? Good, I guess. What else do you say? Figuring there was no drinking culture at Lyrian's work, I asked what they all did for fun together.

'Oh, they all hang around the office late on a Thursday night chatting and drinking cha,' she replied. 'None of them want to go home because they're all in arranged marriages and don't want to have to hang out with their spouses.'

While Lyrian didn't attend these Thursday night cha-drinking sessions, her workmates still took a keen interest in what she was up to. In Bangladesh if you don't enquire in detail about your friends' personal and private lives, people think you don't care. And this inquisitiveness extends to health problems.

'The main problem for me is that the toilet is in a really public sort of area here,' Lyrian said. 'So if I'm having a rough trot, they'll see me run off to the toilet, and 10 seconds later they're banging on the door: "Lyrian, are you okay, can I get you anything?" Then they all sit around and discuss what I could have eaten, and how I can fix the problem. It's so fucking embarrassing.'

Gender equity's not quite what it could be in the workplace either. There are a few women working at Lyrian's NGO, but attitudes are still old-fashioned at best by Western standards.

'Okay, for starters, I'm in my late 20s and I'm not married, so they all want to talk about that,' Lyrian said. 'One time, my boss, who's a really nice guy, sits me down at this meeting with about 15 guys, and he just says, "You know, Lyrian, I think the reason you have not married yet is that you are scared of sexual relations. Really, it is not that big a thing to be worrying about. Relationships are only 10 per cent sexual, and 90 per cent social. My wife and I have a very good time together socially."

'I was dumbstruck. This was in front of all these men! I'm like,

"Um, yeah, my family has a good time together too . . ." What can you say? If I set them straight they'll think I'm a whore. So I just smiled and nodded.'

As the only Westerner in the office, Lyrian had become the sounding board for any issues of a sexual nature for the girls working there. I met a few and they were lovely, shy girls who've obviously been left completely in the dark about a lot of things, including Western culture. One of the first questions Lyrian was asked was: 'Have you ever held a boy's hand?'

'Then there was the girl who was about to get married,' Lyrian said. 'She and her friend came and asked to drink cha with me in my office – no one ever wants to come into my office, so I knew it must be serious. So they sit down, and they tell me the girl who's getting married is really worried about what her wifely duties are, because she has no idea what's going to happen.

'I told them as best I could. They didn't even know men get erections! You should have seen the looks on their faces, seriously. Thank God they found out before the night of the wedding though.'

The office was so conservative that Lyrian had to wear the *salwar kameez*, the traditional Muslim dress, to be taken seriously. She wore jeans to work once and no one talked to her because they thought she looked too Western and were petrified of her. And, like the Chinese, they were also scandalised by the sight of my hairy white legs sticking out the end of a pair of shorts as I wandered through the office that day.

'Yeah, shorts are for little boys here,' Lyrian told me later. 'One of the girls asked me if you'd cut off your trousers! She thought you might have been hot.'

It was true though, I was bloody hot. The temperature was nudging 42 during the day, with about 95 per cent humidity. It meant you'd be soaked through with sweat after just a little walk down the street. Add to that the rivers of raw sewage and mountains of rotting garbage lying by the sides of the road, and you get an idea of the pleasantness of an afternoon stroll around Chittagong.

We spent that evening with Lyrian's old flatmate Tanya and her Bangladeshi boyfriend Ong, who proclaimed themselves: 'The King and Queen of the Rats.' Tanya was working on the UN's disaster relief program, and the disaster she happened to be currently relieving was a rat plague in the dangerous hill tracts above Chittagong. If the genocide doesn't get you up there, the giant rats will.

'God, there's so many there,' said Tanya, who looked like the exact picture I get in my head when I imagine aid workers: long plaited hair, a nose ring, traditional Bangla dress not quite covering the unicorn tattoo on her ankle. 'And they're huge! They've set rat traps around the place, and some of them get caught, and then just wriggle out of them. Makes me shudder.'

Still, Tanya had moved out of Lyrian's flat to live full-time in the hill tracts with Ong, so the girl had guts.

We dined that night at Tava, by far and away the swankiest, most expensive restaurant in Chittagong. The only customers in the entire restaurant, we ordered far too much food, knowing this would probably be the best meal I'd have during my stay. We had *roti* breads, a chicken curry, a *pad thai* (big in Chittagong apparently), a lentil-rich daal, and something with goat in it. Still, our meal cost us $10 each. It's amazing the money you can save when you can't drink.

Over dinner, I told everyone about my bus trip, and the guy with the video camera who'd obviously been shooting a promo clip. The two girls cracked up laughing.

'Are you serious?'

'Yeah,' I replied.

'That's not a promo video,' Lyrian chuckled. 'They do that on every bus trip. It's to make it easier to identify the bodies if there's an accident.'

*

I'd been in Chittagong a few days now, but hadn't seen any evidence of the city my dad had talked about. There were no groups of sailors wandering the streets, or zipping past in CNGs. In fact, Lyrian had only seen one tourist in the whole six months she'd been living there, and she'd approached him to ask, like all the Bangladeshis had asked, what the hell he was doing there.

The port my dad had called into all those years ago still existed, but it was miles out of town, and, according to Lyrian, not worth a visit – just a few jetties with not much going on. And anyway, Lyrian had something far more interesting in mind.

We were back on that very same road I'd come into the city on, only this time in a CNG, swerving to avoid the buses roaring down the road.

'I told everyone at work I was taking you out here, and they were horrified,' Lyrian laughed. '"It is not a tourist attraction," they were saying. Wait till you see it.'

We were going to see the ship-breaking yards, an amazing stretch of coastline where old, unwanted ships are hauled up onto dry land, and systematically torn apart by an army of workers who go over it like ants on a rotting carcass. Within days an entire ship can be pulled apart into nothing, and everything – *everything* – is up for sale in the yards by the street. As we buzzed down the highway in the CNG, we could see stalls selling items from pots and pans found in the ships' galleys (and the kitchen sinks) to entire engine blocks that sat rusting away on the dirt verge. If you ever want to soup up your lawnmower with an extra 40,000 horsepower, you know where to go.

Pulling up at a nondescript blue gate, we told our CNG driver to wait, and walked through a small village, soon picking up a crowd of 20 or so Bangladeshis keen to see what we were up to. At the end of a path we emerged onto a beach, or, more accurately, an apocalyptic wasteland. It was incredible. My dad had come to Chittagong on healthy, living ships. These had come here to die.

They might be called ship-breaking 'yards', but there were no yards to speak of. Up and down the coast as far as I could see, huge tankers had been rammed into the deserted beach, all in various states of disassembly. Some were whole, others sliced in half like a science experiment. Others had just had their panelling torn off, and sat like twisted brown skeletons waiting to be eaten up by the sand.

'They do the wrecking by hand,' Lyrian said, gazing out at the wasteland. 'Just chisels and blowtorches. Some of them are only kids, and they make about a dollar a day. They have a life expectancy of about 10 years once they start the job.'

I could believe it. The tankers were huge, and there was no safety equipment, simply ships and beach. Not even any fences separating the ships from the general public. At one stage a group of 'security guards' approached us, but only because they wanted to take our photo and ask what we were doing in Chittagong.

Something like half the world's super tankers meet their undignified end on the beaches of Chittagong. And if it's not the huge slabs of sheet metal that kill you, it'll probably be the lead paint all the old ships were slathered with, or the asbestos, or the toxic waste. There are only a few countries left in the world that do ship-breaking, and they're not much interested in the environmental concerns of the West.

We chatted to the security guards for a while, then, with our 20 or so Bangladeshis still in tow, walked back to our CNG, and zipped back into town. There, we decided to tempt fate and have lunch at a restaurant. We took our seats, and were immediately surrounded by 20 or so waiters who, rather than serve us, took a seat at the table next to us so they could watch us eat. We'd loved to have eaten, but after half an hour, no food had arrived. Fifteen minutes later, and we were still going hungry. Lyrian rolled her eyes. 'This happens all the time. They take ages so they can keep us in the restaurant longer so everyone can stare at us. I'll try to hurry them up.'

I was impressed with Lyrian's command of Bangla, given

the short time she'd been in the country. With the labels all over the house and constant practice, she could at least make herself understood to the locals. She didn't have much of a choice but to learn the language though – there's almost no English spoken in the country, and as I was finding out, it's a very difficult place to find your way around if you don't speak the lingo.

'Is there a catchphrase you guys have for Bangladesh?' I asked as our meals finally arrived. 'Like, the guy in China was telling me they all say "OIC" – as in, Only In China.'

Lyrian chewed thoughtfully. 'I guess we end a lot of sentences with ". . . for Bangladesh". You know, you'd say, "Wow, that was pretty tasty . . . for Bangladesh." Or, "That's a nice house . . . for Bangladesh."'

About the only Bangla word I'd learnt so far was *shesh*, a catch-all phrase that basically means 'finished', and can be applied to anything that's broken, dead or has run out. Order something on a menu and the waiter will look up, shake his head, and say, 'Shesh.' Try to flick on a light during one of the many power cuts, and Lyrian would shrug her shoulders and go, 'Shesh.' Most things in Bangladesh seemed to be pretty well shesh.

After lunch, we headed to one of the more bizarre attractions around town – not that Chittagong really has attractions. The 'turtle mosque' is a normal-looking mosque with a stagnant and pretty horrible pond in front of it, which is populated by stagnant and pretty horrible turtles. The thing is, some Muslims believe the turtles have been somehow imbued with the spirit of the prophet Mohammed, so the pond and the turtles have become a pilgrimage site. Bangladeshis come from all over not just to feed the gnarled, mouldy turtles, but to douse themselves in the pond water, and occasionally drink from it. Still miraculously healthy, I opted not to taint my guts with scummy pond water.

A slug of turtle poo probably wouldn't have been as disgusting as the street food though. I'm usually a big fan of street food, and had planned to try it in Chittagong too. However, after listening to Lyrian's horror stories, I'd decided to opt out. After all, no one wants to have the trots in Ethiopia. As it turned out, I made the right decision. Even native Deshies don't eat Chittagong street food. It's for the poorest of the poor only.

Most of the street food carts in Chittagong are set up right next to the open sewers that run down the side of the street. And, as Lyrian pointed out, there's a serious water shortage in the city. 'So where do you think they get their cooking water from?' she asked one day.

Lyrian did, however, have some good news. As we were discussing the religious and political situation in Bangladesh, she assured me that despite the recent mutiny and massacre, things seemed pretty stable.

'There is an Islamic extremist party that runs for government,' Lyrian admitted. 'But I guess things are fairly stable. I mean, there hasn't been a suicide bombing since 2007, so that's pretty good.'

I paused. 'Um . . . That doesn't seem like very long ago.'

'Yeah, I guess it's only two years isn't it?'

*

If you've spent any time in a cold climate, you know what it's like getting ready to leave the house. You don't just grab the keys and walk out. You spend 10 minutes or so going through the routine of jumpers, jackets, gloves and beanies. Maybe even boots.

It might have been 42 degrees outside, and humid enough to be able to grab chunks of air and put them in your pockets, but Lyrian still had to go through a similar ritual each morning. The shorts and T-shirt she schlepped around the house in would probably get her lynched on the street, which is why she had to go through the process of changing out of that and into the salwar kameez each morning, topping it off with the traditional *unna*, or scarf. 'This is the most important bit,' she said, draping the scarf low across her chest so it hid the bump of her breasts through the kameez. 'If you don't wear it, people will basically assume you're a prostitute.'

We were preparing to head out to the General Zia museum, dedicated to the man famous for two things: announcing the liberation of Bangladesh through a radio address; and his almost Bono-like dedication to his sunglasses. Zia was a mirrored Aviators man, and was rarely, if ever, photographed without them. That's something I can now attest to after visiting his old residence, which houses the museum dedicated to his life. Its walls are filled with pictures of the general pressing the flesh with world dignitaries, addressing his troops, digging canals, planting trees, kissing his wife – all while sporting his rad eyewear.

The museum really only kicked into gear near the end, though, when we walked out onto the general's balcony. There, lovingly preserved, we found the actual spatters of blood the general had left on the wall when bandits stormed his house and assassinated him during a coup attempt in 1981. There were also a few bullet holes still left in the floor, just for added effect. It almost took our minds off our guide, who hadn't stopped pestering Lyrian to see if she could organise an Australian visa for him.

We managed to extricate ourselves from the guide, and headed to our 'special treat'. 'You have got to see this,' Lyrian said as our CNG skipped through the traffic. 'It's at once the best and worst thing that you've ever seen.'

Our destination? 'Mini Bangladesh', a theme park which was truly an incredible achievement in the art of tourism. While I thought the Bund Sightseeing Tunnel in Shanghai was bad, Mini Bangladesh was without doubt the most spectacularly crap tourist attraction in the entire world. Like the Proclaimers, it was so bad it was good.

Mini Bangladesh was just that – a park filled with miniature versions of the nation's major monuments. Trouble is, Bangladesh being a developing country, and a fairly new one at that, it doesn't really *have* any major monuments. Still, that didn't stop the park's designers from building medium-sized versions (not even properly mini!) of a few very average buildings from around the country. The exhibits included a midi mosque (the full-sized version of which was actually in India), a midi parliament house, a midi fountain from Dhaka, and a midi church, which looked like it would have been pretty small in the first place. There was also an actually mini train to ferry tourists around the mini park – only the carriages were all lying on their sides next to the overgrown track, so we figured it was probably out of action.

While the park was understandably pretty much empty and being gradually overrun by weeds, it did seem to serve one purpose: it was the perfect place for amorous young Deshies to bring their dates. Lyrian and I found several of them *almost* holding hands in dark corners all over the park, whispering sweet nothings into each others' ears. I guess their reasoning was that the chances of their bumping into anyone they knew – or anyone at all – were pretty slim.

For lunch, Lyrian decided to give me a real Bangladeshi culinary experience – in other words, not a very good one. At least it came out with decent speed though. At a small rooftop restaurant near Lyrian's house, we had potato *bharta* and bean *bharta*, the ubiquitous watery daal, a mutton *dopeaza*, and a vegetarian pad thai for Lyrian. 'It's okay,' she said, pointing at my daal and rice, 'but would you want to eat it tomorrow? And the next day? And the day after that?'

She had a point. When she was in town, Lyrian rarely ate out, as the only thing you can get is Bangladeshi food (unless you go to Pizza Hut). Her work with the NGO took her out to the remote villages a lot of the time – as a communications officer, she would check out the work the NGO was doing, then write up press releases and newsletters for the donors to read. In the villages, her choice of food was simple: daal, or rice, or daal and rice. She usually took the latter, and was seriously sick of it.

Before I caught my train that night, Lyrian and I had enough time to finish off her gin while sitting in her lounge room and talking about the gigs she didn't get the chance to see at home, the food she didn't get the chance to eat, the bars she didn't get the chance to drink at . . . We were actually getting on pretty well, having at least a love of indie music in common, and were pretty happy sitting on the little mattresses in the candlelight talking about Fleet Foxes and Death Cab For Cutie.

This was probably the kind of situation the Lawyer had been worrying about. My friends had all brought it up, too. Here you are in a foreign land, just you and a girl you get on well with, who probably hasn't even been on a date in the last six months – what's going to happen? Even I was interested in that one. And in this case: nothing. We stayed up, we drank gin, we chatted, and, when the time came, I threw my bag on my back and headed out into the Chittagong night, leaving Lyrian pretty much as I'd found her, dressed in pyjamas, a smiling white face at the door.

I felt a bit like a prisoner being released from jail, looking back and waving at my cellmate who still had six months to go.

I flagged down a CNG, said, 'Trrrrain a stashion!', and we roared off to the platform. There, I sat on a bench and was admired by 20 or so Bangladeshis – not just the street kids, bored and looking for something to do, but plenty of businessmen who were shooing away the street kids and telling them off for annoying me, then standing in front of me and staring. When the train finally pulled up I jumped on board, slung my pack into an overhead rack, wrapped a jumper around my head, and tried to doze off.

But Bangladesh wasn't finished with me yet.

*

First thing I noticed was the light – or rather, the lack of it. Actually that's not true. The first thing I noticed was the huge smash that threw my head into the seat in front of me, but it was only the lack of light that made me realise that it hadn't been something I'd dreamt.

Since I hadn't been able to book a sleeper, I was in a seated cabin, where the lights blaze throughout the night. I'd had my jumper wrapped around my head, but it wasn't doing much good. After the smash, I unwound the jumper, and blinked in the complete darkness. The train had come to a halt, and people around me were murmuring in Bangla.

I managed to find a few English speakers, and worked out what had happened. The piece of metal holding two of the carriages together had snapped, sending the front of the train off without the back end. The driver had then slammed on the brakes, making the back end smash into the front end. Which left us stranded in the middle of . . . somewhere. Actually, one of my new mates seemed to know where we were. 'This is my home village, just near here,' he whispered. 'It is not good place to stop. Indian border just over there. They have many problems with smugglers here.'

Things were solved quickly though. A train going the other way stopped beside us, we all jumped on and stood in the aisles for 15 minutes until we reached Comilla. There, we all piled out, and my new friend found us a rickshaw to the bus station, where the mob of people started banging on bus doors to wake up the drivers. Hands pushed me onto one of the buses, I threw my pack on a seat, and sat on top of it.

I took stock. The good news was, I would probably still make my flight in Dhaka. The bad news was that I was sitting in a bus which was about to drive down *that* road again, and they hadn't even videoed me.

My new mate, Jonaid – who sounded like he was starting a relief fund for himself – nudged my shoulder. 'Are you all right? You look scared.'

Somehow we managed to make it to Dhaka safely, and Jonaid shared a CNG with me part of the way to the airport. When I say part of the way, it's because 15 minutes into our ride, the CNG started spluttering, chugged a few times, then stopped altogether. I looked over at Jonaid and raised my eyebrows. 'Shesh?'

He laughed. 'Yes, Ben, shesh.'

We hailed another CNG, and finally made it to the airport, where Jonaid and I parted good friends, as I figured I now would with Bangladesh. I'd been pretty taken aback with the place at first, and thought I'd hate it. And most of the time, I had. But despite all the dangers, the big bugs, the grime and the crime, the bad food and the piles of garbage, I found I had really got to like the joint. It may not have been pretty, but I managed to figure out what the hell I was doing in Bangladesh.

Doesn't mean I'm in a hurry to go back though.

5 Ways to Carry a Goat

'I slopped home through the mud, went in my room and closed the door, and stayed there till I decided I liked Ethiopia again.'

I knew this was going to happen. I'd told everyone I was staying with that I was writing a book, so I knew at some point, they'd get shy. Someone would do something funny, or stupid, or embarrassing, and ask me not to include it in the book. And I couldn't deny them.

So I waited for the inevitable as Andrew stared at me bleary-eyed from across the breakfast table. 'Groundy,' he said, 'about last night . . .'

Last night. I groaned. Which bit? The shots? The hookers? The fight? The drink driving? This would be interesting.

'You gotta promise me something,' Andrew continued, rubbing a hand down his face. 'Everything that happened last night . . . it *all* goes in the book. Everything. It was fucking great! How can you not put that stuff in?'

I cracked up laughing, despite the three hours' sleep and the raging high-altitude hangover. 'It's a deal, mate.'

*

I knew I was going to like Andrew immediately. Not because of anything he'd said or done – purely for the fact that he was *there*. I'd arrived at Bole Airport in Addis Ababa at the insane time of 3.15am, and really wasn't in the mood for another debacle like Bangladesh. However, I needn't have worried, as Andrew's email assured me:

> Hi mate, good news is I'll pick you up at the airport. I'll be the
> big white guy.

So when I staggered out of immigration at something approaching 4am, sure enough, a big white guy was waiting for me. The only white guy, as it turned out.

'Ben? Mate! Welcome to Addis.'

My previous feeling about Andrew was confirmed. A Kiwi guy, he had an open, friendly face, and an easy way about him. Still, I reminded myself, I didn't really know a thing about him. So as he led me out to his battered blue Peugeot in the deserted car park, I thought I'd start with what had ever possessed him to move to Ethiopia.

'We're mining uranium,' Andrew told me with a big grin. 'Actually, we're "uranium explorers", although I like to call us "uranium adventurers". Sounds more fun that way. It's my mate – Shep, you'll meet him later – and my business. Basically, we think there's uranium here, so we're going through the process of pegging out plots of land, and finding out whether we're right. It's good fun.'

Well, this is going to be interesting, I thought. I've gone from staying with an NGO-working vegetarian who would occasionally eat fish if it had been 'ethically farmed', to staying with a couple of uranium miners. Very interesting.

I hadn't known Andrew was a uranium 'adventurer', because I hadn't known anything about Andrew. His invitation had been brief, to say the least:

Mate, I realise Ethiopia is a wee bit random, but let me know if you're keen. Cheers, Andrew.

Since then I'd had the email confirming he could pick me up from the airport, and that was it. Regardless, I'd decided to give Ethiopia a shot. It's not like I had a lot of choice. In my quest to visit every continent on Earth, Africa was always going to be a problem. When you're fighting just to survive most days, jumping on your laptop to read some Australian's self-indulgent travel blog is not really a top priority. Of all the invitations I ended up receiving, a grand total of three were from Africa. There was Wendy in Cape Town (tempting), Josh in Nairobi (not tempting), and Andrew, the mystery man in Ethiopia. While a beach holiday in Cape Town would have been nice, I eventually opted for Ethiopia, mainly because I'd never been there, and I was interested.

I wasn't sure what to expect, but I did know one thing – it wasn't going to be the most luxurious destination on my itinerary. In fact, I'd be lucky if it was even a small step up from the rubbish-strewn streets of Chittagong. After all, I'd seen the World Vision ads as a kid, so I thought I knew what to expect: a lot of dust, dirt, and bugger all to eat.

The first inkling that maybe I'd got this wrong arrived as Andrew pulled the Peugeot into a dusty side street marked with signs pointing towards the Norwegian and Sierra Leonean embassies. 'Yeah, pretty much all the embassies are around here,' he said. 'Up the road there's Iran, Malawi, Indonesia – all sorts. Okay, here's our place. Just wait for the guard to get up to open the gates for us.'

'You've got gates?' I paused. 'And a guard?'

'Yeah, fuck yeah! A couple actually, although one of them doesn't seem to do much. Then we've got a couple of gardeners, and some girls come into the house to do all the cooking and cleaning. Not bad, huh?'

Within seconds an African guard, a dark, hooded shape in

the night, opened the gate for us, and we swung into a bitumen drive leading down to what looked like a pretty big house. And it was. The central room was huge, a traditional circular space with a high, conical thatched roof, two dining tables and two sets of lounges around the central fireplace, all enclosed by a curved balcony. Attached to opposite ends of the circle were the sleeping quarters: two identical wings of two bedrooms and a bathroom each. My room was in what I'd decided to call the west wing, and was adorned with Coptic Christian crosses. I had a single bed, which was a fair step up from the cockroach-ridden floor I'd been occupying in Bangladesh.

'Not bad mate,' I said, walking around on the parquetry floor of the central room.

'Tell me about it. It's actually owned by the Anglican church, of all things. So that's why there are crosses and religious shit hanging on the walls. We rent it off those guys for about $600 a month, everything included. That's all the staff working here, plus three meals a day if we're here to eat them. It's fuckin' awesome actually. The only thing is that as part of the deal we share the house with Charles, this English guy who's the local Anglican priest. You'll meet him, he's a decent bloke. Just a bit old.'

'Have you guys got a laundry? I've got a backpack full of dirty clothes.'

'Too easy. Just dump it on the floor of your room in a big pile, and one of the girls will wash it. Seriously, you'll have it back in a few hours.'

I could see I was going to enjoy my stay in Ethiopia. Andrew – despite the fact it was 4am and he'd been woken from his bed about an hour ago – knew I'd been in a dry country for the last week, and figured I'd be keen for a beer. So we sat out in the huge old lounge room and talked about Addis life.

Andrew and his business partner, an Australian guy called Shep, had been in the country about six months, and had committed themselves to staying for another 18. Shep was a mining engineer, so he provided the skills side of the business, while Andrew was an organiser. The pair had identified Ethiopia as a potential place to mine uranium, and were in the process of getting financial backing from South African businessmen, as well as testing the areas they'd managed to peg to see if there really was uranium in them thar hills.

'We're doing some testing for platinum too, and maybe gold,' Andrew explained. 'We've been told the best thing is to diversify. Basically, we're just going to keep this going for two years, and if we haven't found anything, then we'll head back to Singapore, where the company's based. Hopefully, though, we'll find some uranium and we'll be all set.'

As I slugged back the dregs of my beer, an Ethiopian Dashen, Andrew was already heading back to the fridge.

'Another one, mate?'

*

Next morning I wandered out to the lounge room to a highly encouraging sight – a dining table set with breakfast cereal, toast, spreads and coffee.

'That's the standard breakfast here,' said Shep, an Aussie with a broad accent, a face full of stubble, and a love of swearing matched only by Andrew's. 'Get stuck in.'

I sat down, and the two boys started grilling me about my trip so far.

'Did you go to Dhaka?' Andrew asked.

'Yep.'

'Was there a Macca's there?'

'Not that I saw.'

'Fuck! We've been trying to figure out the largest capital city in the world that doesn't have a McDonald's. We thought it might be Lagos or something like that. But yeah, Dhaka would have to be up there then. So who were you staying with there?'

'Ah, an NGO worker who was also a vegetarian.'

They both roared with laughter. 'Mate, we're pretty much the opposite here!' Shep said. 'Was she fat?'

'No, not really.'

'Oh. Andrew has a thing for fat white NGO workers. As you'll see when we go out tonight.'

I spent the rest of that morning doing what Andrew and Shep seemed to be able to do a remarkable amount of, given they were starting up a business: relax. We read books, we threw a football in the backyard, we came upstairs when our lunch of vegetable soup, bread rolls and salad was on the table. This, I decided, I could get used to.

I also had a chance to read Andrew's Bradt guide to Ethiopia, as, once again, I'd arrived in a place with no idea of what there was to see and do. While hopelessly out of date, there were still a few interesting facts in the book. The first was that Ethiopians apparently believe that throwing yourself in front of a moving car and making a narrow escape will bring you good luck – like, not being dead – which would explain the shocking road toll in Addis. The second was the book's assertion that Ethiopia is much different to most people's expectations – something I'd been starting to figure out myself.

That afternoon I figured I should probably leave the cocoon of the boys' house and make it out into Addis Ababa proper. All it took was a quick walk in the sunshine towards the car, and I was in love with the place. I don't know why. I'd barely seen anything. I was just so happy to be back in Africa. I'd spent three months there in 2005, doing one of the budget truck tours from Nairobi to Cape Town. There's something at once beautiful and horrible, peaceful and dangerous about the Dark Continent; the place seems to settle itself in your bones. It has an energy that's hard to describe, but which you feel immediately.

I was always going to love Africa. I grew up reading Wilbur Smith novels, fancying myself as being just like the rugged, gun-toting horsemen he always wrote about, despite the fact my skin was so white it was almost translucent, and I'd never managed to get a horse past a walk. Still, I knew I'd love Africa, and I was right.

Once the car was outside the gate though, I started to realise that Ethiopia isn't like the Africa I'd seen. In fact, it isn't like anywhere in the rest of the world. The roads were the first things that hit me. Actually, it was the roof of our car that hit me, when we drove over one of the many huge potholes in the otherwise smooth roads. Bad roads are an African specialty, but Addis's are something else. A few years back, the Chinese government signed up to build roads in Addis. They made a fair start, but eventually the money ran out, so they just pulled up stumps and left. The result is that you'll have smooth tarmac for a few kilometres, and then suddenly hit a 100-metre stretch of jagged rocks and dirt where the end of the road was supposed to be.

Then you've got people driving the wrong way down separated roads, pedestrians sprinting out in front of oncoming traffic . . . and the traffic itself. From what I could see, you could divide it into three categories. The first was livestock, as even the busiest city roads were full of farmers moving herds of goats or cattle from place to place. The second was the battered blue-and-white Lada taxis that crawl all over Addis, defying the gods of mechanics by not breaking down. And the third was fancy 4WDs with NGO stickers slapped on the side. Throw in our old Peugeot, and the picture's complete.

But it's not just the roads that make Ethiopia different. This is a country that's steadfastly independent, to the point where they're the only nation on Earth with a different system of time. Not just a different calendar – different *time*. Here's how it works. Each 24 hour period is split up into 12 hours of day, and 12 hours of night. What we call 6am is the beginning of their 'day', so the clocks start from 12 then. So our 7am is their 1am, our 8am is their 2am, and so on. Once their clock hits 12 again (at our 6pm), they're beginning their 12 hours of night, making our 7pm their

1pm, and so on. It sort of makes sense, given the country is so close to the equator that there really are 12 hours of light and 12 hours of darkness each day. But it's still a bizarre feeling sitting in a pub of an evening, cracking your first beer, to notice the time is two o'clock.

They don't use the Western calendar either. The Ethiopian calendar has 13 months – hence their tourism association's slogan: '13 months of sunshine.' Confusing? Yes. Even more confusing is that the timing of their calendar meant they celebrated the millennium in 2007/2008, which partially explained all the millennium banners and displays still hung up all over town.

While Andrew headed in to the central enclave for all things Western, the Addis Ababa Hilton, to do some work, I headed to the National Museum, home to Lucy, the 3.2 million-year-old statue of an Australopithecus, whose discovery pretty much changed the way scientists thought about the evolution of man. Or something like that. It cost the equivalent of $1.50 to get in, and, being a notorious tight arse, I opted not to shell out for a guide. Instead, I did what a couple of Ethiopian blokes seemed to be doing, and tagged along at a respectful distance behind an English girl and her guide, catching whatever snippets of information we could. We saw former kings' crowns, we saw ancient bone fragments, we saw terrible modern Ethiopian art, and eventually, we rounded the corner on the bottom floor to find Lucy.

Now, I'm not much of a history buff, but anything 3.2 million years old is pretty cool by me. Unfortunately though, like most of the girls I would come to meet in Addis, Lucy wasn't quite what she seemed. As I snapped away happily at the partial skeleton of this prehistoric marvel, I overheard the English girl's tour guide telling her about it. 'This is Lucy. Of course, the real Lucy skeleton is in a museum in Houston. This is just a replica. But you see the way they reconstructed the bones around the . . .'

Goddamn it. I wandered off to find a decent pub. Fortunately, one of the best attractions at the National Museum is Lucy's

Bar, a pub in the museum grounds. As I had a few hours to kill before meeting up with Andrew and Shep, I settled back with a few Castels and watched CNN on the TV, in between dodging marriage proposals from the girl who was supposed to be clearing glasses.

'So, you from where?' she asked, leaning a slender arm on the bar next to me.

'Me? Australia.'

'Ah, this is very nice country.' There was a pause as she gazed into the distance for a while. Then she turned back. 'You have wife?'

'No, no wife.'

'No wife! Oh. Er, girlfriend?'

'No, no girlfriend,' I lied, interested to see where this was heading.

'No girlfriend! Why not, you don't like girls?'

'Ha ha, no, I like girls.'

'Ah.'

With that, she went back to absently polishing glasses while I turned back to CNN.

'How long you stay Addis Ababa?' she asked.

'Just one week.'

'One week! That is short time.' She paused. 'Maybe, I can be your Addis girlfriend?'

'But I'm only here for a week – you don't want a boyfriend for just a week do you?'

She sighed. 'No. I like Australia though. Maybe, come back to Australia too?'

Even I couldn't bear taking the conversation any further, so I downed my beer, paid my bill, and, already feeling tipsy after just two brews, wobbled my way over to meet Andrew and Shep at the Old Milk House, a rooftop bar with a nice view over Addis's UN headquarters. The pair had already arrived, and had a round of St George beers waiting. I soon found out something about boozing in Addis Ababa: at 2500 metres, Addis is the third highest capital city in the world, meaning you find yourself out of breath just from walking up the stairs, and your tolerance for alcohol is greatly decreased, which was why I was stumbling out of Lucy's Bar after only a couple of lagers.

'So, do you guys like living here?' I asked, watching the sun gradually set in a pool of orange.

'Yeah, fuck yeah,' Andrew said, taking another slug of beer. 'I mean, we're living the life really.'

'Yeah, you did have a moment though, didn't you?' Shep said.

'That's true, I did have a moment.'

'I told him he'd have a moment,' Shep said, 'and he had a moment. Go on, tell Groundy about it.'

'Okay,' said Andrew. 'I'd just got to Addis, like second day or something – Shep had been here for a few months by the time I turned up. And I needed to get some water from the shop up the road. So I head up there wearing my jandles, which was a fucking stupid thing to do, 'cause it'd been raining, and I had to go through the bloody goat abattoir on my way through. So the place is all muddy, there's goat carcasses everywhere, I've got mud and fucking goat entrails streaked down my legs from where the jandles flicked them up on me, and I get to the shop, and it's closed. Lunch time, so the bloke's having a sleep. I was fucking pissed. So I slopped home through the mud, got in, went in my room and closed the door, and stayed there till I decided I liked Ethiopia again. I had a moment.'

Shep nodded gravely. 'He had a moment.'

They made an odd couple, these two. Andrew was only 24, while Shep was 32, and was clearly in charge. Andrew deferred to him on most things – where to go for dinner, which route to take to get there, even what food to order. Still, there was obviously a mutual respect between them, and the guys had their routine down pat: Andrew being the hyperactive funny guy, and Shep playing the gruff straight man.

'I'm allowed to do this,' Andrew explained, wiggling his fingers over Shep's hand in a bizarre handshake, 'three times a day.'

Shep sighed, resigned to having to wiggle his fingers in reply. 'You see what I have to put up with, Groundy? You've gotta be a fuckin' patient man, I tell you.'

From the Old Milk House we jumped in the car and headed to Fasika, a 'traditional' Ethiopian restaurant the guys liked to frequent. This was to be my first taste of real Ethiopian food, and I was excited. I'd heard mixed reports about the stuff – some had described the traditional *injera* bread that's eaten with pretty much everything as having the taste and texture of a dishcloth. Others, like Tanya in Chittagong, couldn't rave on enough about it. I left the ordering to Andrew and Shep.

'Right, we'll have the *shiro wat*,' Andrew told the waiter, 'and . . . *tibs*? Yep, gotta have tibs. Then another *wat*, and . . . the *kitfo*.'

'Sir, you know this is raw beef?' the waiter said.

'Raw? Ooh. Waddaya reckon, Groundy, do we give it a shot?'

Fortified by what seemed like a thousand St Georges by then, I nodded. A few bongo drum numbers from the live band later, the food arrived. Or rather, our injera arrived. The bread is made from teff grains, and is slightly fermented, giving it a spongy consistency and faintly sour taste. When it's served, it's as one giant round pancake laid in the middle of the table; the sauces – or wats – the tibs (fried chicken) and the kitfo (raw beef mince) are ladled on top of the bread in front of each diner. To eat, you just rip off a bit of bread with your right hand, use that to scoop up some meat and sauce, and shove it in your mouth. The result is pretty damn tasty, although the sourness of the injera takes some getting used to. The wats were rich and spicy though, and even the raw mince had its moments.

Next stop on my one-night introduction to Addis nightlife was Champions, a 'sports bar' which seemed to be missing a few important things for a sports bar: namely, any TV screens, sporting memorabilia, or even a pool table. Instead we walked into a dimly lit room full of expats and locals toking on bubbling *shisha* pipes. The pipes are the traditional way to smoke flavoured tobacco in the Middle East, so naturally you'd expect to find them in a sports bar in Addis Ababa. However, there was something else at the bar that had caught Andrew's attention.

'Oh, fuck yeah! Look,' Andrew said, pointing to a group of expats at a table in the corner. 'Fat NGO workers! Boys, I can feel some chat coming on.'

As promised, after forcing us into a couple of sambuca shots, Andrew was off chatting to the group of girls who, it turned out, were in Addis to work for USAID, an NGO from the States. Addis is the major hub for African NGOs, so that's what I'd expected Andrew would be doing too. But I was slightly off.

Sadly, so was Andrew's chat, so once the NGOs had left, we headed to the boys' favourite nightclub, a place called Memo. By this stage I could barely form words, but the boys were still ferrying us around in their battered old Peugeot. 'Mate, no one gives a shit about drink driving here,' Andrew said. 'I guess it's a bit dangerous, but so's taking a cab, when you think about it.'

My first impression of Memo was that it was full to bursting with stunning Ethiopian girls. Think of the most attractive African-American actress or singer you can conjure up – I can guarantee they look Ethiopian.

My second impression of Memo was that it was full to bursting with stunning Ethiopian prostitutes. It actually took me a fair while to form this second impression, since I'm not the sharpest knife in the drawer. But I'm also not the type of bloke who gets approached by hot girls in nightclubs, so by the time I'd fielded my third, 'Hi, where are you from?', I'd started to get suspicious. Turns out Memo is a notorious hooker hangout. Andrew and Shep didn't go there because they wanted to pick up hookers though – they went there because they liked to have a dance, and they liked the attention from the hot hookers. The end of the night is always the same – a shrug of the shoulders, a brief explanation, and a furious Ethiopian hooker.

I can think of things I'd rather do than make idle chit-chat with African sex industry workers, so I eventually persuaded the boys to head home, leaving a slew of angry hookers in our wake. We stumbled through the dirt car park, and back to the car.

'Thash lucky,' Shep slurred. 'I think I jush got booted out anyway. Shome bloke wanned to fight me.'

'You gunna drive?' Andrew slurred back at Shep.

'Nah man, you drive,' he replied. 'I'll sit in the back and make sure you don't go too fast.'

And so began a drive that would have been highly frightening had I not been drunk enough to think it was a great idea. My only memories are the swerving of a couple of parked cars, some senseless beeping at nothing, and Shep in the back screaming, 'Slow down man!' Then, 'All right, go faster than that. Christ . . .'

*

I'm a man who likes his showers. I can rough it with the best of them – I can sleep on floors, or out in the open, and I don't mind a bit of dirt. Even bedbugs don't frighten me that much. Just as long as I can have a steaming hot, waterfall-like shower at the start of the day. In Addis, however, you've got no chance. Rather than a waterfall, what you get is a heart-breaking trickle. You might get hot water. You probably won't. That morning, hung over as hell, with a touch of altitude sickness thrown in for good measure, all I really wanted was a decent shower. But it wasn't going to happen.

Given the fact we were too hung over to do anything vaguely touristy (or work-related for the boys, given it was a Thursday and they were supposed to be uranium adventuring), we decided to catch up on some emails at the Addis Hilton, which is in possession of the city's only broadband connection. It also has a generator, so isn't affected by the twice-weekly, day-long blackouts that the rest of the city has to put up with.

The hotel is also a favourite hangout for expats, and it's easy to see why. Like the boys' house, it's a bizarre cocoon shielding you from the realities of Addis Ababa. The drive there takes you down dusty streets, past mud-and-corrugated-iron shacks filled with hundreds of people going about their daily business of trying to survive. The Hilton, by contrast, is upmarket and relaxing, yet still affordable enough for book-writing backpackers, uranium adventurers, and the odd fat white NGO to while away an afternoon by the pool.

That night, I was introduced to Charles, the boys' 57-year-old Anglican priest of a flatmate, a fantastically dishevelled character with a plummy south England accent, pretty much the exact stereotype of an Englishman eccentric enough to spend 40 years of his life in Ethiopia in the service of the big man upstairs. Dressed in his dog collar but with scuffed shoes, faded, badly repaired trousers and a stained shirt, Charles was cracking his first beer on the balcony overlooking the garden when Andrew and I arrived back from the Hilton.

'Hi, I'm Ben,' I said, sticking out a hand.

'Yes, I rather thought you might be,' Charles replied, his tousled grey hair flopping about as he got up to shake my hand. 'Welcome to Addis. I trust everything has been fine so far?'

'Absolutely.'

Now, you'd expect that sharing your house with a 57-year-old priest would be a bit of a drag, but Andrew and Shep seemed to get along well with Charles. He was almost like the father figure of the house, making sure everyone was getting along okay. On that topic, he was slightly concerned about my plan to fly to Lalibela, a small town in the north of the country, later in the week and then fly back on the day of my flight to London.

'Is it an awful problem if your flight is delayed?' he asked.

'Well, it's certainly not perfect. I'd prefer if it didn't happen.'

'Right, because there's only one plane that flies to Lalibela, and if it's not working, you won't get out.'

'Ah. Well, I'd probably prefer they fix it than pick me up in a broken plane,' I said glibly, with no idea what was in store for me on my Lalibela jaunt.

*

I'd been in Addis three days now, and the sum total of my touristy experiences had been half an hour in the National Museum. So the next morning I decided to check out the Addis Museum, highly recommended by the guidebook, and probably a more authentically Ethiopian experience than hanging out with an Aussie and a Kiwi to throw a football in the backyard.

Turning up there though, I wasn't even sure the place was open – or had been at any time in the last 10 years. The crumbling bitumen pavement had long since been taken over by the marauding garden, and the yellow paint was cracked and peeling from the walls of what I assumed was once the museum. Turned out though, it was still the museum. After a few minutes of poking around outside, a man appeared, took a 10 *birr* note out of my hand, and unlocked the doors.

It was then that I got my first proper look at him, and realised that he was in possession of possibly the most incredible nasal hair I'd ever seen. It was like he had two knots of snot-encrusted steel wool jutting out a good centimetre from the bottom of his nostrils. The hair was so incredible, in fact, that it was all I could look at or think about as the man gave me, unbidden, a tour of the museum, which I soon realised was gobsmackingly bad.

Three dimly lit rooms housed a collection of photos charting the history of Addis Ababa, plus a few ceremonial robes worn by past mayors, and an old telephone. Captain Nasal Hair wasn't helping either, dishing out such gems of information as: 'This first telephone in Addis. This very, very old telephone.'

I left as quickly as I could, and headed back to the house – after all, the cook was about to serve lunch. Once that was done, Andrew and I headed out to get some water, passing the grandeur that is the local goat abattoir just up the road. It's a confronting sight – an empty city block where farmers bring their goat herds in the hope of selling them. It'll cost you around 100 birr for a goat, more if you want to have it slaughtered on the spot. As Andrew and I wandered past, a farmer had obviously made a sale, and was halfway through slicing up a very fresh carcass on the dirt verge by the side of the road. Andrew explained that he and Shep had been studying the market for a while.

'You see loads of people taking live goats away with them,' he said. 'We've worked out five different ways to get them home. Most people go for the one-handed grab, where they just pick up one of the goat's hooves in their hand and walk off with it, so the goat hobbles along with them. Then if you've got two people they can grab a front hoof each and walk it home like that.

'Then there's the wheelbarrow – that's my favourite. You pick up its back legs and walk it along forwards. I've even seen a reverse wheelbarrow! Guy had picked up the front legs and the goat was hopping along behind him. Then the fifth way, if you're really tough, is you can sling the whole goat over your shoulders and walk home with it around the back of your neck. I don't think I'd want to get goat on my shirt though – those things are pretty dirty, mate.'

As our last drinking session was a good 48 hours ago, and we'd only just started recovering, the boys decided it was time to head out again. The Hilton was putting on a British pub night, but we decided to instead hang out in the Bole Road area, about the closest Addis gets to a major shopping strip. We had dinner at Rodeo, a Texan-themed restaurant that didn't seem to serve any Texan food. It was definitely a surreal feeling being served a plate of genuine Russian beef stroganoff by an Ethiopian guy in a cowboy outfit and a Stetson in the middle of Addis Ababa.

We had a short drive to get to the next bar, and the boys had a surprise for me.

'Hey, Shep, I reckon we get Groundy to drive,' Andrew said as we walked through the gravel car park.

Shep paused. 'Get Groundy to drive . . . Yep, let's do it. Here's the keys, fuckhead,' he said, flinging the car keys in my direction.

I grabbed them, jumped in and started the car. Now, driving after a few beers isn't the best idea. But driving after a few beers in a foreign country, which drives on the right-hand side of the road and whose residents like to fling themselves in front of moving vehicles, is definitely not a good idea. Still, I started the car, and pulled out nervously onto the potholed road.

'Show us your horn skills, Groundy,' Shep said from the back.

I gave the horn a tap. *Beep!*

'Mmm, not bad,' Andrew said. 'But you need to give it a bit more in this place. Go on, let it rip!'

I gave it a harder tap. *Beep beeeeep!*

'Nice, Groundy, nice. Still not up to Ethiopians though. Come on, one more try!'

I slammed my hand on the horn. *Beep ba-da beep beeeeeeeep!*

'Now you've got it, Groundy, fuck yeah!' Shep cried, as bewildered drivers stared at the car full of white guys crawling along the main road beeping madly.

We ended up back at Memo that night, drinking Addis's most expensive drinks, and fighting off Addis's most persistent hookers. I don't recall a great deal about it, except that at one stage Andrew and I had an argument over how many points the largest star on the Australian flag has, and the winner would get to wake the loser up at a random time of his choosing, and the loser would have to walk into the kitchen, touch the bench, then go back to bed. We never did figure out who'd won.

*

There are hangovers, and then there's just being sick. When I woke up next morning, I couldn't figure which I had: the world's worst hangover, or the beginnings of some horribly exotic African disease.

When I travel, I obsess over my health. If I'm feeling a bit ill at home, I'll just shrug it off and get on with things. Like most guys, I'd only consider visiting an actual doctor if I started coughing up my pancreas. On the road though, I stress. What if I've contracted some terrible disease? Last time I'd been in Africa I'd ended up having a blood test for malaria in Uganda just because I had a headache. Now, with the added joys of swine flu around, I was doubly paranoid. I didn't really fancy contracting a serious illness in a country with a third-world health care system. Fortunately though, I hadn't arrived in England yet.

Still, I spent most of the day convinced I had all sorts of ills that had nothing to do with the thousand gin and tonics I'd drunk the night before. I had swine flu, I had gastritis, I had food poisoning, I had malaria – when talk turned to dengue fever, I was convinced I had that too. It turned out, of course, that it was just the world's worst hangover. But I was pretty worried there for a while.

I was in quite a state as Charles drove us out to a cafe in the countryside that he knew made meat pies for lunch. While I was trying not to even think about food lest I cause an accident in the back of Charles's Land Rover, Andrew and Shep were like two kids on Christmas Eve.

'What are you gunna get?' Andrew was asking Shep.

'Oh, meat, definitely. It better not just be fucking chicken pies. They're all right, but I'm up for meat.'

'Yep, me too. I think I might get two.'

'Oh, fuck yeah, I'll get three.'

'Fuck yeah. I hope they're not too hot too, 'cause I just want to smash them. You know, you can't put a really hot pie in your mouth. I might anyway though.'

'Yeah mate, I'm just gunna do it. Fuckin' pies, how good is that?'

'Fuckin' good.'

As it turned out, the pies *were* good – as they should be, given they were made by an Australian. Rae Newman is an Aussie expat who runs fistula hospitals throughout Ethiopia, plus has a home for disadvantaged women outside of Addis. It was this home that we were visiting, and the adjoining cafe was where Rae and her band of women served up the pies. She also made lamingtons for an appreciative expat clientele. Another surreal food moment – sitting at the cafe, surrounded by acacia-studded African hills, eating meat pies and lamingtons cooked by a woman named Rae. Unfortunately, I just couldn't do them justice.

'Did I tell you about the deal Shep and I made?' Andrew asked between mouthfuls of *my* pie.

'No, don't think so.'

'Right, we've got this deal that if one of us dies while we're living here . . .'

'The other one will kill himself? Kind of a love pact?'

'No, dickhead. If one of us dies, the other one will make up this awesome story about how we were about to get kidnapped by bandits, and one sacrificed himself to save the other one. You know, put his life on the line for his mate.'

'But isn't it pretty safe here? I haven't seen any bandits.'

'Yeah, but none of our friends know that. Don't fuckin' spoil it, Groundy.'

That night, as Addis was experiencing one of its day-long power cuts, we'd decided to sit around a bonfire Shep had built in the backyard. While Shep roasted canned hotdog wieners on a long fork, Andrew explained the other deals the pair had made (I was beginning to think they might have had too much time on their hands).

'You know how we read *The Economist* sometimes? Right, so I've got to get our company name mentioned in *The Economist*. If I get it in there by my birthday – which is in three months – Shep has to buy me two bottle openers and a didgeridoo. If I get it in by

Shep's birthday – which is in four months – he has to buy me one bottle opener and a didgeridoo. If it's after Shep's birthday, I just get a bottle opener.'

'What are you going to do with two bottle openers?'

'Groundy, you can never have too many bottle openers.'

As the night wore on, I also uncovered a raw wound of Andrew's. It was nothing major – he was just convinced that Bob Marley had stolen the melody for *Redemption Song* from his family's traditional song.

'I don't like to talk about it,' Andrew said.

'Seriously, it upsets him,' Shep added.

'But trust me, he stole the fuckin' lyrics from my family song. It's upsetting, Groundy. Me and Shep do have another deal though. Bob Marley's dead, right? But if I can get Ziggy Marley into our back shed down there, then Shep has to learn clarinet to a second grade level.'

'He . . . what?'

'You know, clarinet? He has to learn to play it if I can get Ziggy Marley into our back shed.'

*

Four days in Ethiopia, and what had I seen? The inside of a few bars, definitely. I'd met a few white NGO workers, been chatted up by a few hookers, and wandered around Addis's two museums. So, despite the fact I was actually going to have to shell out a few birr for accommodation, I decided to spend a few days seeing something of Ethiopia. According to Andrew's guidebook, the holy town of Lalibela was pretty much unmissable, as it housed 13 churches which had been chiselled out from single blocks of stone, like Petra in Jordan. A few days earlier I'd wandered down to the Hilton to book my flights: up on Sunday, back on Monday afternoon to connect with my Monday night flight to London.

I should have twigged that something was awry when I rolled

up at Bole Airport on the Sunday, a good two hours before my flight. All of a sudden, I was being hurried along by panicked security guards who'd seen my ticket. I was pushed through check-in, whizzed through security, and basically thrown through the boarding gate, all with a good hour until my flight was supposed to take off.

'Did you get a call this morning sir?' one of the Ethiopian Airlines hostesses asked me.

'No, I don't have a mobile here.'

'Ah. The flight is scheduled for an hour earlier now – you should have been told that last night.'

It was a good introduction to a very bizarre flying route, where planes seemed to leave (and arrive) whenever they liked, and passengers were forced to work around the changes. There was also the route itself. While I'd booked a ticket that said 'Addis Ababa to Lalibela', I was actually going on a grand tour of the country: from Addis in the south of the country, to Bahir Dar in the west, then to Gonder in the north-west, then Axum in the far north, and finally Lalibela, in the middle of the country. So what would have been a 50-minute flight turned into a three-and-a-half hour nightmare.

It's known as the 'historic route', ostensibly because all of the destinations have some historical significance to the country, but could also have been named after the plane that flies it. Ethiopian Airlines runs a Fokker 50 on the route – a 25-year-old plane that's also used by such aviation luminaries as Aero Mongolia and Sudan Airways. The two-propellered plane looked like it was held together with superglue, and also did a mean landing, smacking into the tarmac like a drunk onto a bar-room floor – and trust me, I did plenty of landings.

There was actual applause from the back of the plane when we landed in Lalibela, a town perched in some spectacular mountains in the middle of the country. Almost inaccessible up until a few years ago (it's a bone-jarring two-day drive from Addis), the town is now the proud owner of an airport, although that's still a half-hour drive through the mountains, meaning you're instantly at the mercy of the city's hotel touts and minivan drivers when you arrive. I managed to fight my way through the throng and get myself a seat in a minivan to get to my hotel.

After a buttock-clenching ride up the mountain, I checked in, sat through the minivan driver's spiel (it turned out he, like everyone else in town, was a guide), then made my way up the hill to the Ethiopian Airlines office to confirm my ticket for the next day. Lalibela was a tiny town, with one long cobbled street winding through the mountainside it was perched on. There's only one tourist attraction – the rock-hewn churches – but there are plenty of people around to pester the tourists.

Of course, it being midday, the Ethiopian Airlines office was closed for lunch. For two hours. As was the ticket office for the churches. Leaving me with a grand total of absolutely nothing to do for the next hour-and-a-half except eat some injera and wat, then sit in the dusty old square that passes for a park in Lalibela and make conversation with the shoeshine kids desperate to give my Havaianas a good buffing.

Sitting there, I had to admit that I was looking forward to the relative civilisation of France. I'd enjoyed my time in the third world, but there are only so many rats and cockroaches and train crashes that a backpacker can go through. Bizarrely, I had two things on my mind: decent sandwiches, and a chemist. It's funny the things you miss – all I needed to make me happy at that point was a baguette and access to multivitamins. Still, that was another 48 hours away. Or so I thought.

Venturing into the Ethiopian Airlines office at two, I was given my check-in time for the next day by the slightly confused man behind the counter: 8am. I raised an eyebrow. 'Four hours before the flight?'

'No, flight has changed. It is at 10 o'clock now.'

I shrugged, recalling Leonardo DiCaprio's catchphrase from the movie *Blood Diamond*: 'TIA broo.' Meaning, This Is Africa.

Some things don't work the way you expect them to in Africa – or *when* you expect them to – but I was determined to go with the flow. I wasn't going to be one of those uptight tourists demanding things happen exactly when I wanted them to. I'd roll with the punches, and things would be all right.

Now that it was two o'clock, I could head down to the churches, where I knew I'd have to fight off a whole town's worth of potential guides. The ticket office was just an old man sitting on a wooden bench out the front, so I paid my 200 birr, and wandered on in. Within five minutes of crawling through the labyrinthine rock tunnels that connect the churches, I was hopelessly lost. Plus, the churches all seemed to be locked up, which was odd. So it was inevitable that I was going to have to employ a guide. Now if only I could find one aro—

'I think you need a guide, friend,' a voice behind me said, startling me with a hand on the shoulder. Of course, I'd been followed in by a few guides going on the seemingly correct assumption that I'd soon be lost. Giving in, I started the negotiation process, and was delighted to hear my man only wanted 50 birr – about a quarter of what you'd expect to pay. You'd think this would have raised some suspicions about his quality, but I gladly forked it over, and commenced what was possibly the Worst Tour Ever Given to a Tourist in Lalibela.

The churches were quite amazing, huge monoliths chiselled with religious fervour from the living rock. My guide's commentary, however, was not so amazing.

'How long did it take to build these?' I asked.

'All 13 churches? Twenty-three years.'

'Wow, that's a very short time.'

'Well, the people of Lalibela, they have help from angels.'

'Oh, that makes sense then.'

'The people, they chisel down two metres,' he said, spreading his hands wide, 'two metres each day. They come back the next morning, angels have dug four metres!'

'Right. Handy having those angels then. Do you think they could sort out the shower at my hotel?'

The tour continued, me scribbling down gems of information like, 'This the inside of church. This very, very old church.'

To get to the final church at a separate location, I had to trail along 20 metres behind my guide as we walked along the road, because he'd had 'argument with policeman a few days ago'. Meaning, I take it, he had no licence to be guiding. We made it to the church of St George together though, and it turned out to be my favourite, a spectacular cross-shaped monolith dug deep into the earth.

'How old is this one?' I asked.

'Um . . . I don't understand.'

'When was it built? What year?'

'This one? I . . . Sorry. What?'

'What year did they build this church in?'

(Uncomfortable pause.) 'Sorry, I do not know this.'

I sighed (it was built in the 13th century, I later found). Despite all this, I paid my guide, with a handy 5 birr tip, and set off back to my hotel, with absolutely no idea how I was going to fill the 14 hours until my flight out, given I'd exhausted every single one of Lalibela's one tourist attraction. Walking down the cobbled street through town though, I heard a familiar noise. The sound of amplified cheering. Of crass songs. Of English men getting overly excited. Football!

Pushing away a few tree branches and stepping down a dirt path, I found what I was looking for. There, in a small square, was Lalibela's one public television, an old push-button set perched on a table and protected by a ripped tarpaulin that had been thrown over a few poles. Crowding the wooden benches in front of it were about 50 locals all in traditional Ethiopian dress: sandals, long pants, and replica Manchester United jerseys. From the blaring commentary that was up as far as it would go, they were watching the Manchester derby from the English Premier League. And going by the shirts and the shouting, you wouldn't want to be a City fan.

Being a football fan – and being a football fan with bugger all else to do – I decided to take a seat on the wooden benches, even though I knew it was going to cause a stir. There might be precious few whites in Lalibela, but there are even fewer prepared to watch football on a wooden bench in the middle of the day. As soon as I sat down, there was kind of a ripple effect throughout the crowd as everyone turned to stare at the *faranji*. I sighed as a guy approached me, but soon felt stupid when I realised he just wanted the 2 birr fee for watching the TV. I settled down and got into the game. Soon, the lads next to me plucked up the courage to make conversation.

'You like football?'

'Yeah, sure do.'

'Who is your team?'

I glanced around. 'Er . . . Manchester United,' I lied. Broad grins broke out all around.

'Manchester United! Me too, I like Manchester United,' said the lad next to me, proudly touching his replica kit.

Fortunately, United won, so with full-time up and no riot in progress, I made my excuses and headed off for dinner, a surprisingly decent 'spaghetti with meat'. I didn't ask what the 'meat' was, and no one offered to tell me. I headed to bed early, harbouring simple dreams of baguettes and multivitamins.

*

It was a big day. I had to get through a frightening minivan ride down to the airport, a flight to Addis via pretty much every town in Ethiopia with a runway, a brief reunion with Andrew and Shep, the possible sacrifice of a goat for dinner, then a stupidly late flight to London, before connecting through to France. And then: civilisation.

Things started off well enough, when my minivan showed up and managed to hold itself together for the ride down the mountain. It was once I was in the terminal, checking in, that the wheels started falling off. 'Just to inform you sir, but we have had bad weather in Bahir Dar, Gonder and Axum, so plane is still in Addis at the moment,' my mate, Joseph, Ethiopian Airlines' one and only representative in Lalibela said to me with a sad smile. I looked around at the perfectly clear blue skies above us.

'Ah, no problem,' I said with a wave of the hand. TIA. I was in no great hurry. When the plane turned up, I'd get on it, and we'd go to Addis. Simple.

Except, after three hours of sitting and wishing, it became apparent that the plane wasn't going to turn up. And we weren't going to Addis. Through one of the wonderful quirks of Ethiopian aviation, the man on the desk informed me that the one flight to and from Addis that day wasn't going to fly, because they couldn't land in Bahir Dar, Gonder or Axum, and as there were only five of us trying to get from Lalibela to Addis, it wasn't worth their while to send the plane on the 50-minute journey to get us. The flight, it seemed, worked like the minivans – they don't leave until they're full.

'What – What about my connecting flight? I'm supposed to be on a flight to London tonight.'

'Very sorry, sir. We will get you on the next flight. It will be okay. You have a room in Lalibela tonight, it's all right.'

I sat down, put my head in my hands, and, like Andrew with streaks of goat entrails up his legs, I had a moment. I fumed. I raged. I cursed Africa and every African. I swore silently to myself. Then, about five minutes later, it had passed. Okay, I was going to miss a day in France. But I'd check in to my hotel, and make the best of it.

Back in Lalibela, I dashed down to the town's one internet cafe, fired up the dial-up modem, and emailed my contact in Nice to let her know I wouldn't be arriving as expected. I then headed back to the hotel to check out the pool I'd seen a sign for. It was the perfect metaphor for my Lalibela stay – a lovely pool set in an African garden, with not a single drop of water in it. I decided to read my book. Tomorrow, I consoled myself, I was going to France.

*

Except, of course, I wasn't. I awoke to blue skies and happy thoughts, but what I didn't notice was the horrifying sight below my mountain perch: cloud. That night, low clouds had rolled in and enveloped the valley where the Lalibela airport sits.

Unperturbed, the hotel manager had us piled into the minivan at 6am, and sent us down the hill and into the goop. It looked fine to me, but Joseph wasn't so sure. 'I cannot say,' he said at check-in. 'The plane is still in Addis at the moment. Hopefully it will come later.'

Hopefully? *Hopefully?* I couldn't believe this.

'Will the cloud clear later?'

He spread his arms and shrugged. 'I don't know.'

And he really didn't. I soon found out that not only does the airport have no weather forecasting equipment (there was a satellite dish on the roof, but that was for cable TV), but it also has bugger all navigational aids, and the old Fokker needed to be talked down by an air traffic controller. If the pilot didn't have a clear view of the runway, he wasn't coming in.

And so another excruciating waiting game began, a nightmare four hours of pacing the airport, turning to Joseph for an update, getting a shrug of the shoulders, walking out to the tarmac to survey the cloud and announce, 'Yeah, they could land in this', before wandering back inside to sit down and stare into space. There were plenty more tourists waiting to leave that day, and the Chinese whispers flew around the terminal as rumours began about where the plane was.

'It's still on the ground in Addis.'

'Apparently it's in Axum now.'

'I heard it's just leaving Gonder.'

'Purple monkey dishwasher.'

Four hours later, we had our answer. Or some sort of answer. The plane had left Addis, and was heading straight to Lalibela. When the pilot got there, he'd decide whether it was safe to land. It was enough for us. We crowded onto the tarmac, staring into the fog, hoping to be the first to spot the lights of our saviour.

Half an hour ticked by. Nothing. An hour. Still nothing. Finally, two hours later, from somewhere high up in the dense cloud above us, we heard the distant buzzing of aircraft engines. Twenty or so of us packed the little waiting area, barely moving, straining our ears, certain we could hear the sound getting closer. Then, heartbreakingly, we could hear it getting further away, until, finally, we could hear nothing but the eerie peace of the African mountains.

A sheepish Joseph appeared a few minutes later. 'I'm sorry,' he said. 'It has gone back to Addis.' Then, by way of an explanation, he shrugged, adding: 'It's a Fokker.'

Oh, it's a Fokker all right, I thought. And if I spend one more day in this Fokking town I'm going to go Fokking insane. An Ethiopian guy put it more succinctly as we piled back into the minivans: 'They have pilots who can land in the fucking Hudson! And this man cannot land here?'

*

I headed back to the internet cafe, only to find all the doors shut. I heard a shout from across the road.

'Hey! Friend! Internet closed, man. Lights are out. Come have a beer.'

Power cut. I should have guessed. With nothing better to do, I headed over to where the guy from the internet cafe, Getaye, and his mate Johannis were sitting out the front of a shop, sucking back St Georges.

'All right man, beer?' Getaye said. I nodded. A beer appeared, and the top was knocked off.

I chatted to Getaye about the things that seem to matter most to Lalibelans: football, and getting sponsored. Getaye, surprisingly, was a Manchester United fan, but could be persuaded to support Arsenal if United weren't playing. He'd finished school, and had been working at the internet cafe for the last six months, making 100 birr – about $13 – a month.

'It's okay though,' he said, popping another beer and passing it to me. 'My boss, he is a good man, he helps me. He'll give me food when he has it, so it's not too bad. I have a room I rent for 50 birr a month, so I don't have much left. Johannis, he has a sponsor, so he is okay.'

'It's true,' Johannis said, nodding. 'I call her my mother. She emails me, she writes, "to my son".'

'How did you meet her?' I asked.

'She came to Lalibela. To see the churches. Now, she is in Denmark, but she sends me money every month. It means I will be able to go to university in Addis Ababa one day.'

Getaye nodded, swigging his beer. 'Me, I have no sponsor. I would like to go to Addis, but my family, they are just farmers. I don't know, maybe one day.'

It certainly put the trials and tribulations of my waiting for a plane to come to take me to my connecting flight to London into perspective. I stayed with Getaye and Johannis most of the afternoon, drinking beers and talking about football, and at no point did either of them directly ask me to sponsor Getaye, but I knew it would have been welcomed if I offered.

I never did, and I'm still not sure why.

*

I slept fitfully that night, constantly staring out the window to see if I could pick out any stars in the sky – an indication, I thought, that the clouds had cleared. When the sun finally rose though, it looked exactly the same as the day before, the mountains wearing a skirt of dense grey cloud. Breakfast was a sombre affair, our little group of potential travellers mournfully eating our toast, trying not to be too pessimistic about the day ahead.

Once again, we piled into a minivan, and once again, made our way down the mountain to the airport, which once again was shrouded in cloud. It was like Groundhog Day. Except this time, Joseph seemed remarkably chipper.

'Visibility is much better today, much better,' he said.

'Do you think the plane will land?'

'I don't know. I hope so.'

After another four hours of playing cards and staring into the distance, a ripple of excitement suddenly went through the crowd.

'There it is!'

Sure enough, there was a plane, like a golden chariot sent down by God himself to this holy city. I was leaving. I was out of Lalibela. I was out of Ethiopia. I was heading for France.

Back to School

'So I'm left there in the middle of the street at nine o'clock in my PJs with this see-through shirt, with no house to go to. Nothing.'

From the start, Katie was true to her word. 'See you at the airport,' her email said. 'Well, actually, I probably won't, because I'm always late. But if I'm not there, I will be soon!'

So as I wandered into the arrivals hall at Nice airport, I half expected to not see someone standing around looking for a strange backpacker. And I was right. A bunch of overly tanned pensioners, a few French girls lounging around, and that was about it.

Fifteen minutes later, Katie came bounding through the door, long blonde hair bouncing about.

'Sorry!' she said. 'I told you I was going to be late. You haven't been here long have you?'

I'd recognised Katie straight away – and her me – thanks to the wonders of Facebook. Rather than just send an anonymous email, Katie had read my blog, then sent me a friend request on the site. Given I was trying to bump up my friend count to win a ridiculous competition with my old flatmate, I accepted, then got a message from Katie inviting me to come stay.

Several things persuaded me to take up her offer. First, she lived in the south of France, which is not a bad place to visit for any reason. Second, I'd been to Nice before, but felt like I hadn't really scratched its surface. It seemed shallow to me, a little resort city with a pebbly beach and a few tourist trap restaurants. But people rave about the place, so I felt like there must be more to discover. And who better to show it to me than someone who called the place home?

As I stepped off the bus with Katie in central Nice, a group of guys almost ran into a baguette stand as they turned to watch her follow me out. (Okay fine, there was no baguette stand – but you get the idea.) It might have been Katie's dress: a yellow piece of fabric that barely covered any leg and was fighting to keep her breasts contained. She also had the classic 'hot girl' hair, and slightly crooked front teeth that could very easily have been dorky, but lent her a kind of cuteness that would drive most guys mad – including, it seemed from the wobbling lumps of jelly on the pavement, French guys.

'Now, I'm a bit worried about you getting lost in my apartment,' Katie said as we picked our way through the gelatinous lumps of man flesh on the Nice pavement. 'So I'll give you a bit of a tour first, show you your wing, then hopefully you'll be able to find your way around.'

I cocked an eyebrow. Ordinarily, this sort of talk would have me excited about the luxurious digs awaiting me. However, Katie being Australian, and in her 20s, and a school teacher living in her own flat in the south of France – I had a feeling the piss was being taken.

Stepping into her apartment in a modern block near the centre of Nice, I saw I was right. I also saw my bed, the lounge room, the kitchen, the dining room and the bathroom. That's because they were all in the one small room, about the size of a normal kitchen. 'That's your bed there,' Katie said, pointing to a futon in an adjoining room which was the exact dimensions of said futon. 'This is the toilet, although I never use this one because you can't actually sit down on it and close the door at the same time. Then we're standing in the kitchen, dining room and living room, and my bedroom and the real bathroom are upstairs. Pretty huge, huh?'

True, it was small. But when you're living on your own in the south of France, it's probably the best you can expect. It turned out Katie had only been in the apartment a few weeks, because her last one had, er, burnt down.

'Seriously, you wouldn't believe it, hey,' she said, flopping down onto a chair. 'It's about nine o'clock at night, and I've just had a shower. So I'm standing around in my pink pyjama pants, this white singlet which is pretty much see-through, and my hair's dripping wet. Anyway, I thought I could smell burning before I got in the shower, and then after the shower it was even worse. So I look outside and I can see sparks coming off the roof. I'm like, "That's not good."

'Then neighbours start banging on my door, and I don't speak any French, so I think they're wanting to come in, so I'm trying to let them in, and they're trying to get me out of there. Eventually I left, and boom, the whole place burnt down. So I'm left there in the middle of the street at nine o'clock in my PJs with this see-through shirt, with no house to go to. Nothing.'

'Wow. Did anyone help you out with a place to stay?'

'Well, one of the firemen said I could stay at his house.'

'I'll bet he did.'

'Yeah, so I decided not to go with that one. But one of the other teachers lives close by, so I stayed with her for a few days, then the insurance company put me in a hotel till I got this place.'

Katie later found out that the place had burnt down because the chimney of the restaurant at the bottom of the building hadn't been cleaned in pretty much forever, meaning all the crap that had built up in there eventually caught fire. It left Katie homeless, but still keen for me to come and stay. Which was Nice. Um, nice.

*

Over my first bottle of French red, we chatted about how Katie had come to live in Nice. A qualified teacher, she'd been working in Qatar for two-and-a-half years, where, amongst other things, she'd taught Saddam Hussein's niece for a year.

'She was such a lovely girl,' Katie recalled. 'No one in the class knew who she was, so one day during a debate someone started saying some bad things about Iraq, and this little girl goes crazy. It turned into this huge argument.'

A year ago, Katie decided she needed a change. Sending applications around Europe, she was eventually hired by an international school in Nice. Or so she thought.

'So the school is supposed to be organising my visa,' she said, sipping her wine and tucking a strand of hair behind her ear. 'And they told me it was ready in August. So I turn up here, go in to work, and the director says, "Well, your situation has changed a bit now, and you'll be working voluntarily for the first few months." I'm like, "What?"

'Turns out they hadn't organised my visa at all. They're useless. And there was no way I was going to work for free. Have you seen how expensive it is here? So I had to negotiate all this stuff with them. Anyway, to cut a very long story short, they sent me to Rome a few times – because you can't pick up a French visa in France – but it then turned out you could only pick up the visa in Rome if you'd been living in Italy. But fortunately the people there helped me out and gave me a visa. Took till fucking January though. January. Can you believe that? And the school still hasn't sorted out my *carte du jour*, which is another thing you need to work here. It's crazy.'

'So all the stories about French bureaucracy are true?'

'Oh yeah.'

Katie was now working and getting paid. She was also tutoring kids on the side, making 50 euros an hour helping a couple of Russian kids in Monaco catch up on their studies.

'I think their parents are mafia,' Katie said, shrugging. 'I mean, come on. They're Russian, they live in this awesome house in Monaco. I know how much rent they pay too, it's about 15,000 euro a month. A month! And they don't seem to do any actual work. The other day I couldn't come and tutor them because they were out on their boat. It costs them 300 euro a day just to moor it in Monaco.'

It turned out Katie spent a fair bit of time in the land of casinos, fast cars and stupidly large boats. On top of tutoring the next generation of Russian mafia dons, Katie had friends she could visit in Monaco.

'What do people actually do if they live in Monaco?' I asked. 'Do they work bar jobs? In casinos? On boats?'

'Nah, most of my friends are cyclists.'

'Oh. Like, good cyclists?'

'Yeah, pretty good. You know Simon Gerrans, who won a stage of the Tour de France last year? Yeah, his wife is a really good friend of mine. Oh, and my ex-boyfriend is [deleted]. You've probably heard of him, right?'

I had heard of him, and the reason I've deleted his name will become clear in a second. (We'll call him 'Brian', hey?) Brian was pretty well known. His name would ring bells with anyone who's into sport. And he was, as Katie said, her ex-boyfriend. The two had been together for three years before Katie went to Qatar, and his now-fiancee was understandably a bit disturbed by the fact Katie had suddenly decided to move into the same area of the world as her ex.

'She fuckin' hates me,' Katie said bluntly. 'I dunno why, it's not like I'm trying to steal Brian back off her.'

'Does she know you well enough to hate you?'

'Not really. I did message Brian once to tell him I'd heard she was a star-fucker, just so he knew, and I think she read the message.'

'Right. That might have something to do with it then.'

'Yeah. Probably. Anyway, it's not like I ever see them. They're in Monaco, I'm in Nice. I haven't seen Brian in, like, six months.'

From what I could tell though, Brian's fiancee probably had reason to be slightly concerned. They might have broken up a few years ago, but Katie still had Brian on her mind. She talked about him – a lot.

In the true Australian way though, I knew the solution. More wine. And maybe some food. I was in France, dammit. I wanted to eat. So the two of us wandered out onto the street, and into Nice's old town. Here was my first chance to see the 'real' Nice.

I'd been to the Riviera four times before, but, like most of Europe, I'd seen it from the inside of a tour bus. I spent a European summer working as an onboard cook for Top Deck back in 2005, ferrying drunk or hung-over-and-about-to-be-drunk tourists between the major European cities. Well, their bars anyway. In the Riviera, our passengers usually got to see three things: the dingy campsite in Antibes, the inside of a casino in Monaco, and the inside of Wayne's Bar in Nice.

If you're a young backpacker in the south of France, Wayne's Bar is pretty much heaven. The bar staff all speak English – in fact, most probably don't speak French. They have happy hours, drinking competitions, and on any given night of the week the place will be chock-a-block full of package tourists trying to ram their tongues down each other's throats. Not that there's anything wrong with that, but I was hoping to see a different side – the locals' side – of Nice this time.

'Have you ever been to a place called Wayne's Bar?' I asked Katie as we walked along the cobbled streets of the old town.

'Ha ha! Yeah, once, but never again. I guess we can go there if you want . . .'

'No, that's okay. I just wanted to see if people who live in Nice actually go there.'

'Oh, God no.'

For dinner, Katie had her heart set on cheeseburgers. Katie wasn't quite the Francophile I'd been expecting. She wouldn't hear a bad word about France, and would defend it every chance she got, but there were certain things she didn't quite dig. The language was one of them. 'I know,' she said, 'I should learn more. I used to think French was such a beautiful language until I came in and started butchering it.' The food was another. 'To be honest, I don't eat much at all,' she confessed, 'but these cheeseburgers are awesome.'

Walking up to the restaurant Katie had picked on a cobbled pedestrian mall, she suddenly stopped in her tracks. 'Oh, hi,' she said, as a guy at one of the tables looked up with an equal amount of shock.

'Er, hi,' he said, pushing his chair away from the table, and coming to give Katie a kiss.

'Ben, this is Brian; Brian, Ben,' Katie said as I shook the hand of the slim, good-looking bloke that I immediately realised was *the* Brian. 'And this is Marie,' Katie continued, gesturing towards the highly unimpressed but also highly attractive blonde Brian had been sitting with. He asked Katie what she was doing.

'Well, I'm going to South America in four weeks.'

'What, for good?' Brian asked.

'No! For a holiday. Although I bet you guys wish it was for good.'

Marie nodded enthusiastically. 'Yep.'

Brian laughed. 'Well, you know, if you want to send me a care package from Colombia, you go for it, okay?'

'Er, okay . . .'

With that, Katie urgently signalled for a waiter, then urgently signalled for a table as far away from Brian and Marie as possible, and we retreated into the darkness of the inside of the restaurant.

'Oh my God,' Katie said, her hand on her forehead. 'Oh my God.'

'What are the chances, hey?'

'Oh my God. We need to get some wine.'

'Agreed. So what happened with you guys?'

'Oh, I dunno, we were never really that serious. Well, I was kind of serious, but faithfulness wasn't one of Brian's strong points. And he has a massive recreational drug problem, of course.'

'Ah, so that was what the Colombia comment was all about?'

'Yep. Not just cocaine though, anything he can get his hands on. He's fucking mad for it. I don't know how he hasn't been caught by the drug testers.'

We spent the rest of the night eating our cheeseburgers and chatting away about, well, Brian for the most part. He might have been sitting outside, but he had a seat at our table, too. I was happy enough to call it a night and head back to Katie's flat once the red had run dry.

*

The bed was terrible. Worst so far, and that included the thin mattress on the rat-infested floor in Bangladesh. Large wooden slats seemed to stick out at odd angles, so you had to manoeuvre your body into strange positions that worked around the lines of the slats. I couldn't exactly complain though – I was in Nice, and I had a full sunny day ahead of me. Except, of course, it wasn't sunny. It was raining: the first time in months.

Katie stumbled out of bed, an act which pretty much put her in the centre of the lounge room, and made a breakfast of instant coffee and stale *pains au raison*. Not exactly the rich *cafe crème* and dripping fresh *pain au chocolat* I'd been picturing, but again, I wasn't going to complain. (Not out loud, anyway.)

We'd decided to spend the morning in Cannes – where Katie had never been in her eight months in the Riviera – before heading to Monaco in the afternoon, so Katie could nurture the future of the Russian mafia while I wandered around looking at boats, cars and houses that I could never afford. We caught the train out, me with my head pressed to the window admiring the white beaches, blue sea and red Ferraris zipping past.

'It's funny, after a while you just start getting used to that kind of stuff,' Katie said. 'At the start I was blown away by everything, but then you just start thinking, "Yeah, there's another super yacht . . . Was that a Ferrari? S'pose the beach looks good today . . . That's a nice enough house." But I still love the train trip up to Monaco. You never get used to that.'

The train trip to Cannes was pretty spectacular too. As I'd been to Cannes before and Katie hadn't, I ended up playing tour guide, walking her down to the beachfront and past the theatre where all the Hollywood stars had been out for the film festival just a week earlier.

'I should really have come down for it,' Katie sighed. 'I just didn't get around to it, you know?'

Cannes was just as I remembered it. The streets were lined with designer stores, the pavements packed with perma-tanned people wearing ridiculous outfits. There were middle-aged women in hotpants, guys with slicked back hair and all-white ensembles. Money can buy lot of things, but taste isn't one of them.

We grabbed a lunchtime baguette, before Katie called a few friends of hers who lived in the area. 'They're going to come down and meet us for a coffee,' she explained. 'They're lovely. English, too. Emma's a teacher, and Paddy teaches but he also plays for the Nice rugby team. He's pretty good.'

I spotted the pair before Katie did, and they were exactly what I'd expected, given the company Katie had been keeping so far. Both were ridiculously brown, in the annoying way that supposedly white English people seem to be when they get some sunshine, and Paddy had an equally ridiculous shock of bleached blond hair, with a tight white shirt and billabong boardies. In short, he looked like an NRL player.

However, Paddy – and Emma – were, indeed, lovely, and also extremely funny – mostly in that they spent all of our time together taking the piss out of Katie for her continued infatuation with Brian the cyclist.

'You're not still on about him, are you?' Paddy asked as we sat down at a sidewalk cafe.

'It's not like that, I hadn't seen him in ages before last night,' Katie said. 'About the only contact I've had with him is when I emailed him a few months ago because I was thinking about getting a cat.'

'What? So why did you email him?'

'Well, he had a cat once, so I wanted to get his advice.'

Paddy laughed. 'You what? Katie, that is ridiculous. "Oh, I'm getting a TV, I should email Brian, he's got a TV. I'm taking a shower, I wonder if Brian's taken a shower before." Please.'

'Fine. Whatever. Shut up.'

'Okay. So Ben,' Paddy said, turning his attention to me, 'tell me about this trip. How many invitations did you end up getting?'

'About 400,' I said.

'Wow, that's amazing. And you chose Katie as one of them? Why?'

'I dunno, she sounded nice, lived in a nice spot . . .'

'You probably just saw her photo on Facebook and accepted straight away, didn't you?'

I laughed awkwardly.

Paddy and Emma had been in France almost a year, and they loved it. I'd read a survey in the *Times* a few weeks previously that said 94 per cent of Britons who moved to France reported being happier in their new country. Good statistic – although it seemed to me that if you weren't happier in France, you'd have moved back to the UK before someone came trying to survey you. What those 6 per cent were up to, I don't know.

Still, Paddy and Emma were firmly in the 94 per cent. They'd vowed to trade in their British passports for French ones if they got the chance, and were embracing continental life, living in a small village called Mougins outside Cannes, and taking on French customs.

'The French guys in my rugby team love it,' Paddy said. 'You know, I drink *pastis*, which is the French liqueur, I speak French, I kiss my French friends to say hello, I play boules . . .'

A couple of *cafes noisette* later, Paddy offered to show me around their little village, so we hopped in their very French little Peugeot and headed up into the hills. This was the France I'd been hoping to uncover in an area that seemed plastic and vain. Mougins was set on the top of a hill, and was all winding circular streets, quaint cafes, art galleries, little shops, and churches. Walking around taking photos of absolutely everything, I comforted myself with the knowledge that, being an old town, Paddy and Emma's house was probably pretty rundown and miserable. We'd seen it on the way in, a little stone balcony with a barbecue and a couple of chairs. Inside, I figured, it would be falling apart.

Only it wasn't. Not even close: tiled floors, modern furniture, white-washed walls, and views as far as the snow-capped mountains on the horizon. I was in awe. I'd enjoyed staying at people's houses all around the world so far, and had had a pretty good time, but there was no one I was particularly jealous of. I've got a pretty good life in Sydney, and I couldn't see myself chucking it in for a small flat in Seoul, or even a mansion in Addis Ababa. But this . . . I was so jealous of this.

'We were going to have the bedroom over here, overlooking the street,' Emma said, 'but the old men are out there playing boules until three in the morning sometimes. It's noisy! So we sleep in the back room instead.'

I shook my head, wandering around the beautiful old flat mumbling, 'You're living the dream' over and over again to no one in particular. Paddy decided to save me by forcing me to try pastis, pouring us each a shot mixed with warm water. Now, I don't like sambuca. I don't like ouzo. And I don't like licorice. So why I thought I'd like a spirit which tastes like a mixture of them, I don't know. But anyway, it was horrible. The warm water diluted it slightly, but each gulp was still a serious effort of will. I only finished it for Paddy's sake – the guy was just so enthusiastic about it.

'We're so jealous of your job,' Emma said to me as I winced my way through the pastis.

I looked around their stone house in a French village, surrounded by patisseries, Michelin-starred restaurants, art galleries, and old men who played boules. 'Oh yeah,' I said. 'Wanna swap?'

Katie and I headed back to Nice for dinner (the Russian mafia had cancelled her lesson – something about some 'business' to deal with), and then walked back to her house, passing Wayne's Bar on the way. It was full as usual with expats and backpackers, a Basement Jaxx song blaring from the speakers. I had to admit, even though I'd spent a few nights living the local life in Nice, it didn't seem that different to what the backpackers were doing inside Wayne's Bar. I'd come hoping to get underneath Nice's skin, to find something different and interesting about it. What I'd found was that same beachy resort town, only with a few more cyclists than I remembered.

Turning onto Katie's street, we passed an old beggar, who Katie explained was her favourite in the area. 'I don't know what it is about him, but I just like him,' she said, dropping a 10-euro note into his cup on the way through. The old guy looked up through rheumy eyes, smiling the smile of the not-quite-there. 'I know you're not supposed to give to beggars, and I don't know what he does with it, but I always give him something. The poor guy. I almost want to invite him back and let him use my shower or something, but you just can't do that, can you?'

*

Christ. Classrooms were bad enough, but this was plain frightening. I was stuck on Katie's school bus, making our way in for the morning lesson. Part of me was wondering whether I'd remembered to get my lunchbox from Mum, while another part reassured me that there'd be no little punks calling me 'Benny Toiletwater' at this school.

I was due to take the train to Paris that day, but I'd decided I had time to visit Katie's international school before I left. 'Don't expect too much,' she said as we took a seat behind the driver, avoiding the stares of 40 sets of schoolkid eyes. 'The parents pay about 13,000 euro a year to send their kids here, but it's a bit shit for what you get. Sixty per cent of the teachers aren't even qualified, for starters. And they don't have any tests at the end of the term. So there's no way of telling how well your kid is going. It's bizarre. It took me a while to get my head around that. They do have a fete each year though, which is pretty fun. You know it's actually pronounced "fet", not "fate"?'

'Really?' I replied. 'Typical French, ruining their own language.'

Despite Katie's assertions, the school looked fine to me. It was like any other in Australia, with bags hanging on nails on walls, and little desks in the classrooms. 'Most of the teachers have been here, like, at least 30 years,' Katie said as she started setting up the classroom. 'It's like having about 20 mums, seriously. Everyone keeps trying to get me a boyfriend.'

As Katie's Year 2s and 3s filed into class at nine o'clock, I realised I had no idea what to do. As previously mentioned, I don't know how to handle kids. And given the fact I was back in a school, I was just petrified that they'd think I was uncool. I needn't have worried, though. The kids were incredibly friendly, and smart – too smart. Rather than give the scheduled maths lesson that morning, Katie had decided to use me as show and tell. So I got up in front of the class, and conducted a lesson on my favourite topic: me. We talked about my trip, where I'd been so far, where I was going.

A boy named Alex put his hand up. 'With all those countries you've been to,' he said, 'how many languages have you learned?'

'Um,' I replied, embarrassed, 'just the one.'

Alex was shocked. 'Really?'

Katie jumped in. 'How many languages does everyone here speak?'

We went around the class – three, two, three, four, two, three, five – basically, all of the kids spoke many more languages than I could ever hope to massacre in my own special way. Being an international school, Katie's kids were from around the world. There were three Australians, an Italian, a Lebanese boy, a German, a couple of Dutch, and a few English. The only things they had in common was that their parents had moved to the south of France, and they had a lot of money. During the lesson, Katie asked everyone what their preferred method of travel was: train, plane, or automobile? Alex, again, piped up.

'Well, I think I like flying first class best, but if I can't do that, then I like to take the boat.'

'You lucky little shit,' I briefly considered saying.

'Does anyone here have a private jet?' Katie asked. Fortunately, they all shook their heads.

I stayed for two lessons in all, and left to a chorus of lovely goodbyes.

'Ben has to go now,' Katie announced.

'Noooo!' they all cried, looking genuinely disappointed. It was probably only because I was getting them out of maths lessons but I must say, I was touched. Coupled with the time I'd spent with Ariya and Marisah in Thailand, I was actually starting to really enjoy hanging out with the kids.

*

Some people dislike stereotypes. My blog readers, for example, hate stereotypes. I get shot down by the baying masses if I ever mention anything about obnoxious Americans, or stingy Scots, or bath-shy Englishmen. It smacks of lazy journalism, of a lack of ideas, and of lots of other things that journalists aren't really bothered by. So it was with a small hint of satisfaction that I looked out the window of the train as it pulled into Gare de Lyon and saw my first Parisian standing on the platform. Dressed in black linen slacks, a horizontal-striped sailor-style T-shirt, and puffing heartily on what I could only imagine was a Gauloise cigarette, he was the Frenchiest Frenchman you could possibly imagine. I could have kissed him, only I'm not French, and I don't do that sort of thing.

My Gauloise-puffing Parisian wasn't the last stereotype I'd encounter. There was another I'd been looking forward to seeing – the chic, sexy Parisian woman. See, I have a weird thing for French girls. It's 'weird' because I don't actually know any French girls, nor have I ever knowingly engaged one in conversation. But that doesn't seem to have dulled the attraction.

For starters, there's the accent. That throaty husk, and the slight mangling of English words that can be so sexy. My infatuation might also have come from my exposure to French films, which all seem to be of the art house variety, meaning my only impression of French girls is that they're intelligent, arty, sex-obsessed and prone to taking their clothes off a lot. I mean, what's not to love?

So I was all wandering Australian eyes as I boarded the Metro to meet up with my Parisian contact. I wasn't disappointed. I was surrounded by catwalk-like models, cute girls in tight jeans and sophisticated sweaters, Eva Green lookalikes, Audrey Tautou doubles. I didn't talk to anyone of course – my French is appalling and it was the Metro, after all, home to another Parisian stereotype: no one smiling.

Parisians are meant to be snooty, to never break into a grin. And if they weren't smiling on my carriage, they were never going to smile. Because down one end was a black man dressed in white pants and an orange sports coat, wearing a Goofy hat complete with long floppy ears, rapping to a beat from the mini keyboard slung around his neck. Every few verses, he'd hold up a Superman puppet, and start rapping in falsetto, all the while bouncing around the carriage. It was without doubt the funniest thing I'd ever seen on a train.

I looked around at my fellow passengers. Nothing. Not even a smirk. Long faces fiercely concentrating on something – anything – else. Finally, I saw what I was looking for: a woman, head in her hands, shoulders shaking, trying to contain gales of laughter. We exchanged smiles. This place could be okay after all.

I was to meet Stephane outside his local Metro station, Censier-Daubenton, around eight. Unlike most of my hosts, whom I'd meticulously planned dates with months in advance, Stephane and I had been in contact a grand total of 48 hours. My plans for Paris had gone somewhat awry. I'd originally had two contacts who'd persuaded me to visit the French capital. The first was Sam, who sounded like a winner from the start:

> I'm an Australian journo/writer in Paris. I live in the Marais with two hot girls, one of whom works for Nestle. We have one sofa bed and a free fridge shelf of gourmet yoghurt products – Ever tried pistachio yoghurt? – both of which you're entitled to.

A month before I was due to arrive, however, Sam emailed to tell me we had a problem: his parents had decided to visit over the exact dates I'd be there. So there was no more couch, and no more gourmet yoghurt products. Still, I had a fallback option. Jen, another Aussie expat, was also offering a couch, although she warned that she had a 'slightly strange French housemate'. Sounded fine to me, so we agreed to meet up. Only problem was, Jen hadn't answered any emails for the two weeks leading up to my stay, and I eventually had to assume she'd decided having a complete stranger stay on her couch wasn't such a good idea after all.

So I had a problem. I had a logical route planned out through Europe, which would take me from Nice, up to Paris, on to Munich, and then the Czech Republic for the wedding. So I had to go to gay Par-ee. But now I had nowhere to stay. As a last resort, I put out a plea to Parisians on my blog that week, hoping someone would take the bait. I was desperate. I'd take anything.

Bingo. 'I just stumbled on your call,' someone called Stephane said in an email.

> I don't have a couch but an actual spare bed for you. My location is pretty central, in the fifth arrondissement, just near the Latin Quarter. About me I'm a 40yo male who worked in Sydney back in 1999 so I know I usually get on well with Australians ;) Safe journey.

I'd have taken a spare cardboard box on the banks of the Seine, but a whole spare room in the Latin Quarter? Sign me up. The dates worked for Stephane, so my problem was solved.

Stephane spotted me straight away (most Parisians don't wander around with giant backpacks). He was slim, suited and booted, balding slightly, and with short stubble pretty similar to mine. We shook hands firmly, as good Anglo-Saxons should – I resisted the temptation to go in for a Parisian kiss.

'Ben? Welcome to Paris,' he said in flawless English. I breathed a sigh of relief. Anyone can write an email in English, but speaking it is sometimes a different matter. I was excited to be staying with someone who wasn't Australian for a change, but also worried Stephane and I might not be able to communicate well. It turned out his English was almost better than mine. There was a reason for that.

Stephane was one of those annoyingly cosmopolitan, well-educated Europeans. Born in Switzerland to Austrian parents, he'd gone to school in Luxembourg, university in New York, had started working in law in Sydney, before eventually settling in Paris. English wasn't his only skill. He spoke German, Spanish, and, of course, French, with consummate ease. Once again, I was left feeling like the thicko colonial I probably am.

Stephane led me back to his house, which wasn't, as I'd secretly hoped, one of those beautiful old Parisian buildings, but a relatively new apartment block in the trendy fifth arrondissement.

Ever since Stephane's original email, I'd had a feeling he might be gay. Not that he sent emails in a gay way, but you don't often find single, 40-year-old straight men living in Paris's trendier areas. So I had an inkling. My gaydar was emitting a few soft blips.

By the time I'd taken a tour of Stephane's house though, it was blaring like an air-raid siren. In case you're ever in the same situation, here are some of the pointers that might indicate the owner of a flat is gay: it's very clean, stylish and thoughtfully decorated; the only photos up are of the owner with other men; and there's a diamante-encrusted mouse next to the computer. A diamante-encrusted mouse? It seemed Par-ee was going to be gayer than I thought.

'Tonight,' Stephane said, 'I will take you out to eat in my area. Then tomorrow night, we will go to Montparnasse. I like food, but I am a terrible cook, so we will go out. Does this sound okay?'

'Fine with me. Is this where you would normally go for dinner?'

'Yes, definitely. I don't really go to the tourist areas. I haven't been to Champs Elysees for two years now! Or the Louvre, too. And last time I went was only to show my friends from Australia around.'

Stephane hadn't lived in Sydney for 10 years, but he'd kept up a healthy interest in the place, which was the reason he'd been reading my blog in the first place. 'When I was in Australia,' he explained, 'people would always ask me to stay with them. Friends, friends of friends. So many people. So now I like to, you say, return the favour. And I like hearing your accent. Listening to you talk, it makes me homesick to Australia.'

From the Harbour Bridge fridge magnets in the kitchen, and the library full of Australia-focused Lonely Planet guidebooks, I'd already got the impression that Stephane was quite into Australia.

He still had plenty of friends from his time there, who'd all come to visit him in Paris, and he tried to get back there for a holiday every year. As with a lot of Europeans, he'd seen more of the place than I had.

But we were in Stephane's territory now, so I let him take me out to see his neighbourhood. Like Nice, I'd seen most of Paris through the glass of a tour bus window. I knew all the touristy highlights, but that was it. I'd literally done about 50 night tours of the city, cruising past the Louvre, the Eiffel Tower, the Musee d'Orsay, the Bastille and Sacre Coeur over and over again on the Top Deck training trip: a six-week mock tour around Europe's highlights. Crew members take turns to do their respective jobs – driving, tour leading and cooking for the other trainees – in each destination, which means a lot of driving around Paris.

So on this trip, there would be no Eiffel Tower. There'd be no Sacre Coeur, and no Moulin Rouge. I was staying with a local, and I wanted to do as the locals do. And that, I assumed, meant eating.

Just a few blocks from Stephane's house, we were into the Paris of my dreams. A small cobbled street led up a hill, and was lined with charcuteries, boulangeries, fromageries, poissonneries – all the 'eries' you could hope for, really. Plus, up the top of the hill was a little square lined with bars and restaurants, each overflowing with Parisians enjoying the last of the evening light with beer or wine in hand. It wasn't all perfect though.

'You see this shop here,' Stephane said, pointing to a hideously bright Subway store wedged between the bars and patisseries. 'This was a second-hand book store up until a few months ago. Then Subway came in. It's very sad. There's even a Starbucks around the corner now.' He shook his head with disgust. 'I think my favourite bar is this,' he said, pointing at a quaint little place on a corner. Stepping inside, Stephane ordered pints of a local beer called Delirium, plus a saucisson, or dried sausage, which we had to slice up ourselves on a little cutting board. You know you're in a friendly bar when you're handed a sharp knife by the barman.

Something tells me the concept wouldn't catch on in, say, Glasgow.

The saucisson was delicious – a herb-encrusted sausage studded with large chunks of salty fat that melted in your mouth and made their way directly to your love handles as you chewed it. I loved it.

From the bar we moved down the street to a little restaurant where two courses and a bottle of wine set us back 50 euros – not bad considering I had duck livers to start, then a beautiful chicken dish. The chicken breasts were served with a few strips of bacon, and actual potato chips, like you get out of a packet. The whole thing was then brought together with a thick lemon- and chicken-flavoured sauce.

'Sauces are very important to French people,' Stephane said, watching me swirl a slice of baguette through the leftover sauce on my plate. 'The chefs spend hours just making a good sauce. This one I think is very good.'

The other 'very good' thing about the restaurant was our waitress, a blonde French girl dressed simply in jeans and a black singlet. The waitress, as attractive as she might have been, represented my extreme disappointment in French wait staff on my trip so far. I knew what to expect from the bastards. They were going to be snooty. They would refuse to speak English. They would serve me ridiculously large coffees and charge me 10 euros a pop for them. They would fling my food on the table and walk away in a huff. They would demand a whopping tip for the trouble of putting up with me.

But the rot set in at the first restaurant I visited in Nice. Approached by a young waitress rambling a stream of French at me, I'd reacted with a tentative, *'Parlez vous Anglais?'* I was stunned to see her break into a wide smile. 'Of course! Please, 'ave a seat, I will bring you a menu in English.'

And it had been the same everywhere: people magically switching to English; menus in English appearing. Smiles all round. I'd bought a bottle of wine the day before, and the lady in the store, realising I had no idea what she was saying, immediately switched to English, and explained the type of wines that come from each region. It was terrible. Where were my snooty Parisians? Where was the attitude? Goddamn it, this place was positively *friendly*.

Stephane was doing the team no favours either. We'd known each other an hour and he'd already given me his spare room, handed me a set of keys for his house, bought me dinner, offered to give me a shirt to wear to the wedding I'd been invited to in the Czech Republic, and a bottle of wine from his cellar as a present, and offered to have me come back to Paris and bring the Lawyer for a longer stay.

Damn Parisians.

There was a moment of awkwardness at Stephane's that night, more on my part than his. I just didn't know what to expect. It was the same situation as with Lyrian, only slightly tweaked – would *he* try to hit on me? As it turned out, I'd been flattering myself. Stephane poured a glass of water, handed it to me, said good night, and walked off to his room. I'm an idiot.

*

I was on my own the next day, as Stephane was off to work at his very important, but apparently very boring, job as an in-house lawyer for – ironically, given Sam's gourmet yoghurt offer – Nestle. Stephane had been with the company a few years, and lamented the fact that despite working in international law, the closest he came to travelling these days was sitting in a room and making conference calls to people in Argentina.

With Stephane joining the rat race, I had the chance to explore Paris on my own. Stephane had mapped out a route of his favourite Parisian haunts, taking me up through the Jardin des Plantes, along the Seine up towards Notre Dame, across the Ile de la Cite into the Marais, and then north up Boulevard Richard-Lenoir to a long canal.

I walked with the sheer joy of a Top Deck prisoner set free, a stupid grin on my face that no true Parisian would ever be caught dead displaying. I practically skipped through the gardens, took photos of Notre Dame, dipped my hand in the Seine, and sat for an hour watching boats move through the locks in the canal. I also realised I'd become an old man. Who spends an hour watching boats go through locks?

Eventually though, I cracked. Goddamn it. I couldn't do it. I couldn't come to Paris and not see the Eiffel Tower. As it was, I'd been straining to catch just the tiniest glimpse of it while I walked down the Seine. Who was I kidding? So I took the Metro to Trocadero, jumped off, rounded the corner, and joined half the world's population staring at that famous tower. I snapped off about a thousand photos, then wandered down to the Champ de Mars to relax in the gardens among French couples doing what they do best: getting it on in public.

I'd never realised the extent to which the French enjoy a public display of affection. But they love a pash. All around the city, couples embraced on street corners and park benches, hands groping, tongues down throats. They sat on top of each other. They lay on top of each other. They giggled, squealed and slurped. To me, it all seemed like a big game of 'Ha ha, I have a sexy French girlfriend and you don't'. But if you're young and in love in the French capital, there's only one way to let everyone know: get it on.

Thus I sat down on the grass below the tower, while all around me French men canoodled with their girlfriends and erected towers of their own. It's a pretty demoralising sight when your own girlfriend is a good 10,000 kilometres away, so I decided to move on. I wandered back down the Seine, watching the tourist boats, or *bateaux mouches*, glide by, thinking how I'd rather bateaux myself in the balls than ever go on one of those things again.

I headed back through the sixth arrondissement, and then into the fifth, feeling very proud of myself that I knew the difference between the sixth and the fifth. ('Yes, I much prefer the fifth, more character,' I could hear myself pretentiously telling my friends at dinner parties in the future.)

That night, Stephane had planned for us to go to a *creperie* in Montparnasse. Crepes are the food of the Bretons, and there's a large Breton community in the area. The reason is simple. 'You see,' Stephane said, 'the Montparnasse train station services the south-west of France. So when the Bretons moving up to Paris arrived at Montparnasse station, they just stayed there. They obviously did not want to move any further.'

Also in Montparnasse is the only building even mildly resembling a skyscraper in inner Paris: the Tour Montparnasse, or Montparnasse Tower. It sticks miles out of the skyline, and is seen as something of an eyesore by most Parisians. 'I like it though,' Stephane said. 'It has the best views of Paris from the top, much better than the Eiffel Tower. There are two good things about the view from here. First, you can see the Eiffel Tower, which you can't when you're on top of the tower. And second, from up there, you can't see the Montparnasse Tower.'

Stephane's crepe meal involved two courses, a savoury and a sweet. My savoury crepe was stuffed with a huge Breton sausage, plus fresh tomato and cheese, while the sweet serving was dripping with blueberries, ice cream and Chantilly cream. It was incredibly good, and traditionally should have been washed down with a few mugs of apple cider, although Stephane wasn't drinking, as he'd had a bad hangover that morning from the few pints and half bottle of wine we'd shared the night before.

Now sober, our dinner conversation was stilted at best. Once we'd covered all of the travel-related topics, and even made a foray into law talk, we'd pretty much run out of things to say. I guess there's only so much I had in common with a gay 40-year-old European lawyer.

'I have an idea,' Stephane said, emerging from the toilet after the meal. 'How would you like to have a very Parisian experience on your last night?'

'Um . . .' I wasn't entirely sure what he was getting at. A baguette fight? Snail eating competition? Dancing in a cabaret?

Stephane continued: 'We should ride home on the bikes! If you want to?'

I breathed a small sigh of relief. He was talking about the hire bikes you can see all over Paris – since 2007, Parisians have been able to rent pushbikes that are owned by the city. The parking stations are dotted all over the place. Basically, if you have a transport pass, you swipe that, take a bike from the rack, and when you return it to another parking station, you'll be charged for the amount of time you used it. It's a brilliant idea, and one plenty of other European cities have since taken up.

After a few goes trying to find a station with two spare bikes, we finally found our ride, and pedalled our way back to the fifth arrondissement.

'Is this a tourist thing, or is it mostly locals?' I asked as we zipped through the busy streets.

'Locals, for sure. It is too hard to some tourists to work out how to use them,' Stephane said. 'For Parisians, it is perfect. You might be out late at night, too late for the Metro, and you don't want to pay for a taxi, you just hire a bike, and drop it somewhere close to home. And you just swipe your transport card to get one. It's a very good idea.'

*

I was up early the next morning, ready to catch my train through to Munich. About the only problem I had was how I would say goodbye to Stephane. Shake hands, or get all continental and go for the kiss? Ultimately, I went for the good-old-fashioned, stiff-upper-lip English handshake. One day, I decided, I would make my man-kissing debut. I just didn't want to make it with a 40-year-old gay guy.

Raving Mad

'When was the last time you were surrounded by this
many men?'

I must have this wrong, surely. A couple of days with Stephane,
and all of a sudden I'm convinced everyone's gay. But still, I
couldn't shake the nagging feeling that maybe, just maybe, my
new host Callum was batting for the other team as well. I don't
mind either way – but still, how do you ask without offending
anyone?

    We were riding the S-Bahn train out to Herrsching, a town
about 20 kilometres outside Munich. Callum had just introduced
me to his friend Pedro, and the three of us were going to spend the
evening at a monastery that brewed its own beer. The train ride
gave me some time to get to know the two guys, and pretty soon
I felt the familiar tinkling somewhere in the deep recesses of my
brain.

    The signs were there. Both Callum and Pedro were immacu-
lately dressed, for starters. And when I'd mentioned that I used
to work for *FHM*, the two lads had looked at me blankly and

asked, 'What's that?' Plus, they were now bickering like a married couple.

I asked Callum: 'So do you have loads of Armani clothes now, working at a cafe that's owned by Armani?'

'Ah, no, not really,' he said.

'You do so!' Pedro jumped in.

'I do not.'

'You do! Every time I see you, you're, like, wearing more Armani.'

'I do not.'

'Oh come on! Especially when you go out. It's like, maybe jeans, or a jacket. Always something.'

Okay, so we'd established Callum had some Armani clothes. The guys then started telling me that they didn't usually buy tickets for the trains in Munich, as no one ever checks, and there are no gates to get through at the stations. I asked if they'd been caught many times.

'Um, no, probably only twice,' Callum said.

'That's such a lie!' Pedro yelled. 'You get caught, like, all the time.'

'I do not.'

'You do so! I know you've been caught with me at least twice, and you've been caught on your own before too.'

'I've only been caught with you once, remember?'

They were still going at it as we got off the train and set off on the hour-long walk through the forest to get to the monastery. Callum and Pedro, by now, were arguing about whether there was a slowdown in construction going on in Dubai, where some friends of Pedro's were moving.

'There definitely is,' Callum was saying. 'See, my ex-partner was living there for a couple of years and . . .'

Okay, this was it. He could now describe this person as 'she' or 'he'. I was about to get my answer. There'd be no awkwardness, no wondering. We could just have it out in the open.

'. . . and he had to move because there was no more work there for him.'

Yes! I had an answer. While Stephane and I had studiously avoided the topic of his romantic life for my entire stay, Callum had let slip, probably on purpose, within the first hour or so. That cleared some things up. Pedro, I assumed, was possibly Callum's boyfriend, or maybe just a friend.

It was going to be a gay week, I decided. First Stephane, now these guys.

Not that there's anything wrong with that.

*

Angela had sounded perfect. In fact, if she delivered on everything she'd promised, I might just apply for asylum and stay forever.

I hadn't really planned on going to Munich on this trip – of all the German cities, it was the one I'd visited the most, and the one I was least interested in going back to. I'd been there four or five times before on Top Deck tours and had enjoyed it, but seen pretty much all there was to see (and drunk all there was to drink on one trip that ran through Oktoberfest).

But then I looked at my itinerary. I was definitely going to Paris, and I was definitely going to the Czech Republic for the wedding, and I needed to travel between the two points. I could probably have jumped on an EasyJet flight to Prague, but then Angela's email dropped into my inbox.

'I am an ex-SMH journo, so of course you can stay with me in Munich,' she wrote.

I am married to a German journalist, and he says you are welcome to stay as long as you help him sample his cellar of wine and bier. The only setback is that you may find our inquisitive dachshund, Strudel, in your bed in the wee morning hours. Warm fuzzies, Angela.

Really Angela, you had me at 'cellar of wine and bier', but throw in Strudel the inquisitive dachshund, and I was prepared to book in for a solid fortnight. Unfortunately, I only had a few nights, so we agreed on dates, and I was all set. However, with three days to go before I arrived, I checked my email, and disaster had struck, much more for Angela than me, by the sounds of it:

Dear Ben. I have been called back to Australia on urgent family matters and will have to cancel on your visit. I am terribly sorry about stuffing you around like this – there is nothing I can do.

Bugger. No more wine and bier cellar. No more fun times chasing a German sausage dog around the house. Still, I had a fallback option. Callum, like Katie in Nice, had got in touch with me via Facebook a few months earlier. My plan had been to stay with him for one night after staying with Angela for two, but as she'd had to take off, I shot Callum a quick message, and he was happy for me to stay the extra nights.

As usual, I didn't know much about him, just that, like Katie, he was pretty good-looking (his Facebook profile photo was an arty black-and-white shot). I also knew he was a chef at a local cafe, and if I was going to stay with a stranger, I figured that stranger might as well have a career I could benefit from. Masseuse would be good. Travel agent, handy. Chefs were definitely up there, too, so I was pleased when Callum asked me to meet him at his work, a place called 'Armani Caffe'. This was promising, I thought. Pretty wanky name for a cafe, but still, promising.

I've always been into food. As a kid I used to hang around the kitchen, bugging Mum to show me how she made things. I never had the patience or skill for baking, but I could whip up a mean pasta dish long before I'd mastered long division. I took a high school job cooking at McDonald's (if you can call that food), then put myself through journalism school by working nights at a seafood restaurant. Now, I watch the Food Channel with the sort of guilty joy that some guys reserve for porn. I also do all the cooking at my house, although if Callum was prepared to whip me up a few delicacies during my stay, I wasn't going to knock him back.

Just before I arrived in Munich, I got a short message from Callum:

> There's just one thing I'd ask of you. When you get to the cafe,
> ask one of the service staff to come and get me, rather than try
> to drag your bag through the store.

Okay, that seemed a little strange, but I could accommodate. I immediately realised why he'd asked that, though, when I emerged from the U-Bahn in the middle of the city and found his cafe on the bustling Theatinerstrasse. It wasn't just any old Armani cafe, it was *the* Emporio Armani Caffe, a restaurant out the front of the way-out-of-my-price-range Italian clothing store. There was no way I was wandering through there with a giant backpack. I was even intimidated about approaching a snappily dressed waiter, but eventually found a guy who said he'd give Callum a call. Soon, I felt a hand on my back.

'Ben? I'm Callum.'

Dressed in dark chef's clothes with a little cloth Armani cap, Callum shook my hand. For the first time, my host seemed as nervous about meeting me as I was about meeting him. Still, he suggested I sit down and have some lunch.

I looked around. 'Ah, I don't know if this is in my price range . . .'

'Don't be silly. It's all good. Sit down, I'll bring you something. A Caesar salad maybe?'

'Sure, sounds good.'

And it was. First, I got an entree of chicken mince fried with lemongrass, curry paste, fish sauce and oyster sauce, drizzled with fresh lime juice and served in a lettuce leaf. Next was the Caesar, which was just as good. This was a chef I was going to enjoy staying with.

A few hours later, Callum was finished work, had changed out of his chef's coat into jeans and a T-shirt, arranged his hair so it flopped stylishly across his face, and was ready to take me out to the monastery.

'We're going to meet up with my friend Pedro too, so I hope that's okay,' he said.

When Pedro arrived, all smartly dressed and Latin-looking, he shook my hand briefly, then turned to Callum in mock outrage. 'They wouldn't take my fucking bone marrow!'

'They wouldn't?' Callum asked.

'No, because I'm fucking allergic to aspirin. What difference is that going to make? They know I'm allergic to aspirin, so they don't give me aspirin. I don't need aspirin. They're so stupid. This is good fucking bone marrow they're missing out on. It's half South American, half German, so it would match so many people. Pfft.' Pedro threw his arms up in the air.

Pedro, I later found out, was doing a PhD in microbiology at Munich's University of Technology, and had been trying to get on the bone marrow donor list. Thanks to his aspirin allergy, he'd been rejected. This rant about his potentially awesome cellular tissue was just one in a series of long, completely one-sided conversations about all things microbiological from Pedro. I barely understood a word most of the time, and by Callum's muted responses, neither did he. Still, Pedro didn't seem to mind.

The dynamic between the two was pretty clear – Pedro was the talker, the outgoing one, while Callum was the quiet achiever, not saying much and taking it all in. They'd known each other a few years. 'We moved over here together,' Callum said.

We ditched my backpack at the cafe, then the three of us jumped on the S-Bahn and headed towards the monastery, Andechs, which, in the glorious tradition of Germanic religious institutions, had been brewing its own beer since the 18th century. When the local monks have set up their own brewery, you know you're in a place where beer is appreciated. The place was once the site of religious pilgrimages, although the groups of young people now taking the hour-long hike through the Bavarian woods with us probably weren't in search of religious enlightenment. They were going for the beer, and by the time we all made it, huffing and puffing, to the hilltop monastery, we felt like we'd earned it.

Bavarians each drink 170 litres of beer per year – although I'm sure I've seen some of them smash that in a single session at Oktoberfest. Contrary to popular perception, not all Bavarians drink from a *mass* – the one-litre beer steins with huge handles that everyone tries to souvenir from Oktoberfest – they're more of a festival thing, or a tourist thing. So, being tourists, Callum, Pedro and I got ourselves a round of them at Andechs, brimming with foamy *weissbier*, and took a seat in the beer garden overlooking the hills.

This is what Bavaria's all about, I thought, as the three of us clinked our huge glasses together and took a slug. A group of locals sat at a table next to us, singing beer songs and spilling precious amber ale on their lederhosen (seriously). The sun was shining, life was good. And Callum had come prepared – he reached into his backpack and pulled out cheese spread, prosciutto, pickled peppers and a few different packets of crackers.

Pedro, meanwhile, was still talking, beer and crackers be damned. He was 23, he explained, born in Venezuela to a Venezuelan dad and German mother, making him the proud owner of two passports, which was half the reason he'd moved to Germany, as he had plenty of aunts, uncles and cousins in Munich.

It was while he was talking about his family that I made one of my trademark conversational gaffes. I'd managed to avoid making an arse of myself on the trip so far, but I was about to jump right back into action. See, when I'm listening to someone, especially someone whose first language isn't English, I have a tendency to fill in the gaps occasionally. When I don't quite hear what someone's said to me, my fallback option is to smile, laugh a tiny bit, and say, 'Yeah.' So when Pedro said what I thought was 'My cousin and I get along all right,' I smiled, nodded, and said, 'Oh yeah.'

There was an awkward silence. Pedro looked over the table at me. 'Did you hear what I said?'

'Um, no, not really,' I confessed.

'I said, my cousin was on that Air France flight.'

I gulped. 'The one that crashed a week ago?'

Pedro nodded. I felt terrible. Here was the guy confessing to me that his cousin had plunged to her terrible death somewhere in the Atlantic Ocean just days ago, and I'd reacted by smiling, nodding, and saying a casual, 'Oh yeah.' Fortunately, Pedro didn't seem too concerned.

'Have you seen her photo in the papers?' he asked Callum, who nodded. 'I mean, she so does not look like that. It's a really hot photo. I don't know where they got it from. Maybe my aunt gave it to them.'

Pedro and Callum had lived briefly with the cousin when they first came to Munich, and had still been pretty good friends with her. She'd been visiting family in Caracas for the last few weeks and had been trying to get home to Germany via Rio de Janeiro. Pedro was taking it well, he explained, because he had a funny attitude to death. His mother died when he was 19, so no loss, in his eyes, could possibly top that. And anyway, he was soon back talking happily about his cells.

'What do you want to do when you finish your PhD?' I asked.

'Well . . . I actually want to get out of science. This will sound silly, but I want to be a TV presenter. I want to, like, present science segments on a news channel. You know, science is so boring for some people, and they just don't get excited about it, so they need someone charismatic to present it to them, make it interesting. So that's what I want to do. I'm thinking about starting my own YouTube channel, to try to get things going now.'

I had to admit, Pedro had the personality to pull it off. And with his slim Latino good looks, he'd be a hit on screen. However, there was one topic he'd probably be best avoiding when he eventually cracked it on CNN: his love of killing experimental mice.

'Oh I love it, it's so much fun,' he confessed as Callum smiled uncertainly. 'I don't know why. I didn't even work with mice until, like, this year, but killing them is great! You can do it tomorrow if you want to,' he added, nodding at me. 'Do you want me to teach you how to do it?'

'Ah, probably not actually.'

I breathed a sigh of relief when we stopped talking about massacring cute little mice, and started talking about Pedro's sexuality, which came up, strangely enough, during a conversation about the movie *Titanic*.

'You know, I looked pretty good in a nude painting too,' Pedro said, referring to the scene where Kate Winslet poses for a very lucky Leonardo DiCaprio. I laughed.

'He's not joking,' Callum said. 'He actually posed nude. For his cousin.'

'Your cousin?'

'Yep, in Venezuela, when I was, like, 16. It was so funny. Her dad came along when we were in the middle of it, and he's like, "What are you doing?" And my cousin's like, "It's okay, he's gay!" Like that would make it all right. I don't know how she knew. My girlfriend at the time didn't know.'

'You had a girlfriend? And she didn't know?'

'Nope. I didn't even, really.'

'Hang on,' Callum said. 'Hadn't you already had sex with the headmaster's son by then?'

'Well, yeah . . .'

'And that didn't give it away for you?' I asked.

Some of Pedro's family had taken the news of his sexuality better than others. His Venezuelan dad took a few weeks to get used to the idea, but was then okay. His conservative sisters weren't too happy about it, but let him do his own thing. He barely talked to his brother anymore, and his aunt in Munich wasn't impressed with it either, although she was still holding out hope that he could be turned the other way.

'She hates me, pretty much,' Callum said.

'How come?'

'Basically, she thinks I'm the reason Pedro's gay. What happened was, Pedro's cousin – the one who died in the plane crash – made the mistake of telling her Pedro was bisexual.'

'To soften the blow,' Pedro added.

'Yeah, so now she thinks he's bisexual, and basically if I wasn't around then Pedro wouldn't be gay anymore.'

I nodded, still trying to figure things out. 'So you guys are together then?'

There was a slight pause while the two of them glanced at each other.

'No, no, no, no,' Pedro said, shaking his head and clicking his tongue. 'We were, but we broke up a few months ago. It's complicated.'

I had to agree. Finishing off our beers, we made the trek back to the S-Bahn and in to the city to pick up Callum's bikes and my backpack from the cafe. While Pedro went home to his apartment, Callum and I cycled to his new flat. The combination of giant beers, a giant backpack and cycling certainly wasn't a good one, but we made it there in one piece. As we cycled along Munich's paved bikeways, I thought about what a gamble it must have been for Callum to invite a random travel writer to come and stay with him. It had turned out fine, but what if I'd been violently homophobic? Maybe I was overreacting, but it seemed pretty gutsy to me, especially for a mild-mannered guy like Callum.

Callum's house was in Maxvorstadt, a trendy up-and-coming neighbourhood just north of the city centre. The flat, like Callum, was neat and stylish. The furniture all looked new, there were modern, thoughtfully chosen pictures on the walls, and a giant flat screen TV in the lounge, where I'd be sleeping on the big, comfy-looking couch. Callum shared with a German-Italian guy called Fabio, who played guitar in a rock band successful enough for him to pay the rent and not have to work. Fabio wasn't home, but I did get to see his vast collection of Absolut vodka bottles lining the walls.

'You should see when Fabio has parties,' Callum said. 'Most of those bottles are just filled with water now, but what he usually does is buy some cheap vodka and pour it into the Absolut bottles, so the girls all think he's splashed out for them. Funny guy.'

'Is he a bit of a ladies' man?'

'Oh yeah. A few months ago his ex-girlfriend from Berlin came to stay here. So Fabio went out, and she went somewhere else, then she came back to the house, so Fabio didn't have any keys. Anyway, at about three in the morning he calls me to come let him in. So I let him in, and I'm about to close the door, and he's like, "whoa whoa, hang on," and two more girls follow him into the house. I don't know how he does it.'

*

The clank of pots and pans woke me up. It should have, really, given I was sleeping about a metre away from the kitchen.

'You up for some breakfast?' said Callum, already showered and dressed. 'There's muesli, fruit, or bacon and eggs, something like that?'

'Just muesli is fine,' I said, trying to be as accommodating as possible. Callum looked disappointed.

'I went out to get the bacon and eggs this morning – it's okay to have them.'

That was all the encouragement I needed. And, just as I'd hoped, staying with a chef was freaking awesome. We had crispy strips of bacon. We had creamy eggs scrambled with fresh basil leaves from the little herb garden on the window. We had thick, crusty slices of toast. We had mushrooms sauteed in garlic and rosemary.

'Keep this up,' I said, trying to talk around a mouthful of mushrooms, 'and I may hire you to follow me around the world.'

It was a Saturday, but being a chef, Callum had to go to work, leaving me to spend my day in the dubious care of Pedro, who'd once trained to be a city tour guide in Munich, but had failed the test because, 'I just seem to have trouble with names and dates.'

We met up in Marienplatz, the central point in Munich, but immediately had to jump on the S-Bahn out to Pedro's house, because he'd accidentally turned his phone off and couldn't remember his PIN to turn it back on. Then Pedro needed a haircut, which he got done not by the thousand-dollar-a-trim hairdresser he claimed Callum frequented, but by an Egyptian guy who charged 8 euros – and did a pretty decent job.

A few hours later, we finally started our city tour. Emerging at Universitat station, we wandered across to the side of the Englischer Garten, the large park that dominates Munich's centre. Running through that park is an artificial river, which serves two purposes – the water is the right temperature to keep beers cold if you stick them in there while you're having a picnic, and, at the outer edge of the park, it has to flow under a bridge and down a sharp concrete slope. The shape of that slope creates a surfable wave almost a metre high, making it probably the single spot in all of Germany where anyone would want to go surfing.

Even the day we were there, when it was still very early in summer, and, as I said, the water was cold enough to keep a crate of Löwenbraüs cold, there were eight or nine guys in full wetsuits, lining up to take their turn on the wave. Most riders lasted a good minute or so slashing up the little wave before falling off and getting washed down the river, ready for the walk back to the wave.

Pedro and I sat watching them for a while, before we headed into the town proper for Pedro's tour. To be fair, it was quite a good tour – although given the standards of tour guides I'd had so far on this trip, I'd have been happy with anyone who could talk. Pedro did, however, show a shocking disregard for the golden rule of visiting Germany (care of *Fawlty Towers*): don't mention the war.

Pedro mentioned the war all right. Loudly. In crowded places. We walked down busy streets and through bustling squares with Pedro yelling valuable information at me about 'NAZIS!' and 'HITLER!' and 'THE HOLOCAUST!' Half of the war memorials in Munich aren't even marked, so you wouldn't know they were there unless you had a half-Venezuelan, half-German, very forgetful gay tour guide to show you around. We saw a small plaque commemorating the street where Kristallnacht – the Night of Broken Glass – began, a critical moment in German history that happened in . . . Actually, Pedro couldn't remember. We saw a cobbled street near Odeonplatz with a small river of gold running through it – a memorial, Pedro explained, for the people who deliberately walked that way to avoid having to kowtow to a shrine for Hitler in the main square. That happened in . . . Well, sometime back then.

Pedro was full of facts, but, as he'd warned, not a lot of names or dates. 'Now this was where King . . . Well, one of them, was first crowned,' he said, 'which was back in . . . ah . . . a while ago.' He also regularly interrupted our tour to answer his mobile phone, usually with a joyous, 'What's up, homo!'

The highlight of the tour though, and the bit Pedro had clearly been looking forward to showing me the most, was one of Munich's *hundeparkplatz* – literally, 'dogs parking place'. Muncheners are allowed to take their dogs pretty much anywhere – on trains, in cafes, even to the cinema. The only places they're not allowed to take them are supermarkets and pharmacies. So, with true German efficiency, these shops have a hundeparkplatz out the front – a place for you to park your pooch while you go shopping. It's usually just an iron ring which you can tie the lead on to, but some have an official council sign with blue 'P', a picture of a dog, and the sign 'hundeparkplatz' on them. Brilliant.

Last stop on Pedro's grand tour was a walk around the Englischer Garten, which was something I'd been looking forward to. Not because I'm a great admirer of Germanic flora, or because I wanted to take in the magnificent landscape architecture in the 3.7-square-kilometre park.

See, the Englischer Garten is known for a few things. It's known for its lovely open spaces, for its acres of greenery, and for the fact that a lot of Germans like to go there to take their clothes off to sunbake nude. ('Oh yeah,' Callum had told me earlier, 'Germans don't need much encouragement to nude up.') As it was a bright sunny day, I was pretty sure we'd see a fair bit of naked German flesh on the south side of the park, which is traditionally where you go if you want to shed your keks. And I wasn't disappointed – the huge field was dotted with Muncheners sunning parts of themselves that don't often see the sun.

However, like any nationality, there are some Germans you'd like to see nude, and some you definitely would not like to see nude. On the day Pedro and I visited, it was a little from column A, and a little from column B. For every group of 20-something girls, there were the inevitable acres of wobbling, wrinkled German man-flesh on proud display. It was at once exciting and highly frightening.

Of course, if there's one thing Germans like more than public nudity, it's drinking beer, which is why it was no surprise to find a huge beer garden in the middle of the Englischer Garten. It was there that I realised the true beauty of Bavaria: Bavarians do exactly what you'd expect them to do. There are no huge surprises. It's cliche after cliche.

You'd expect them to drink a lot of beer. That's what they were doing. You'd expect them to be doing it while wearing lederhosen. That's what at least a few of them were doing. You'd expect them to eat large, doughy pretzels while they drink their beer. That's what they were doing. You'd expect an oom pah band to be playing somewhere. That's what was happening. You'd expect the drinkers to occasionally break into song. That's what they did.

I later mentioned this phenomenon to a Bavarian friend of Pedro's, who snorted in disgust. 'Oh yes,' she said, 'and before work every day we drink a beer and then do a *schuhplattler* dance [the silly German slap-your-thighs jig]. Then at lunch time we do another dance. And for dinner we have a beer and a pretzel. Every day.'

It seems Germans have mastered the English art of sarcasm. And admittedly, of the people I saw in lederhosen at the Englischer Garten, a group of them turned out to be a bunch of pissed-up Poms on a buck's weekend.

Over the jaunty boom-crash of the oom pah band, Pedro finally told me the story of him and Callum. They'd met in Melbourne, where Callum was working at the time, and had lived there together for a few months. Callum then moved to Ireland, before joining Pedro on a trip around the Middle East, and then moved with him to Munich.

'I liked Callum's hours much more in Melbourne,' Pedro lamented, taking a slug from his *mass*. 'He was doing normal kitchen hours then, so I would hardly ever see him. He'd come home, we'd have sex, and go to sleep. It's not like I had to talk to him or anything. Here, he is around all the time . . .'

'How did you go travelling around the Middle East as a couple?'

'Oh, fine, we just said we were friends. We had to make sure we had sex really quietly though. We could have been in a lot of trouble. But Jordan has a good gay scene, and Beirut even has gay bars. They're fine.'

We spent that night at Pedro's science lab, not killing mice as I'd feared, but hanging out at a going away barbecue for one of the lab workers. I was kind of interested to see how a German barbecue would work. As it turned out, it was pretty much the same as in Australia: someone brings in a few crates of beer, everyone snacks on chips and dips, and I get stuck doing the cooking.

I'd made a conscious decision not to get stuck doing the

cooking; however, I was standing near the barbecue, and no one appeared to be looking after the *weisswurst* that were slowly sizzling away, so I was left with no option but to give them a quick twirl. Pretty soon I'd taken over the place, adjusting the temperature, throwing on some beer, flicking sausages this way and that.

Pedro was working the room. The youngest of the group by a few years, he was also clearly the favourite. I, on the other hand, had managed to extricate myself from the hotplate, but in a 'fry pan to the fire' moment, had soon got stuck talking to Tommy and Reinhardt, two of the lab's bosses not known for their conversational skills. ('I thought you might need saving,' Pedro later confessed, 'but I was too busy.') Sitting down with the two, I thought to myself, what the hell do I have in common with two middle-aged German scientists?

The answer was obvious: beer and football. Fortunately, these were two of the topics closest to Tommy's and Reinhardt's hearts, so we chatted for hours about all things Oktoberfest and Bayern Munich FC. It sounded immediately like my Oktoberfest experience had differed wildly to theirs. While I'd just hung out at the Hofbrauhaus, the party place for foreigners (read: Australians), it turned out proper Germans went to the festival as well – they just hung out somewhere more sedate.

'I always go to Oktoberfest,' Tommy told me in between mouthfuls of my lovingly cooked *weisswurst*. 'We 'ave a beer, a pork knuckle . . . actually, we 'ave a lot of beer. If you come next time, I will take you to the Lowenbrauhaus. There we will have some fun.'

'Everyone here goes,' Pedro said, having overheard the conversation. 'Most people's companies here will give them a day off to go, and they'll organise a day out together. We all went this year. We didn't see Callum though. His work had to get into the "exclusive" tent because they're Armani. We just went to whatever one we could get in to.'

While the barbecue was nice, it did have the unfortunate effect of ruining one of my stereotypes about Germans: that of the gruff, unfriendly bunch running around screaming at people for being inefficient. I couldn't have been more wrong. Germans aren't just friendly, they're ridiculously friendly. Painfully friendly.

I'd approached a few strangers on the street earlier to ask for directions, and they'd all been happy enough to help. At the barbecue, though, I'd been there about an hour before people started offering me places to stay for my trip. Reinhardt wanted me to stay with his family in his little village outside Munich, while sarcastic Nina wanted me to go stay with her brother in Cologne (I got an email from him a few days later). Munich's supposed to be the most conservative and unfriendly of the big German cities, but even their town motto is 'Munich loves you'. I was shattered. If the party guests hadn't all been wearing lederhosen, it would have ruined my impression of Germany.

*

I didn't get a cooked breakfast the next day. In fact, I didn't get a breakfast at all, because by the time I dragged my sorry arse off Callum's couch, it was 11am, and Callum had already gone to work. That didn't mean the house was empty though.

'Morning,' Pedro said, emerging shirtless from Callum's room.

'Morning mate,' I said, raising my eyebrows.

Pedro just shrugged. 'Shall we go and get some coffee?'

While yesterday had been the sort of warm sunny day that had inspired Germans to go to the park and take off all their clothes, today was the opposite. Munich's notoriously fickle weather had turned, and it was cold and rainy. Pedro, desperate for a cigarette, made us sit outside the local cafe anyway, wrapping ourselves in blankets while he sucked back some nicotine and ordered a round of cappuccinos.

'Your German's pretty good,' I said to Pedro. 'Did you learn when you were a kid?'

'No, I've just picked it up since I moved here. I actually learnt a lot from watching episodes of *The Simpsons*. You know how they dub all the American TV shows into German here? Well, I know most of the English words of *The Simpsons* by heart, so I just watched it in German and translated for myself.'

Pedro was going to spend the afternoon with his family, who were in the midst of making funeral arrangements for his cousin, so I had the day – or what was left of it – to myself. As I'd seen pretty much all of the town on Pedro's tour the day before, I decided to head out to the city's outskirts to take a tour of Alliance Arena, the huge football stadium that looks a bit like a giant tyre from the outside.

I made it out to the stadium by four o'clock – a solid three hours too late for the final tour in English.

'Is it worth taking a German tour anyway?' I asked the girl behind the counter.

She shrugged. 'Yes, I think so. You can still see everything, and maybe you can ask some questions in English.'

So I took the tour, and, of course, didn't get to ask any questions in English, and didn't have a clue what was going on most of the time. I laughed when the Germans laughed, frowned with concentration when the Germans did, and basically just followed everyone around as we moved from grandstand to grandstand, being treated to what I imagine were some fascinating titbits of information from our guide. About the only times I was sure I knew what was going on was when she mentioned a footballer's name, and when someone sneezed and she said, '*gesundheit*'.

That night I had my first chance to spend time with Callum, who was still a bit shy, but slowly coming out of his shell.

'What do you want to do tonight?' he asked as we got ready as his place.

'Well, I guess we've done all the touristy things . . . How about we just go to the places that you guys would actually hang out in on a normal night?'

'Okay, that sounds good. You sure you know what you're getting yourself into though?' he said, smiling.

'Yep, I'm ready.'

We decided to have dinner at a traditional Bavarian restaurant near the house Callum used to share with Pedro. The place was like a time warp, with old wooden tables and chairs covered with gingham tablecloths, deer antlers hanging off the walls, fake plastic tree branches stuck to the ceiling, and gruff German *frauleins* in traditional dress running the floor. The menu was traditional too, in that it contained lots of meat items at genuine 1972 prices. Given it was the season for white asparagus (which we'd seen stacked out the front of every grocer in town) we started with white asparagus soup, followed by half a pork knuckle with *knoedel*, and strawberries and cream to finish.

Callum was joyfully shovelling food into his mouth, but I was struggling. I'd ordered a *Franziskaner weissbier*, one of my favourite beers in the world, but it was going down like broken glass. I'd been on the road about seven weeks by now, and had been drinking pretty much every night. It was starting to catch up with me. My body seemed to be staging some sort of revolt, probably under the stern stewardship of my liver.

I was also feeling the strain of having to be 'on' all the time – staying with strangers, on couches, you don't really get much time to relax by yourself. I almost yearned for a night on my own couch watching *Family Guy* reruns on Foxtel. Sad, I know. I was also struggling with the pork knuckle, which probably tasted amazing, but I could barely get down. The accompanying knoedel was an even tougher task – a big squidgy mass of mashed potato about the size and consistency of a cricket ball. And about 20 minutes after you eat one, it feels like you've swallowed a tube of Spakfilla.

'You all right, mate?' Callum asked as I lay down my knife and fork with more than half the pork knuckle still on the bone, clutching my aching stomach.

'I'm struggling a bit, mate. Might have to make it an early one tonight.'

'Reckon you can do one more beer somewhere? I was going to meet up with some friends later.'

Everything in me said no, except, of course, my mouth. 'Yeah, sure.'

While we waited for the strawberries to come out (please, no more), Callum told me about his own coming out episode.

'I decided I just had to tell my parents,' he said. 'So I went back to see them in New Zealand one time while I was living in Melbourne, and broke the news. My mum was okay, but Dad didn't take it very well. He just didn't talk about it. I had a long-term partner at the time, and he refused to talk to him. He even came to stay once, and Dad made him stay in the cottage next door, not in the actual house.

'But then one day Dad just suggested he come over for dinner. That was like the turning point. He's been a lot better since then.'

From the restaurant, we had to figure out where Callum's friends were.

'Well,' said Callum, punching a message into his phone, 'I think they're at this bar I know in town. It's a gay bar though . . .'

'No problem,' I said. 'Let's do it.'

So we jumped on the bikes and cycled to Munich's gay district, which was in the centre of town and seemed to consist of two gay bars opposite each other.

It's strange being a straight man walking into a gay bar. The bar was packed wall to wall with stylish, muscled men, and there were two large plasma screens playing an Aussie Bums underwear commercial on a loop. I was introduced to Callum's friends, who I don't think even bothered checking me out, then we settled down with a few of those drinks that are all the rage with gay Germans: beer. Soon Pedro arrived, his family commitments over, and we started chatting.

'Wow, there really aren't many girls here, are there?' I said to Callum.

'No, all guys,' he said. 'Germans don't really do the concept of fag hags. It's kind of practical, I guess. The way they see it, if they're not going to get anything out of it, there's no point. So you only get guys hanging out here.'

If there weren't many girls at the bar though, there were even less at the rave we later found ourselves at. (My second wind had arrived by this time, liver be damned.)

'You don't mind going to a gay bar do you?' Callum had asked.

'Well, not really, given we're already in one. I just don't like doof-doof music.'

Held in an old building on an island in the middle of the Isar River that runs through the centre of Munich, the place was a seething throng of mostly shirtless – and mostly hairless – men. A DJ was spinning techno tunes on the floodlit dance floor, which Pedro led us straight over to.

'SO,' he shouted at me over the thumping electronica as he started shedding layers of clothing, 'WHEN WAS THE LAST TIME YOU WERE SURROUNDED BY THIS MANY MEN?'

I thought for a second. 'PROBABLY THE LAST TIME I PLAYED RUGBY!'

Not being gay, and not liking dance music, the place wasn't ideal for me. But I did my best to writhe around, shuffling my feet awkwardly, and at least looking like I was having a good time. Strangely enough, no one hit on me, so we eventually left a few hours later and cycled – in a wobbly fashion – back to Callum's place.

Pedro was last seen shirtless, making his way towards the DJ booth.

*

Once again, there was no cooked breakfast from Callum the next day, as I was due on my train to the Czech Republic stupidly early. We cycled out to the station – me with my entire backpack again – did the usual stiff Anglo-Saxon handshake, and waved goodbye, two fairly different people who, I'm pretty sure, had managed to have a great time together.

'See ya, mate,' Callum said. 'Hope you had fun. Hope we didn't go to too many gay bars.'

Here Comes the Bride

'The blogger is going to get blogged, I think.'

I don't really like weddings. I know you're supposed to love them and everyone gets all excited and teary and it's so beautiful and moving and you get loads of free booze – but I just don't dig them. My gut instinct whenever I get invited to a wedding is to try to figure out how I can get out of it. After all, they cost lots of money, they're usually a pain in the arse to get to, and I only own one suit, so the more weddings I go to, the more chance I have of everyone realising that I only own one suit.

And that's for people I know. So you'd think an invitation to attend a wedding full of complete strangers in a foreign land wouldn't be a very attractive offer. And you'd be right, which is probably why I turned it down the first time. Besides, it wouldn't just be painful for me. What about the couple tying the knot? I mean, it's enough of an imposition to put up with having my fat arse on your couch for a few nights, never mind having me rock up on the most important day of your life to drink all your booze and leer at your bridesmaids.

Originally, a guy called Peter had just invited me to stay with him and his wife Fran at their home in Budapest. That sounded pretty interesting to me, so I'd shot him a quick email to let him know I was going to be in Europe in early June, and it'd be great to come and see him then. His reply was swift:

A bit closer to mid-June would be better, mate, as we will be very busy before that; our daughter Maggie will be getting married to her dream man in his country, the Czech Republic, on June 9. Unless, you want to join the party at an old chateau in a faraway Czech village, which will never be the same again after a whole lot of Aussies (plus Serbs, Hungarians, Yanks, Canadians) descend upon it for one big day. It should give you a taste of expat life at its most raw :)

I was flattered that he'd invited me, but immediately sent back an email saying I didn't want to impose, and that I'd just try to get to Budapest to see him another time. Then I told the Lawyer about it.

'Are you mental?' she asked politely. 'You're writing a book, you've been invited to a wedding in a chateau in the middle of the Czech Republic, and you're not going to go? You're crazy.'

She had a point. I reread Peter's email, and followed the link he'd given me to the chateau in which his daughter was tying the knot. It looked incredible – an old Habsburg-era mansion in the middle of the Czech countryside. I was on board. I shot Peter another email, this time saying that, if it wasn't too much of an imposition, and, crucially, he actually ran the idea past his daughter, I was in.

Once again, the reply was swift:

Just asked Maggie and she said – why not? Why not, indeed. We are about to walk out the door, leaving on a road trip to Sopron in western Hungary, so let's get onto the details when we return at week's end. But, I assure you, you will be treated like a member of our very international family.

Hearing about my plans, most of my friends then began asking the same question I'd secretly been asking myself: what sort of person invites a complete stranger to his daughter's wedding? An extremely friendly one? An extremely crazy one? An extremely inconsiderate one? Probably a little of all three, I figured.

I'd originally planned to turn up in Nove Hrady, where the wedding was being held, on the Monday for a Tuesday ceremony. The chateau was in the country's north-east, about a three-hour train ride from Prague, so I'd spend a night in the capital, then head into the countryside the day before the wedding. But that plan soon changed when Peter talked me (electronically of course) into turning up a day earlier and staying the night at the groom's farmhouse in another little village.

'If you are interested,' he wrote,

Sunday evening there will be a general festivity in Sudislav, complete with a whole pig on a spit and open fire, where the entire village is invited to celebrate Maggie and Den getting hitched. You should really be there.

Well hell, if a pig was being roasted, I reasoned, I'd better be there to witness it.

I took the train from Munich to Prague, and then changed to get to a small town called Ceska Trebova. Even without any border control, it was pretty easy to tell when we'd passed into the Czech Republic. Suddenly, the orderly neatness of Germany was replaced by the character-filled decay of the former communist state. Where German train stations had been spotlessly clean and modern, here I could see peeling paint, cracked concrete and hand-painted signs flashing past my window.

Pulling into Prague, passing by the endless rows of miserable, identical apartment blocks, we crossed the Vltava River, and suddenly I had a small pang of regret that I wasn't hanging around in the capital more than my allotted 20 minutes. From the rail bridge you can see the whole of the old town – the huge Gothic church on the hill, the beautiful old buildings, the Charles Bridge . . . But somewhere a few hundred kilometres north-east, a wild boar was slowly being spit roasted, and at least a small bit of it had my name on it.

The train to Ceska Trebova was another step down in comfort. There was no plush restaurant car like the TGV that had brought me to Munich – not even a bar, like the Bavarian train, just a whole bunch of screaming kids, and a man mournfully pushing a rusting trolley of snacks through the carriages. My attempt to pay in euros was turned down with a bored shrug. Fortunately, Czechs to the rescue. The slightly bizarre-looking couple in the seats across from me suddenly leapt up, grabbed my 10-euro note, counted out 260 Czech *koruna*, slapped it down in front of me, and called the food cart man back. Having no idea of the exchange rate, I figured I was probably getting done over pretty badly. I also figured that I was starving, and had no choice, so I ordered a chicken roll and pocketed the change.

Curious, I jumped on Google later and found out the official exchange rate: 26 koruna to the euro. They'd given me the perfect amount. Czechs, I decided, were a helpful bunch.

They weren't, however, the most stylish. I was noticing a strange predilection towards shockingly ugly trousers on my train. The pairs of pants attached to the legs getting on at each station became gradually more bizarre, from simple army camo pants to grey baggy things with flowery patches stuck on them, and a few little numbers that may have been in fashion in the 70s, but I seriously doubt it. These were mostly coupled with glorious Eastern European mullets, and – even more strangely – a few people carrying large medieval swords. It was a little frightening: here I was, sitting on the train with people carrying swords.

No one had challenged me to a duel by the time the train pulled up at Ceska Trebova, so I hopped off and made my way through driving rain to the waiting room to sit it out until Peter and Maggie turned up. It took a while. For a brief moment, as I walked out to the crumbling platform to have a look around for them, I wondered if I'd even come to the right city. He did say Ceska Trebova, right? I'd just hopped on a train. I actually had no idea where in the country I even was.

Fortunately, a few minutes later they arrived, Peter in shorts, T-shirt, running shoes and a Chelsea FC cap, and Maggie in shorts and a hoodie. Slightly embarrassed to be meeting Maggie, given her possibly bonkers father had gone and invited me to her wedding without her knowledge, I introduced myself to her first, and she gave me a wide smile and a shake of the hand.

'Welcome Ben, it's so great you could come,' she said.

'Okay, we have to hurry,' Peter added in a faintly familiar European accent. 'My German friends are waiting in their car and the pig is ready to go.'

We piled into Peter's Ford, which had Hungarian plates, and made our way into the countryside.

'So where are we going, exactly?' I asked.

'We're going to Sudislav,' Peter said, in what I now figured was a Hungarian accent that still sounded naggingly familiar. 'Population: 109. Although tonight, it's about 125!'

'Got a few people staying?'

'Oh yes, all of Maggie's friends from Australia are here already. It's going to be a big party tonight.'

Parties I could handle. Maggie was marrying a Czech guy called Den – short for Zdenack – whom she'd met a few years earlier in London. 'You'll never guess where we met,' Maggie said. 'The Walkabout! Classic, I know.' The pair had been living in London and Australia together, but had moved to Sudislav (bumping up the population from 107 to 109) a few months ago to save for the wedding. As tradition goes in wherever the hell we were, the local hunting club had gone out and shot a wild boar, and were roasting the thing in Den's honour. Tonight was like Den's buck's night – only with girls, family, and a giant dead pig.

'I should tell you something about the people from the village,' Peter said while steering us up through the heavily wooded hills, through towns that were gradually getting smaller and smaller. 'Sudislav is only a small town. One street. If you want to send a letter to Den there, you would write Den's name, then "Sudislav 9". That's it! There is also one very big family in the village, with about eight brothers – some of them will be cooking the pig today. Because it's a big family and a small village, I think some people might end up marrying people they might be related to. So it's a bit like Tasmania.'

Maggie nodded. 'Some of them are a bit "special".'

We still had a good 20 minutes before we arrived, so the conversation flowed on and inevitably fell to sport – as it does with me – and it was then that I finally pegged Peter's accent. It was the word 'football' that got me. It sounded something like 'foootaball' – and it sounded exactly like the only other middle-aged Hungarian I'd ever heard in my life: SBS commentator Les Murray. With his floppy greying hair and Hungarian features, I could even persuade myself that Peter looked a bit like Les. I briefly considered asking Peter to say 'Welcome to the World Game', but figured this would be pushing the friendship.

Although he'd spent the bulk of his life living in Sydney, Peter was born in Hungary, and had moved back to Budapest with his wife, Fran, about five years ago to run a business as a manager of female basketballers. He'd been a sports journalist in Sydney, and had even edited the *Jewish News*. Although Maggie shared the same dark skin as Peter's wife Fran, I later found out she was adopted, plucked from the streets of Bogota when she was six months old. Another Peter, the German who was following in the car behind us with his wife Rita, had been on the same boat from Trieste to Sydney that Hungarian Peter had originally caught about 50 years ago. Quite a few of Peter's Budapest friends, he explained, were also making the trek to Czech for the wedding.

Sudislav really was as small as Peter had made out. Coming through town, we passed a house, and another house, and another house, then a tiny church, a small town hall, a pub, and then we arrived at Den's place. Next door to Den's place was another house, and next door to that was an endless stretch of absolutely nothing. Den's place was old – a large stone farmhouse with concrete floors, and a huge old wood-fired oven in the kitchen that must have been from the 20s or 30s, but which Den was still using. I asked Maggie if she liked living there.

'It's okay,' she said, picking her way through the old barn towards the house. 'You get a bit bored sometimes, but I've been doing a lot of work in the garden, you know, stuff to keep me busy. At least we're moving to London in a few months though, so it's not like I'm here forever. It hasn't been too good lately though. I think we've got a weasel in the house that we can't get rid of. Oh, and you're sleeping on the kitchen floor tonight too. Hope that's okay?'

Maggie had been taking Czech lessons twice a week, so she could at least communicate with the other 108 villagers, and a few, including Den's best man, Lubos, could speak good English. Once I'd dumped my bag, we trudged up the road to the hunting club, which was just behind the church, and thus, just behind Den's place, and everything else in Sudislav. But where I'd expected to hear hearty roars, the sound of country folk clanking tankards of beer together and tearing large hunks of animal off the bone to stuff in their mouths before going off to marry their sisters, I was disappointed. The only sounds coming from the hunting club were emitted by Peter's wife, Fran, telling us to hurry up. 'The pig's almost gone,' she yelled.

Incredibly, she was right. The pig *was* almost gone. I could count about 30 people in the club, and they'd almost managed to devour an entire swine. I grabbed some shreds of meat left in the bottom of the tray, and sat down with the Australian contingent: five of Maggie's school friends from Sydney, plus three of their boyfriends.

As well as my plate of swine I was also enjoying one of the things I'd most been looking forward to in the Czech Republic: a cold pint of Czech beer. At the Sudislav Hunters Club, the beer of choice is Gambrinus, and if you arrive on a pig-roasting night, it's free. The Gambrinus was being poured by a chap I later came to know as one of 'the special brothers' – the 'close' family Peter and Maggie had been warning me about. They weren't too hard to spot: they were country boys through and through, with dirty hands, bushy red moustaches, and faces that looked like they'd been rearranged just slightly.

With the help of best man Lubos as translator, I managed to have a conversation with one of them over the bar. 'Don't worry,' Lubos said. 'He say after 10 beers, you'll be speaking Czech to him.'

I asked if there was much lady action in Sudislav for single men like Lubos and the special brother.

'Well, not really much, but tonight we see, eh?' Lubos said with a grin.

'Maybe you could pick each other up,' I said jokingly, pointing between the two of them.

The smiles slipped from their faces. 'No,' said the special brother. 'No, no.' There were some Czech mutterings between him and Lubos, then some angry staring at the floor.

I also finally got the chance to meet the groom, Den, a blond-haired, good-looking lad with none of the facial rearrangements of some of his fellow villagers. A farmer, carpenter and all-round handyman, Den had been spending a year living in London when he ran into Maggie at the Walkabout. He also turned out to be one of the nicest guys on the planet, running around making sure everyone was enjoying themselves while he tried to organise his wedding with only the dubious help of a drunken Lubos.

From the first time I was introduced to him, Den referred to me as 'Mister Ben'. Thinking this was just his way, I ran into him later in the night, while a few of us were standing outside the club drinking beers and looking over the endless fields, and I casually said, 'Hello, Mister Den.'

He looked at me seriously. 'How do you know to call me Mister Den?'

I had no idea. 'Oh, you know, I just do.'

'In Czech Republic, this is a deep sign of respect. To call someone "mister", it means you think you can learn something from them. I call Matt [one of the boyfriends] "Mister Matt", because he has studied a lot, and I can learn a lot from him. And I call you Mister Ben because you are a good writer, and so I can learn something from you. So to call me Mister Den, this is very nice.'

'Well, you know, you're a handyman, good at making things, and I'm not, so that's why I call you Mister Den,' I said, trying to cover my embarrassment at having paid him an unintentional compliment.

As the night wore on I noticed something shocking – this was no raging Czech beer-drinking fest. Most of the guests were trickling off to bed by 9pm, particularly the Australian girls, claiming they had to make cupcakes for the wedding the next morning, and didn't want to be too hung over. Even Maggie had gone, and before long we were left with just Ian the Pom (another of the boyfriends, who'd politely vomited up all of his pork and beer in the grass next to me a few hours ago, but was manfully soldiering on), Lubos the best man, Den the groom, one of the special brothers, and a couple of local girls. The Czechs decided it was time to break out the 'plum vodka' – a hideous local brew that tastes like neither plums nor vodka, but could probably power a jet aircraft. They seemed to love it though, and the bottle did the rounds a few times.

'I used to smoke a lot of pot,' Lubos confessed, apropos of

nothing. 'But now, I don't do it anymore. It makes you too lazy. You make your own world, and you don't leave. And I want to get into the immigration police now, so I don't do it anymore. Do you smoke pot?'

'Yeah, sometimes,' I admitted.

'Oh. Okay. Well, I will get us some pot.'

True to his word, Lubos was back about a minute later with one of the special brothers, who was clutching a plastic tube filled with pot. 'No joints here,' Lubos said. 'We're not that rich, you know.'

Lubos lit up the pipe, took a few lungfuls, and passed it around. I sucked deeply on it, and, used to only smoking the occasional joint, was immediately so stoned I could barely see. I sat giggling at the huge full moon for what could have been hours before Den announced that he'd found some leftover wild boar in the kitchen, and we could all tuck in. What had hours ago been a pretty decent meal had suddenly become the best thing I'd eaten in my entire life. I sat there on the grass in the moonlight, wolfing down my boar, drinking my Gambrinus, listening to the rapid-fire Czech words bouncing around the empty countryside, and decided life was good. Just as long as I didn't have a midnight run-in with the weasel.

*

If the weasel did pay me a visit during the night, I didn't notice it. In fact, a 747 probably could have paid me a visit and I wouldn't have noticed it. I'd fallen into a deep slumber, warmed by the wood oven still burning away next to my spot on the kitchen floor.

First thing I registered that morning was the flash of a camera, a few soft footsteps, and another flash. I had a feeling I knew who it would be. Peter was obsessed with his camera. It was the lead-up to his only daughter's wedding, so fair enough, but I was yet to see him not in possession of his chunky Canon, happily snapping or videoing away.

Maggie's group of Australian friends were all staying at the house as well, and as everyone gradually rose and started making use of the only two mod cons in the house – an electric kettle and toaster – Peter soon had two of the girls, Chris and Lana, and me cornered for a slide show viewing on his computer.

We saw Maggie and Den visiting Peter and Fran in Budapest. We saw them snowmobiling in Italy. We saw them eating in Bratislava.

'So I take it those flashes this morning were from your camera, Peter?' I asked.

'Oh yes,' he smiled. 'The blogger is going to get blogged, I think.'

I groaned. 'You have your own blog?'

'Oh yes.'

So there you go: somewhere out there in cyberspace, if you Google it hard enough, you'll find pictures of me trying to get some sleep on a Czech kitchen floor. Exciting, no?

As I sat around watching the Australian girls baking cupcakes, churning out batches and running them over to Den's neighbour, who had the village's only electric oven, I realised I was missing my own friends. Everyone in Sudislav, Czechs and Australians, had been nice enough to me, but I was a stranger amongst a close-knit group. As the laughter and easy conversation reverberated off the kitchen's stone walls, I sat there and thought about my own version of this group, who were in a galaxy far, far away.

To cheer myself up, I stole a few cupcakes and headed out to the back garden to have a go at firing Den's air rifle at pieces of wood. 'I will give you five pellets,' Den said, digging into his ammunition tin. 'I keep two for me, because maybe I have to scare the weasel.'

Den then drove me down to my hotel in a nearby town called Litomysl, which may not have been a sprawling metropolis, but felt like downtown Manhattan compared to Sudislav. Technically, this hotel stay was cheating. The idea of this trip was to stay at people's houses, experience life from their couch, but, as I'd been invited to someone's wedding in a chateau in the middle of nowhere, I could make an exception.

I was pretty keen to check Litomysl out, too. After all, this was untouched Czech Republic. Anyone who's been to Prague knows the capital city has been well and truly 'discovered'. It might have been an untouched gem of central Europe 10 years ago, but now frequent EasyJet flights and regular Contiki tours mean its Gothic streets are awash with vomiting English bucks wearing tutus. Litomysl, I thought, would be different. I'd be the only tourist in town, free to experience a real Czech city filled with manly Czech men and, probably, attractive Czech women.

It was a five-minute walk into town, which, in turn, was a mere 20 years away from everywhere else in the Western world. I'm sure Litomysl's tourist board would be happy to hear the place described as 'like stepping into a time warp', but I don't necessarily mean that in a good way. Sure, there were beautiful old churches and an impressive castle on the hill. But the rest of the town had made it about as far as the early 80s, and then everything stopped. Another possible explanation is that as the Czech Republic was a communist country up until 1993, the place is only just recovering and it's really not their fault and I shouldn't be so insensitive and uneducated as to want to pick on them, but I'm going with my time warp theory.

The clothes shops' windows displayed spectacular examples of what not to wear in the 21st century. If you're ever wondering where the clothes you chucked in the St Vinnie's bins went to, it's not to the op shops in Australia, but on a direct flight to Litomysl, where your flowery blouses, safari suits and bright, baggy pants are relabelled and stuck in the shop windows.

I was pretty excited to see that the local Italian restaurant had six pasta dishes on the menu, until I actually read what they were. The discerning diners of Litomysl could choose between spaghetti bolognaise, ravioli bolognaise, farfelle bolognaise, rigatoni bolognaise, penne bolognaise, or, for the really adventurous, lasagne bolognaise. Yum.

And my search for a supermodel was fruitless. Where I'd expected to find tall, slim women with Slavic features and piercing, icy stares, I instead found myself walking through groups of stocky farmers' daughters who looked like they'd be much more at home throwing bales of hay around a barn than striding the catwalks of Milan.

Litomysl also rated highly on my staring scale, with the sight of an obvious out-of-towner wandering the streets not going unnoticed. If Bangladesh had a stare factor of 10, then Litomysl came in at about five. I didn't attract a pied piper–like crowd of followers when I walked the streets, but people still had a good gawk.

One thing that was in Litomysl's favour, however, was the price of beer: you can get a pint for about two Australian dollars. Compare that with the painful $14 a pint I'd had to pay in Paris, and I could admit that this place did have its charms.

Back at the hotel, I was having my own fashion problems. Throughout the trip, I'd had in the back of my mind the knowledge that I needed to buy something decent to wear to the wedding before I hit the Czech Republic. I'd brought a shirt, a tie and decent shoes along with me, but I hadn't wanted to drag a suit all the way around the world, so I figured I'd pick something up in Europe. I hadn't, of course. The best I'd managed to do was buy a cheap jacket from H&M in Munich, which I planned to pair with my jeans. ('Jeans!' the Lawyer texted. 'To a wedding?! Benji!') It wasn't ideal, but hey, no one knew me, so if everyone was secretly shaking their head at my sloppy dressing, at least I'd never find out. And besides, Peter hadn't seemed troubled. 'Ben, this is not something to worry about,' he'd said. 'Czech weddings are very informal; a lot of people will be wearing jeans.'

My main problem, then, was ironing my white dress shirt, which had been balled up and stuffed into the bottom of my backpack exactly eight weeks previously. As expected, it had more creases in it than Paul Hogan used to, so I wandered down to reception to borrow an iron, doing a little pantomime for the girl behind the desk for a good five minutes before she figured out I wanted an iron, and wasn't having a heart attack. What she handed me, though, didn't look like an iron. As with everything else in Litomysl, it was proudly presented to you by the year 1970. A weird red-and-silver contraption, it had no water spout, no temperature gauge, just a flat silver surface, and a frayed cord hanging out the end of it. Apparently, there was no board to go with it.

I headed upstairs, laid a towel on the TV stand to use as a makeshift ironing board, and plugged the old beast in. We stared at each other warily for a few minutes while I let it warm up, then I awkwardly laid my shirt down on the towel, and gave it a rub with the iron. Disaster. I'd smeared a glob of black soot across the back of my shirt. It was ruined. I stood staring at it for a while, silently cursing the iron, wondering what to do.

I was way too much of a tight-arse to go out and buy a new shirt, and after all, my only choice in this town was something in the shade of paisley. And there was no time to take it to a drycleaner, if Litomysl even possessed such a thing. I'd just have to iron the shirt as best I could, and then, as only the back of it was dirty, I just wouldn't take my jacket off all night, and no one would know. ('Great plan,' the Lawyer texted sarcastically.) I sighed. What had started off as a clean, hopelessly creased shirt had been rendered a dirty, hopelessly creased shirt. At least it would take the focus off the fact I was wearing jeans.

That night I shared a lift with the Germans, Peter and Rita, who were also staying in Litomysl, across to Nove Hrady, where the rest of the wedding party was staying. It was in this half-hour that I realised that German Peter, who spoke quite good English, was obsessed with Australia. After taking the boat across with Hungarian Peter in the 50s, he'd lived in Melbourne, Sydney and then Longreach for a few years, before heading back to Germany.

His love for all things Australian had stayed with him though, and, in between fighting with his malfunctioning GPS ('I turn him on, and he turn himself off!'), he never missed an opportunity to tell me a story about his time in Oz.

'When I was in Australia,' he'd start, 'there was a tram to Bondi Beach. And now I go back, and it's not there!'

'Mm hmm.'

'And when I was in Australia, I moved to Longreach. Do you know were that is? That's where I learnt English. But it's bad English I think! They speak bad English there.'

Rita, for her part, barely spoke a word of English, so I had Peter's stories all to myself.

We finally made it to the other hotel, where Ian the Pom and Dom – a stocky bloke in a NSW Waratahs shirt who had truthfully proclaimed the night before that he was, 'pretty farkin' Australian' – had been drinking on their own all afternoon. Ian was a quiet sort of guy whose tongue loosened considerably after a few drinks, and who was prone to the odd shocking drunken confession.

'Werra you been?' he slurred when I walked in.

'Oh, you know, hanging with Peter and Rita.'

Ian nodded thoughtfully. 'Right.'

Soon, Hungarian Peter had come over to join us, and was asking where everyone's favourite place in Europe was.

'Amshderdam mate, fuckin' great,' Ian said. 'Not jush the red light district though, the 'ole thing, like.'

'I've got a friend in Amsterdam who lives in the red light district,' I said. 'You can see the hookers' windows from her place. It's great. You can sit out there and watch the blokes go in, time how long it takes them.'

'Mate, they don't muck around in there,' Ian said, throwing off his life vest and diving into a deep ocean of trouble. 'Seriously, you walk in there, hand over yer money, and bam! They've whipped yer keks off, and they're washing the old fella with soap in a basin.

Like, in a proper basin. Then they slap the johnny on, and away you go. Finish the job, and you're out. Seriously, man.'

Peter's eyes had been getting wider and wider during this story. There was a long pause as the rest of us decided what to say next.

'You know,' Peter said, 'I really like Vienna . . .'

*

Wedding day. After a painful breakfast with Peter and Rita – 'When I was in Australia, I could not get a good coffee anywhere! Now, it is not so bad, I think' – I headed up to my room to don my jeans and dirty, wrinkled shirt, and headed back down to reception to wait for our taxi. Peter and Rita had beaten me to it.

The three of us shared a ride out to the chateau, which was stunning. Built in 1777, it's known as the 'Versailles of Central Europe', which may be a bit fanciful, but it's still an amazing building to get married in. Still, some traditions aren't allowed to be observed. Throwing rice in the wedding hall was strictly forbidden, as were real flower petals and plastic flower petals. There weren't enough seats for everyone at the ceremony, but the owners refused to add any more, lest the chair legs damage the carpet. The whole show was directed by two gruff Czech women – the gatekeepers, as I liked to call them – who herded guests around like formally dressed cattle.

As the guests started wandering in through the chateau's carefully trimmed gardens, I was struck by a horrible realisation: this was going to be a small wedding. I'd figured, given the fact they'd invited a weird travel writer, that there would be at least 100 people there. Maybe 150. In fact, the number was closer to 50, meaning my jeans and crumpled shirt – and the fact that I didn't know anyone and really shouldn't be there – would be much easier to spot. And, despite Peter's assurances to the contrary, I noticed *all* the men were in suits and ties. The bastards.

These suits and ties, though, ranged from the well-fitted and stylish (the bride's side), to the high-pantsed and dowdy (the groom's). Watching everyone pile in, I saw some spectacular examples of northern Czech fashion. The first were the 'cousins' – a pair of men with identical large square glasses perched on identical large square noses, wearing almost identical 70s houndstooth suits. Hanging off one of the cousins' arms was Cyndi Lauper – a woman of about 40 with bleached blonde hair that was being harassed by some dark regrowth, wearing a loose, flowery blouse tucked into a white, almost see-through micro-skirt, and white heels. She also had the same nose as her identical chaperones, making me hope one of them wasn't her husband (one was). She was showing the sort of spectacularly garish fashion sense – and will to show off bits of her body that really shouldn't be – you see in a lot of the post-communist Eastern Bloc. After a lifetime of being told what you can and can't wear each day, I suppose it's a natural inclination to go a bit nuts when you're given the opportunity.

Cyndi Lauper, though, had nothing on the mayor. We'd all filed up to the wedding hall on the second floor of the chateau, and waited while the string quartet played Peter – teary-eyed and beaming – and Maggie into the room. Then, clearly intent on giving himself an even more dramatic entrance than the bride, the mayor of the local town emerged from a side door, bursting into the middle of the room ready to conduct the ceremony, as is the Czech custom.

He looked like Alice Cooper probably would if he ever had to appear in court. His gray, wavy hair reached well below his shoulders, and was being allowed to flow free, as only hair that spectacular should be. His face was hollow and waxen, his eyes small puffy balls set into dark, sunken sockets that sat above a bushy grey goatee beard. He wore a cream suit and tie, partially covered by the giant medal that hung around his chest – what I could only assume was the mayoral medal.

Sadly – for me at least – the heavy metal mayor conducted

the ceremony with practised aplomb, giving a moving speech about the importance of marriage in modern society that was ably translated into English by one of the gatekeepers. Mercifully, as I'd had two pints of beer before the ceremony and was about to explode, the vows were short and sweet. Do you? I do. Do you? I do. Bam, let's get out of here. The certificate was signed, the heavy metal mayor shook a few hands, then disappeared back through his side door – and possibly back to 1982 – and everyone else headed down to the reception, which was being held in one of the side wings of the chateau.

Peter was still a mess, hugging everyone he could get his arms around. 'She's come a long way from the slums of Bogota,' he said to me, smearing tears of joy on my cheek. It was a sweet thing to watch, and showed something I love about all Europeans – their pure passion for life, be it hatred of a political party or football team, or a fierce love of family and friends and a willingness to show it. Pretty much all of the Hungarian contingent were dabbing at their eyes by the end of the ceremony, while us rough, tough Aussies just took it in our stride. Wedding? Yeah, cool.

After the photo session we headed in to the reception. It was one big long table, and I wandered around it, looking for my name on the placards. There I was, between Chris, by far the craziest and most fun of the Australian girls, and, of course, Peter and Rita. I braced myself. It took about 10 minutes before I felt a familiar tugging on my sleeve.

'You know,' Peter leant across to me, 'when I was in Australia . . .'

I was saved by the bell. Normally, speeches are the part of a wedding I hate the most, but this time, the prospect of long speeches sounded better to me than a cocaine sandwich. And I thought I'd heard long speeches before; this time, they had to be translated into three languages, given most of the guests were either Australian, Hungarian or Czech.

Den kicked things off in Czech, before switching to English, and then letting Peter translate into Hungarian. His speech done, it was Peter's turn, and he decided to basically thank every single guest individually – in Hungarian, then English, then Den translated to Czech, although he told me later that he might have 'summarised a little'. Twenty minutes later it was Maggie's turn, and she backed up most of what her father said with a little extra thrown in. By the time it was all over the rush to the toilets was like the queue for micro-skirts probably was back in town.

After a dinner of roast duck and bread dumplings, which tasted fantastic but settled in my stomach like a sack of billiard balls, I realised the reception, like the first night's party, wasn't going to be the giant Czech booze-up I'd been picturing. The cousins were sitting at a table silently sipping their beers, taking things slow; Cyndi Lauper had gone to slip into something more comfortable; the Australians, most of whom had stopped drinking, were dancing to the same cheesy tunes you hear at every wedding the world over; and I'd just heard we would be getting kicked out by 10pm. About the only group holding their end up were Peter's old Hungarian mates, who were getting stuck into what looked like a huge jug of kerosene, but was actually his friend Yuri's homemade *palinka*.

Palinka's a fruit brandy, which tasted about as good as you would imagine strong homemade spirits would taste. Yuri was adamant that the stuff was 'medicinal' though, so I did my best to drink it down. Peter, camera still attached to face, seemed to be enjoying it, and was launching into a few stories about his homeland.

'You know what the true international language is?' he asked everyone.

I had a feeling he wasn't going to say English. 'No, what?'

'Hungarian. Everywhere you go, all around the world, you'll always bump into a Hungarian.'

I considered arguing the point, before remembering I had a Hungarian friend in Sydney. Damn. And besides, Peter had launched into the next story.

'This winter,' he was telling everyone, 'we had the best time in the snow. Oh, it was so good. My friend Les, he's been in Australia so long, but he came back to get in touch with his roots. The food was amazing! We ha –'

'Wait a minute,' I said. 'Your friend Les?'

'Yes, you know Les Murray? He is on TV in Australia.'

I couldn't believe it. 'Les Murray? As in, *the* Les Murray? You're friends with him?'

'Yes, of course. He came to Australia from Hungary around the same time as me. You know, he worked in sport while I was a journalist, so we became very good friends. He always comes to see me when he is in Hungary now.'

This was the greatest news I'd ever heard. It's not like I actually know Les Murray – although I did interview him over the phone for *FHM* once. But as a lifelong foootaball fan, I feel like he's my best friend.

'You know, I have a video of Les and me tobogganing in Budapest,' Peter continued.

'You do?'

'Oh yes. Two old men on a sled! I will show you some time.'

(I did see the video a few days later and it was everything I'd hoped it would be: two old men, one very stylishly dressed in a fitted black coat and pants, shooting down a snow-covered road on an old toboggan. Les Murray, getting in touch with his roots. That made my night.)

By kick-out time at 10pm, most people had stopped drinking anyway and were gravitating towards the mini-buses. Even the Hungarians looked ready to leave, and all approached me to offer the solemn Anglo handshake they thought would be appropriate.

'No, no!' Peter cried. 'We will do this the Hungarian way.'

As he leant in, I realised what was about to happen. Peter had warned me by email that Hungarian men like to kiss each other once on each cheek to say hello and goodbye. Here it came. I was about to make my man-kissing debut with a slightly sozzled, but very happy father of the bride. I closed my eyes, and thought of England.

Peter, if you're reading this, you were my first. Thanks for being so gentle.

Meanwhile, best man Lubos had stolen a bottle of whisky from behind the bar, which he planned to smuggle back to the hotel room where some of the girls were staying. The girls, of course, weren't drinking anymore, so they just sat around on their beds while Lubos, Ian and I passed the bottle between us. Ian, having briefly broken free of Claire's iron rule since she'd gone to bed, was doing a few warm-up stretches before launching himself once more into trouble land.

'I fucking love drugs,' he announced, belly-flopping into a pool of no-going-back. 'I mean, reality's shit, you know? I love getting out of me head, and I'm not afraid to admit it. If there were no drugs, life'd be shit.'

The girls looked shocked. 'And what does Claire think about this?'

'Well, we don't see eye to eye on it, you know what I mean? But fuck it, man. You're here to live and die, nothin' else. Might as well get wasted every now and then, right?'

That kicked off a long argument that was saved by Lubos – or, more specifically, Lubos's phone.

'Hey, do you want to see a video of the weasel?' he asked.

I was impressed. 'You guys found it?'

'Yes. This morning we make a trap, and we catch it in the roof. Watch.'

Lubos passed the phone over to me. The video showed Den out in a field with a large trap, which he opened to set the weasel free. And this wasn't any old weasel, not the guinea pig–sized rodent I'd been expecting to have seen scurrying around the farm's roof. Out from the trap bounded an animal at least the size of a house cat, which took a quick look around, then fled into the long grass.

'We thought about shooting it,' Lubos said with a shrug. 'But, we let it go.'

*

Maybe it was the 'medicinal' homemade palinka I'd been drinking, or possibly the half bottle of whisky, but I had some weird dreams that night, the strangest of which involved me meeting my favourite Australian travel writer, Peter Moore, who was being a complete wanker to me. I have no idea of its significance – if any – but it did serve to jolt me back into the reality of the fact that I'd done a lot of drinking lately, but not a lot of writing. I had some catching up to do.

I'd woken up in the spare bed in the girls' apartment to the beautiful sight of Lubos in his boxer shorts, snoring away on the floor next to my bed. I threw my jeans on, plus my stained, crumpled shirt that no one seemed to have noticed, and crept outside to have breakfast with Peter, Fran and the Hungarian crew. As a parting gift, Peter drove me back to the hotel in Litomysl, and gave me a bottle of Hungarian wine to drink when I got to Poland.

'There's just one thing you have to do first though,' he said as I stood bleary-eyed in the hotel car park, clutching the wine and still wearing last night's clothes.

'What's that?' I asked.

'Just pose for one more photo.'

Click.

Girls, Girls, Girls

'When Maccas first came to Warsaw, schools used to come here on field trips from the country. It was like a status symbol.'

'Warsaw? Good luck with that mate, it's a hellhole.'

So said my mate Jamie from back home when I sent him a quick email update on where I was going next. It wasn't exactly a rave review, but he hadn't put me off. I was happy enough to be going to a hellhole. When you travel the post-communist Eastern Bloc, you want a dose of harsh reality. That's what travel's all about. I was okay with seeing mournful rows of decaying apartment buildings surrounded by hulking men in dark coats talking into their cufflinks. I wanted to see wizened old women in shawls lining up in the cold for bread. If that's what I was getting myself in for, then fine.

Only, I found Jamie might have been wrong, or at least things had changed a lot since he was last there, about four hours into my stay. I had a bottle of Heineken in one hand, and an empty shot glass in the other. I'd lost my two new mates, Chris and Pablo, but I wasn't worried. I was a few floors underground in a dingy bar where a thriving mass of people shook around on the dance floor, sprawled on the couches, and jostled each other for room at the bar. Everyone was well-dressed, stylish, happy, drunk, enjoying themselves.

But it was the girls who had caught my attention. They were stunning. Every single one of them. It was like I'd busted in on a casting for a catwalk show. I kept waiting for a giant bouncer to politely throw me out on to the pavement for not being good-looking enough. I'd never seen anything like it in my life. If this is a hellhole, then I decided I was a pretty big fan of hellholes.

I'd always been interested in going to Poland. A few people I'd talked to had been slightly more complimentary about it than Jamie, and had said that it was at least worth a look. This was the old Europe; plus, it fitted well into my itinerary, as Ceska Trebova in the Czech Republic is right near the Polish border, and on the train line that runs up to Warsaw.

I'd been hoping to get an invitation from someone in Krakow, of course, because it's supposed to be amazing. 'Like a medieval Disneyland,' someone once told me. So I waited in vain for an email to drop in with Krakow in the title, but it just didn't happen. However, I had invitations from someone in a place called Katowice – which was also on the Ceska Trebova train line – plus a couple in Warsaw, so I decided to lock it in.

Once again though, a few weeks out from my arrival, I ran into trouble. While I'd been in Ethiopia, an email from Andy in Katowice had dropped into my inbox:

> Hi mate, can't remember when you said you were going to be here. Anyway, any time except the weekend of the 15th of June will be fine, because it's a long weekend here and we'll be away. Other than that, you're still right to stay.

I checked my diary. Sure enough, I was due to chug in to Katowice station on the 15th of June exactly. Fortunately, I had my

Warsaw contacts, and much as I thought five nights in the one city might be a bit of overkill compared to the whirlwind visits I'd had in most places, I decided to go for it.

After all, Chris and Jay sounded like they'd make the visit worthwhile. Chris got in first:

> Hey Ben, I'm from Sydney, living in Warsaw. Feel free to crash on my couch if you are in the area. Come April, I'm afraid the girls will have taken off their furry hoods, but the mini-skirts may just be out already!

How the Lawyer didn't find that one and veto it, I'll never know. Jay sounded much different, but just as interesting:

> Hi there, my husband's a diplomat, and I'm what's known in the trade as a 'trailing' wife. This is our first diplomatic post – we put down Hanoi and New Delhi, so of course we got Poland. Warsaw is bizarre, amazing and above all, nothing like I expected. You are welcome to come and visit.

So that was sorted then: five nights in Warsaw, starting with Chris and the mini-skirted girls, and ending with Jay and the diplomatic community. Taking the train from Ceska Trebova, we called briefly past Katowice (it looked crap anyway), then a few hours later I stepped off at Warsaw's Centralna station, and heard a shout: 'Ben!'

I looked around to see a big, smiling bloke striding towards me, who then wrapped a giant hand around mine and pumped my fist. 'Mate! How are you? Welcome to Warsaw.'

Chris looked like a North Shore rugby boy. He was wearing smart shoes, well-cut Diesel jeans, and a polo shirt with collar unashamedly in the position of popped. He was also a good talker, and nattered away in a booming voice as we made our way out of the station, across the road and over to the tram stop.

A rickety old communist-era tram pulled up and we climbed in, ignoring the ticket machines and taking a seat as it rattled through the intersection. Normally, this initial meeting is my time to grill my new host. I ask them what they're doing in their city of choice; I ask how they got here, how long they'll stay. With Chris, I barely got a chance to speak. He was on a roll, and was genuinely interested in everything I'd done. I finally got a chance to ask him a few things as we hopped off the tram and made our way down a slightly potholed street towards Chris's flat.

'You been here a while?' I asked.

'Three years, mate.'

'Like it?'

'Mate, it's awesome. I came over to Germany for the soccer World Cup, watched that, then thought I'd come over here for a few weeks. And here I am three years later.'

'What do you do here?'

'Develop wind farms. I'll tell you about it later, but it's pretty awesome.'

Chris's parents were Polish immigrants to Australia, and he was now completing the circle, coming back to the homeland to start his own business. It also meant he got to use his aunt's flat, so he was living rent-free in the centre of Warsaw. He'd also been speaking Polish from a young age, and was now fluent, which was a handy asset for his two main pursuits in the city: running his business, and picking up girls.

'Yeah it helps, mate, it helps,' he admitted. 'I'm fluent, I know all the words and everything, and my accent is pretty much right. The only trouble is, I just get a few words wrong every now and then, like maybe the tenses or something like that, and people have got no idea why I've done it. Because my accent is perfect and everything, so they just assume I'm Polish, but I'm getting these words a bit mixed up. So I've had a few people who've actually thought I was a bit mental. It's pretty funny really.'

The stairs leading to Chris's place were brilliant in their

rattiness, and exactly what my friend Jamie must have been talking about from his time there. There were graffitied walls, cracked concrete stairs, and piles of rubble on either side of the dark entrance. This was the Warsaw I'd been expecting, and I wasn't disappointed. Even the tram we'd got here was probably older than my dad, and the central station looked like it hadn't been touched since World War II.

Chris's apartment, however, was disappointingly nice. Poles don't live in large houses – if you've got anything more than a bedroom and a lounge/kitchen, you've done well. Chris had a pretty standard flat, although quite modern, with a small bedroom, plus a lounge with two couches, and a kitchenette. It was a typical bachelor pad, too, with clothes strewn on the floor, dirty dishes in the sink, and what looked like a Russian copy of *Playboy* sitting on the bench under a set of headphones. I was going to be sleeping on one of the couches, Chris told me, while the other one was going to be occupied by a few different people during my stay.

Chris was doing pretty well for a 24-year-old. He'd studied finance in Australia while working at PricewaterhouseCoopers, then done a year's exchange in the Netherlands, before arriving in Poland. He'd been developing wind farms since he arrived three years ago, and one project had now reached the building phase. Chris, like Pete in Shanghai and Pedro in Munich, was prone to going off on long monologues about things I didn't understand, although in his case it was all things finance and wind-farm related. I did my best to follow these conversations, but usually failed miserably. He did explain the whole process of developing a wind farm to me, but I'd be lying if I said I remembered any of it. About the only facts I came away with is that each huge turbine you see piercing the horizon in Europe costs a couple of million euros to erect, and it was Chris's job to not only finance them, but to find the best places to put them.

Chris was also, as I'd thought, a rugby boy. 'I've been playing for the expats' team here,' he explained. 'It's pretty good craic, good bunch of blokes. We just had a trip to play in the Ukraine actually. I hooked up with this fucking beautiful chick . . .' He trailed off, then flipped me the *Playboy*. 'Check this out – *Playboy* in Ukrainian!'

I flicked through it. 'Bet you bought it for the articles, right?'

Chris grinned. 'Of course. Mate,' he added, 'is this your first time in Poland?'

I nodded.

'Oh man, the fucking chicks are unbelievable. Seriously. You wait till we go out tonight. I guarantee you've never seen more beautiful girls. This place is fucking paradise.'

As Chris had promised, Polish girls were indeed the most beautiful on the planet. Polish girls might own track pants, and their hair might occasionally be unbrushed, but they sure as hell don't leave the house in that state: every girl I saw was immaculately made-up, with perfect hair, stylish tops and tight jeans. And the more Chris and his mate Pablo talked about the girls, the more I talked about them. And the more I talked about them, the more I thought about them. And the more I thought about them, the longer I spent staring creepily at them on the streets, in the restaurants, and at the nightclubs. To the Lawyer, I apologise.

Eager to hit the town, I dumped my stuff on top of my couch of choice, and we headed in to the main part of the city, about a 10-minute walk from Chris's apartment. 'I'm going to take you for a quick tour of the touristy area,' Chris explained, 'then we'll get the hell out of there and hang out somewhere you'd actually like.'

I was immediately disappointed with downtown Warsaw – it was actually kind of nice. The sun had come out. The streets were clean and safe. The buildings were old, with character, but looked in good repair. About the only thing amiss were other people. The place was an absolute ghost town, except for a few struggling buskers and the odd tourist.

'It's a long weekend here,' Chris explained. 'So everyone's

gone out of town. There's not really anything to look at in Warsaw, so no one spends their long weekends here. They go to Krakow or Gdansk or something like that. But I've never seen it this bad. I hope the clubs are okay tonight.'

The touristy centre of Warsaw is the Old Town which, like a whopping 85 per cent of the city, was completely destroyed during World War II. It had to be rebuilt from scratch, which explained why all of the buildings seemed to be pretty well looked after. Rather than take the Germans' post-war approach and rebuild everything to look new, the Poles attempted to return things to the way they were before the war, using old paintings of the city as reference material for the designs of the buildings.

'There was one problem with that,' Chris explained as we wandered down the empty cobbled streets. 'One of the main artists they used as a reference, his trademark was to draw little pictures of monkeys on the walls of the buildings in his paintings. So the people rebuilding the city thought the original houses actually had pictures of monkeys on them, and they painted them onto the new buildings.'

It was a good story. I didn't actually see any of these monkeys, so I can't vouch for its authenticity, but still – good story.

'It's also a bit of a tourist trap, no one really goes here,' Chris added. 'We're going to go to a bar in the newer area, should be much better.'

The bar was modern and very un-communist. We met up with Chris's friend Pablo, a half-Portuguese, half-Spanish finance consultant who'd just been made redundant and was trying to figure out a way to extend his stay in Poland. Pablo, nicknamed 'Drunken Pablo' by the rugby team, was a kindred spirit of Chris's, a man who liked to drink, chase Polish girls, and . . . Actually no, that's about it.

'So what should we have,' Chris asked Pablo and me, as we drained our beers and decided it was time for dinner. 'Indian? I know a great Indian place. Or do we feel like Italian? There's that place down the road. No, let's do Chinese. Pabs, you know that place over near mine – really cheap, awesome food?'

I certainly wasn't excited about the food in Warsaw. I'm not a fan of stodgy Eastern European food at the best of times, and I figured Warsaw was not going to be the best of times. I was preparing myself for slabs of meat with bread dumplings. And for dessert: slabs of meat with bread dumplings. But I soon discovered that in Warsaw, people don't bother with Polish food when they eat out.

Chinese it was. Sadly though, our Chinese friends didn't know we were coming, and had closed early. Instead, I had my first Polish meal at a traditional establishment called McDonald's. Sigh.

The time was ticking past 10pm, but the night was young. Chris's plan was simple: we'd meet up with his Polish cousin, Rafa, we'd go to the local casino and pretend to play on the tables so we could get as many free drinks as possible, then we'd hit a club. I didn't have the heart to tell Chris that I don't really like casinos, and I don't really like nightclubs, so I just tagged along.

The Warsaw casino is inside the Hilton, a smallish place filled with flashing lights, depressed Chinese people and absolutely stunning drinks waitresses. If you're playing on the tables – or at least look as if you're playing on the tables – those waitresses will ply you with free drinks. As this is Poland, your drink choices are a glass of beer, or a shot of vodka.

'What will you have Ben?' Pablo asked.

'Well, probably just a b—'

'Four vodkas thanks!' Chris interjected, sending the mini-skirted waitress scurrying behind the bar to rack up the shots.

I groaned. Again, I didn't have the heart to tell Chris, but I don't really do shots. I can drink beer until the sun rises, but I usually try to steer clear of straight slugs of the hard stuff. I have this reputation among my friends for not ever getting really drunk. And that's because I don't do shots. I can't handle them. They all taste terrible, so I try to avoid them. I was quickly realising, however, that I'd have to harden up if I was going to survive with Chris and Pablo.

As Chris explained, the nightclubs aren't that cheap in Warsaw. In fact, nothing's as cheap as I'd expected it would be. The aim of Chris and Pablo's game was to get as loaded as they could on cheap booze – usually vodka – before hitting a club at about midnight. By the time we were hailing a cab outside the Hilton, we'd necked five free shots of Polish firewater.

Starting to feel the vodka take hold, we headed to an artfully dingy underground nightclub, a place filled with Warsaw's young and beautiful (at least, those who hadn't gone to Krakow for the weekend). And when I say beautiful, you know I mean *beautiful*. I could see why Chris had found it easy to spend three years here.

While I fumbled around the dance floor, doing my own unique impression of dancing, Chris and Pablo got to work, scouring the room for girls to talk to. I couldn't keep up with their progress, but I saw them with blondes, I saw them with brunettes, I saw them on the dance floor, and I saw them canoodling on the old couches (not with each other). Ultimately though, we left alone. At about 6am.

*

I'm never drinking again. Never, never, never.

These were the first words that came to me when I eventually opened my eyes and figured out where I was at 1pm the next day. My couch may have been comfortable, or it may have had rusty nails sticking out of it. It wouldn't have made a difference. Chris, I could vaguely see through blurred vision, was already up and moving.

'Mate, Pabs is up, we're going to meet him at Pizza Hut. Cool?'

Great, I thought. The sum total of my Polish meals so far was one McDonald's and one Pizza Hut. Authentic. Still, I dragged my sorry arse off the couch, through the shower and into the Old Town for debrief and pepperoni pizza.

'Man, I got that 19-year-old girl's number,' Pablo greeted us.

'Awesome man,' Chris said, slapping him on the back.

'Look at her name though,' he added, passing his phone to Chris, who burst out laughing.

'You fucking idiot!'

'I could not remember her name,' Pablo said, showing me where he'd typed in the girl's name as '19' on his phone.

As we settled into the big booths inside, giving our order to a ridiculously attractive waitress, I asked Chris if there was any other reason to live in Warsaw other than the lady folk.

'Yeah man, for sure,' he said, sipping a Pepsi. 'Like, I started getting the shits with Sydney a bit, you know? 'Cause I've got all my friends from high school, but once I got to uni, no one wants to meet any new people any more. Poland's totally different. Everyone's keen to meet you, up for having a good time. It's really good like that.

'And people are into different things here. You can have a conversation about politics, or about business, and people will actually get into it. Plus there are the business opportunities too. This place is going nuts. Here and Cyprus are the only countries in the EU that still have positive growth. It's a good time to be getting in, man.'

After Pizza Hut, we took the bus ('Don't bother buying a ticket,' Chris said, 'no one ever checks'), to the Lazienkowski park, a beautiful area in the middle of the city that hosts live Chopin piano recitals every Sunday during summer. Once again, this was far from the post-communist hellhole Jamie had been describing. The park was lovely – so lovely, in fact, that Napoleon apparently spent a whole week riding around it on his horse while his army went to fight in Russia (another good story about Warsaw which was a tad dubious in its authenticity). We lazed on the grass and wished our hangovers away as peacocks squawked and squirrels ran around us.

'Right,' Chris said, raising his head after a few minutes. 'Beer?'

Somewhere deep within me, my liver groaned. But I was here to do as the locals do, so back into town we went and back into the swing of things. This time we were joined by Chris's next-door neighbour, Carlos, a Mexican immigrant with the improbable profession of violinist in Warsaw's premier mariachi band (Warsaw's *only* mariachi band). And apparently, there's plenty of work for a mariachi band in Warsaw.

'Oh man, we get so much work,' Carlos said, adjusting his ponytail. 'Too much. I've been here 12 years man – 12 years! I can't believe it. But we play parties, at restaurants, at private functions. All around Poland.'

Carlos had taken a predictable path when he'd originally moved to Warsaw for a year, falling in love with a Polish flight attendant and eventually getting married. He was now divorced, but had no plans to move back to Mexico. 'Why would you,' he said with a wave of the hand, taking in the cobbled streets, quaint buildings and table of beer, 'when you get to live here?'

*

For dinner that night, we finally got out of the fast food rut, and went to an old Polish-German restaurant, where the steins were cheap, an oom pah band played in the corner, and the giant slabs of meat were served on large wooden boards, untarnished by such things as vegetables. I started with *zur*, a sour rye-bread soup with slices of white sausage and egg in it. It was delicious. I ate so much of it that there was no way I was ever going to finish my 'plate of dead animals'. Okay, it was actually called an 'officer's dinner', but it included hunks of pretty much every edible Polish animal. I had no chance.

As was tradition in Chris's Poland, we then headed back to Pablo's tiny apartment to drink our way through a bottle-and-a-half of the cheap Ukrainian vodka Chris had brought back from his rugby trip. Drunk ice cold straight from the freezer it wasn't too bad, although I couldn't believe I was doing this for a second night in a row. I just closed my eyes, knocked it back, and tried desperately to look like I wasn't dying a little inside each time.

'Tonight,' Pablo said, red-faced and grinning, 'we go to one of my favourite clubs. There are four clubs I like in Warsaw. This one is in my four. There are no students at this place. You will notice the difference.'

The place was called Platinum, and I'd had to wear my wedding shoes and still-crumpled shirt to make sure we'd get in. Pablo was right: I did notice the difference. I didn't think it would be possible, but the girls there had gone to even more effort, dressed in painfully skimpy dresses or skirts, showing endless inches of flawless skin and long, slim legs. Chris and Pablo were well into their element, working the room.

If I didn't have a girlfriend, I thought to myself. Then I realised: if I didn't have a girlfriend, I'd be doing exactly what I was doing now, wandering around and not talking to anyone. As Chris explained, he only ever went for the most beautiful girl in the room, which in Poland was a considerable effort. I, on the other hand, have never had that kind of confidence, so I just stood, staring like the creepy old bloke I was apparently rapidly becoming, and took it all in.

Once again, despite Chris and Pablo's best efforts, we all left alone. At 6am.

*

I'm never drinking again. Never, never, never.

This was becoming a familiar refrain for me, chanted to myself like a prayer when I woke up each afternoon in Warsaw. How much can one person drink, I wondered, before his body eventually gives in? I had to be close to that limit. I'd been fighting off a cold for weeks, and I could feel it slowly enveloping my worn-out body. No more, I silently cried. No more.

'Right, mate, up for some breakfast?' Chris said, bounding out of his room like he'd spent the previous night at home on the couch with a DVD. The bastard.

We decided to eat breakfast (lunch) at Warsaw's new shopping mall, a bastion to everything communism was not, a place of rampant consumerism and, hopefully, something good to eat.

'Man, Warsaw's changed so much,' Chris explained as we walked into the city, wrapped up against the rain and cold that had suddenly taken over the city, lending it that post-communist misery I'd been hoping for. 'When communism fell, there were hardly any restaurants or bars, nothing. You just wouldn't eat out, people thought it was a waste of money. It's even changed a lot since I moved here three years ago. Now, you can eat pretty much anything, and it's really good food. You can do anything you want.'

'Winters must be tough though,' I said. 'Are there ever times when you just think to yourself, "Man, it'd be nice to be on a beach in Australia right now"?'

'You can't think like that man, it'll drive you crazy. You've got to see it as an experience. You have to enjoy it.

'You know,' he added, zipping his jacket up to his chin, 'I used to hate the wind here. Then I remembered I'm supposed to be developing wind farms. So, the more the better really.'

The food court at the mall was like any in the Western world – a whole bunch of small stores with a few people eating at them, and about a thousand people lined up in front of McDonald's.

'When Maccas first came to Warsaw,' Chris told me as we walked past, 'schools used to come here on field trips from the country. It was like a status symbol. Kids who went there would keep their receipts so they could wave them around in the playground, like, "Nah nah, I went to McDonald's and you didn't." Crazy, man.

'So anyway,' he said, glancing at his watch, 'I've got some mates watching the rugby at an Irish pub just around the corner. You up for beer?'

Oh. My. God. How does this kid do it? My insides were

hurting just at the thought of drinking again. Still, I couldn't look like a wuss in front of my new mate, so I agreed, and forced myself to walk to the pub and drink a pint of Guinness that went down like arsenic-coated needles. Then it was time to head back to Chris's place to prepare for another night on the town. I don't know why I'd even entertained the possibility of not drinking that night: this was a Saturday night in Warsaw, and Chris and Pablo hadn't showed any signs of letting up yet.

Sitting around Chris's dining room table with a few more of his rugby friends, we drank a pale yellowy vodka called Zoladkowa Gorzka, which cost less than a bottle of mineral water. Chris lined up the first shot.

It was like being in a duel. I stared down the glass. It sat patiently on the table, taunting me. I breathed in, picked it up, and let the stuff slide down my throat. I waited for the inevitable pain. Nothing. I felt fine. It didn't even taste too bad. Was I becoming Polish? Was the secret to liking straight vodka just to force it down your throat every night? Whatever I was doing, it was working, and I didn't even wince as the 10th shot went down, we grabbed our coats and set out into the late evening.

Half an hour later though, I was so drunk I could barely move. It didn't come on slowly. It hit me like a front-row forward, turning my legs to jelly. With no medi-cab to drive onto the Platinum dance floor and stretcher me off, I crawled towards a seat and tried to gather myself. I could see Chris and Pablo off in the distance, working the room like pros. I could see a girl in an incredibly short skirt that didn't *quite* cover her lacy underwear gyrating on the podium in front of me. Then I have a feeling I fell asleep.

*

Pablo summed it up best. It was about 2pm, and he'd just woken up and was talking to Chris on speakerphone.

'Thank God it's Sunday today,' he was saying.

'How come?' Chris asked.

''Cause it means I don't have to drink tonight, man.'

We both laughed. 'True man,' Chris said.

I had another reason for not drinking, besides the fact my veins were probably now coursing with straight vodka. I was switching abodes, and, in effect, switching ways of life. It was time to bid single Warsaw goodbye, and say hello to married life. I was off to spend two nights with Jay, the 'trailing' diplomat's wife. It would be, I imagined, a much different experience to the one I'd been living out for the last few nights.

I had no idea how few Australians there were in Warsaw. When I got two invitations from the same city, I assumed it was like any other European capital: full of Aussies. But as soon as Chris found out I was staying with someone else, he wanted to know who it was.

'Someone called Jay; her husband's Simon.'

'Yep,' Chris nodded. 'I know 'em. Met Simon at the Anzac Day bash we had.'

Something weird was about to happen now. Chris had offered to drop me around at Jay's house that afternoon, meaning two of my hosts would meet each other for the first time. This wasn't part of the plan. What if they got together and talked about what a weirdo I was? What if they didn't get along?

There was no need to worry, of course. Chris stormed into Jay and Simon's house in his usual confident style, pumping Simon's hand and giving Jay a kiss before I'd even got through the door. Simon stuck his head through the doorway and beckoned me in with a broad Aussie accent. He was tall, with close-cropped hair, rectangular glasses and bare feet. Jay had a pair of fluffy ugg boots on, and bounded out of the kitchen in a wave of energy to greet me.

'Hi! I'm just making some dinner! Do you want some?'

God did I want some. It's weird the things you miss when you're travelling. It might sound glamorous hanging out at Polish nightclubs and dancing till dawn, but for a few weeks now my idea of heaven had been a home-cooked meal and a night on the couch.

It was exactly what I needed, and from the smells coming from Jay's kitchen, this was going to be a good place to do it.

First though, Simon and Jay had to chat to Chris. They asked him about his favourite places to go out ('Nope, haven't heard of that one . . . Or that one . . .'), his favourite things to do in Warsaw ('We have a rugby team?'), and his favourite restaurants. The three of them agreed to organise an Aussie expats' get-together soon, although Simon stressed that his embassy couldn't get officially involved. His drink finished, Chris shook everyone's hand again, and headed off for home, leaving me to get to know my new hosts.

'Now, your time with us could be a little different to your time with Chris,' Simon said. 'We've got dinner coming up, but, you know, I s'pose we could go somewhere to get a drink first, if you want?'

'Oh God no,' I said, looking around the flat. Compared to Chris's place, Simon and Jay's place was a mansion, paid for by the Australian taxpayer, of course. Set in a gated community of high-rise apartment blocks, it was brand new, with two bedrooms, a study, a huge kitchen, balcony, and flat screen TVs sprinkled throughout. I could see myself staying here for a lot longer than my allotted two days. Simon was a diplomat at the Australian Embassy, one of a staff of three; he and Jay had been in Warsaw for a year, with two more to go on his posting.

'Warsaw wasn't top of our list when we applied for a foreign posting,' Simon explained, 'but we're so happy we ended up here. It's just such a great quality of life. You know, I can walk to work here, we've got this great apartment . . . I don't think all diplomats live this well.'

I'd never met diplomats before. In fact, I didn't even really know diplomats existed. I knew we had ambassadors, but I had no idea what they did. I thought it was just what former politicians did when they were looking for a cushy semi-retirement.

'Well, it might be like that for some,' Simon chuckled. 'But no, it's pretty interesting. It's not all cocktail parties and soirees. You do all sorts of stuff. They're big into climate change at the moment, so a lot of my job has to do with that – you know, gathering information about what Poland and the Czech Republic are up to in regards to that, monitoring the politics, trying to interpret what the governments are thinking and relaying that back to Australia. We also lobby on behalf of Australia too, advising the governments here on our position and what we'd like them to be doing. It's a lot of work, actually.'

'And what do you do, Jay?' I asked.

Simon and Jay exchanged looks. 'Well, not very much at the moment,' she laughed. 'It's a strange life, being a diplomat's wife. You can't really work, because you're in a foreign country, so you have all this time on your hands. Simon doesn't understand, but it's amazing how quickly the day goes. I love it though. There are some wives that don't like it. We don't hang out with them much, but you hear them sometimes, and all they do is whinge: "I hate this, I hate that . . ." It's like, how could you not want to be here? This place is amazing.'

Jay and Simon had done some serious backpacking before turning to the diplomatic life. 'I was thinking about how you would write about us,' Jay said over her excellent home-cooked dinner, 'and I reckon it's something like, what do backpackers do when they grow up? Because you can't backpack forever. But I reckon we've found something that's just as good.'

Simon's career began in IT, before he was struck with the realisation that he didn't really like working in IT. So he went back to uni, studied international relations, got his masters, and joined DFAT. He and Jay had been waiting three years for their first posting, and had had to wait an extra 18 months after being told they were going to Warsaw. That was long enough for both of them to pick up rudimentary Polish skills – although Jay already spoke Vietnamese and Indonesian. Jay had been working for the government in Australia too, and had managed to get three years' leave without pay.

'So now I just have to get used to being a housewife,' she said. 'In the first week Simon was going out to work, and he asked me to pick up his dry-cleaning. I'm like, "I've got a masters, I don't think I really need to be doing your dry-cleaning." But I did it anyway. I also travel a lot by myself during the week while Simon's working. I've been to Hungary, all around Poland – some of the other wives can't believe I go by myself.'

Jay was also writing a novel, had made a few short films on travel destinations in the area, and had joined a book club which only studied Polish literature.

'Geez it's good to hear an Aussie accent,' Jay exclaimed, digging into her nicoise salad as I resisted an urge to leap onto the couch and turn the TV on. 'I mean, we don't seek out Aussies here. We really try to live the Polish life, have Polish friends and everything. But it's great to hear an Aussie every now and then.'

It was fun for me too, but all I could really think about was that couch, and that huge TV. Eventually though, I just said goodnight, had a shower under the sort of incredible feat of plumbing that I could only have dreamt about in Ethiopia, and hit my big, cosy bed. In my own room. With a large map of the world on the wall. And my own telly. Just two nights?

*

In married Warsaw, you don't sleep in. You get up in the *morning*, of all things, and you actually partake in activities that don't consist of nursing a hangover or eating at Pizza Hut. For my last full day in Poland (and, in truth, my first full day in Poland), the ever-excitable Jay had a little tour planned, taking in some of the city's lesser-known attractions. Jay was worried that I might have seen a few of them already with Chris, although I assured her that, as long as her tour didn't take in the casino or the dance floor at Platinum, we should be pretty safe.

The minute we left the house and I actually began to take the city in, I realised what a feat of linguistic genius it was for Jay and Simon to have picked up the amount of Polish they had. Simon wasn't bad, but Jay was very impressive, asking for directions and reading street signs, most of which contained words that looked more like booking reference numbers to me. Just going in and out of train stations was difficult enough – remember, you go in the *wejscie*, and out the *wyjscie*. Then you have to figure out if you're after *wyjazd* (arrivals) or *przyjazd* (departures). And make sure you don't mistake the *krajowy* for the *miedzynarodowy*, or you could get on a domestic train instead of an international one.

I'm no linguist, clearly. I have a good ear for sounds, I can repeat exactly what someone's said to me in a perfect accent, but I can never remember anything. (Of course, I could always remember pointless but hilarious sayings. The one phrase I retained from my visits to the Netherlands is *'neuken in de keuken'*, which, until such time as I actually do manage to have sex in a Dutch kitchen, will remain pretty useless to me.)

So I resolved to let Jay do all of the talking on our tour. She seemed quite happy with that, anyway. In her late 30s, Jay was one of the most enthusiastic travellers I'd been around, and it was impossible not to get swept up in her bubbly enthusiasm for her adopted city. I already liked the place, but as we wandered the old streets, past drab communist office blocks and new, ultra-modern shops, I began to think I could easily grow to love it.

Sure, there were the remnants of the bad old days – the stark, brooding buildings with social realist art still sculpted into the sides of it. But that just gave the place character. There was real history here. There might have been trendy cafes lining the pavement at Plac Konstytucji now, filled with students drinking coffee and using the free wifi, but it wasn't hard to picture tanks rolling down the wide avenues, or soldiers marching down the footpaths. It's a blend of history and modernity that you can never hope to find in Australia.

Over a coffee I got the chance to ask Jay more about being a 'stringer', the slang for a diplomat's wife.

'It's weird, because you come with your husband, but then you lead completely separate lives,' she explained. 'Simon goes to work all day, and he comes home tired and ready to watch a DVD on the couch, whereas I'm sitting around all day, and I'm full of energy when he gets home. It's the same on weekends – he's tired from a long week at work, but I'm ready to do things. That's why you have to get out on your own.'

'How do the other wives deal with it?'

'There are a lot of affairs, definitely. If you've got nothing else to do, apparently they happen. But the worst thing I find is almost this loss of identity. You know, at home I was working with the Department of Families, actually doing something. Here, I'm just Simon's wife.'

Jay had been finding plenty to keep her busy though. As well as everything else, she'd helped out with translating a few foreign TV shows into Polish. I'd seen a few shows like this at Chris's place, and they were hilarious. Rather than delete the English soundtrack, the Poles just add their voices on top of it – sometimes with just the one person doing all the characters' voices.

'Oh my God, the funniest thing was when they got me to help out with dubbing *Rex Hunt's Fishing World*,' Jay said. 'They had to ring up the Australian embassy, because the translator had no idea what Rex was saying. So Simon sent me along to help. The poor guy, he's like, "What is this meaning when he says a thing is cactus?" I'm like, "It means it's broken." I mean, I didn't even understand some of it, I had to google Australian slang! You try explaining to a Polish guy what "yibbida yibbida" means.'

As we had a lunch date, we jumped on the Metro (actually buying a ticket this time) and headed to the Australian Embassy to meet Simon and his boss, the Australian ambassador to Poland, Ruth. I'd seen a few embassies already in Warsaw – the walled-in American embassy with big 'no photo' signs out the front, and the giant Russian embassy, with a massive fenced garden. The Australian embassy was a little less imposing. In fact, if it wasn't for the Australian flag on a pole out the front of the office block, you wouldn't even know it was there.

'Yeah,' Simon grinned as he greeted us, 'it's a bit small. But hey, there's only three of us that work here, so what do you expect?'

'You know,' Jay added, 'on the anniversary of Steve Irwin's death, a wreath of flowers appears under that flagpole. No one knows who puts it there, but every anniversary, it appears, stays for a few days, then disappears again. No one else's death is marked here. Just Steve's.'

The two introduced me to the friendly and entertaining Ruth, and I spent most of the lunch listening to her stories of her time as ambassador in Moscow, being trailed 24 hours a day by guys in dark sunglasses and suits.

Simon also broke the news that, despite his previous assurances that the diplomatic life wasn't all cocktail parties and genteel soirees, we'd been invited to a 'summer drinks' night at the Irish ambassador's house that evening. Simon looked me up and down. 'You haven't, er, got a nice shirt or anything do you?'

'Yep, no worries,' I said, secretly wondering what state my one decent shirt was in, given the fact I'd worn it out to Platinum a few nights ago and hadn't paid it any attention since. And there were still black marks on it from the Czech incident. I just had to hope the Irish ambassador had had plenty of Guinness by the time I arrived.

With Simon and Ruth heading back to the hard slog of deciphering Polish politics under a staff of three, Jay and I hopped on a tram and headed across the river to Praga – the 'bad' side of town. Praga is where most of Warsaw's immigrants have gone to live, and it's also the area most locals will tell you not to visit. However, Jay had a few reasons for taking me across to the bad lands. The first was that, like most cheap, rundown neighbourhoods in big cities, Praga was now home to a thriving arts community, and a heap of cool cafes and restaurants tucked into small corners of crumbling buildings. The second reason was one that I doubt even some locals knew about – the Jewish Cemetery.

I don't mind visiting cemeteries, but I don't find them that interesting, apart from giving me the chance to make corny dad jokes about being in 'the dead centre of town', that people are 'dying to get in to'. However, Warsaw's Jewish Cemetery was something else. Sitting on the tram, Jay wasn't even quite sure where it was, as it was certainly not marked out for tourists. Thinking we were close, Jay asked an old woman on the tram if we were in the right area. The woman glared at her for a second, then gave a gruff '*tak*', or 'yes'.

Stepping off the tram, we walked past a service station, and then through a large set of gates with no markings, just an old graffiti-covered guardhouse with smashed windows. The cemetery, unlike most, was covered in large trees, long grass and thick underbrush. After a few minutes of walking down the cracked pathway through the middle, I began to realise that the place was missing something you tend to find in a lot of cemeteries: graves. There were none. It was just a huge empty block of land that had long since been taken over by the trees and weeds and undergrowth. 'Just wait,' Jay said, pulling out her camera. 'Wait till we get to the middle.'

The pathway led to a round concrete platform in the middle of the cemetery, and we were about 30 metres away from it when the trees started thinning out, exposing an incredible sight. On each side of the path were hundreds of gravestones, some broken, some still intact, stacked horizontally against each other and overrun with weeds. I couldn't count how many there were, brutally left to slowly weather away.

'It's exactly as it was when the Nazis walked out of here,' Jay said softly, snapping off a few photos. 'There are mass graves here that are completely unmarked, but this cemetery is hundreds of years old, so there were plenty of marked graves here before the war. The Nazis tore up all the headstones to use to pave roads. This is as far as they got before the war ended, and it hasn't been touched since.'

'Why don't they do something to fix it up?' I asked, amazed.

Jay shook her head. 'I don't know. It's weird, I guess. I mean, there are barely any Jews left in Poland, so they don't have the resources to do anything about it. And the other Poles . . . They're not anti-Semitic, but I guess in part they blame the war on the Jews. You know, if the Jews hadn't been here, it never would have happened. So they're never going to do anything to harm this place, but they're not going to pay to fix it up either. And besides, can you imagine how much work would have to go in to figuring out where each headstone belongs? The Nazis destroyed all of the records – it would be almost impossible.'

That inaction has served to leave a pretty amazing snapshot of World War II hysteria in place. There can't be many other places in the world that have been left absolutely untouched since Nazi occupation.

'It just gives you an idea of the insanity that came over people,' Jay continued. 'Even now, look at this,' she said, pointing out a crudely graffitied swastika on one of the headstones. 'That's recent. People still come here and do this now. I don't know why.'

*

Back over on the safe side of town, Jay had something more to show me. 'You probably haven't witnessed Polish "customer service", so I'm going to give you a demonstration,' she said. 'We're going to go to my local supermarket, which must have the worst service, even in Warsaw.'

Jay wandered through the aisles, picked up a few things, and then took it to the cashier, a surly but obviously attractive girl (this is Poland, after all), who glared at the two of us as she ran the items over the scanner, twirling her hair a few times before pointing at the amount on the screen. Jay handed it over, and the girl grunted and went back to filing her nails.

'I try not to let it get me down,' Jay said as we walked out. 'I always think to myself, "It's not me, it's them, it's just the way they are, it's not because they hate me." Jean, our Irish neighbour, has a different approach. She's just ridiculously cheery to them to see if she can get a smile. She's like, "Wow, thank you so much, have a great day." It never works though.'

Getting home, I realised the dire situation my clothing was in. Here I was going to my first diplomatic soiree in smelly jeans and a shirt that had travelled from backpack to nightclub to backpack again with no detour anywhere near a washing machine. I decided to use my old trick: iron it clean.

'These events can be so surreal sometimes,' Jay said as I attempted to iron a beer stain off my sleeve. 'We had to go to a conference in Poznan a few weeks ago, and there was this speaker there, a guy who survived the Holocaust and has gone on to be a human rights campaigner and all this other stuff, really eminent guy, and he gave this amazing speech at the conference, so moving. Anyway, at the lunch later on, Simon and I got to sit at the table with him as VIPs. It's like, "I'm just this girl from Melbourne! I don't deserve to be here." I kept thinking I'd be found out some time.'

I had the same feeling as we rolled up to the Irish ambassador's house, a huge place with marquees set up out the front shading Warsaw's diplomatic community, who were all standing around sipping warm glasses of Guinness and Kilkenny. It was time to press the flesh. I was introduced to the Japanese ambassador, the Venezuelan ambassador, and, of course, Mr Ireland. I made small talk. We chatted about, well, football and beer. I met an American diplomat from Washington DC who advised that if I was to go there, to stay away from the northern suburbs as, 'folks there don't look like you and me.'

'You mean they're black?' I asked.

He shuffled his feet. 'Well, yeah, I guess so.' Not very diplomatic for a diplomat.

A couple of glasses of wine later, I began to notice that Simon and Jay weren't handling their alcohol with the aplomb of, say,

Chris and Pablo. Jay had come over to me first, slurring her words a bit. 'Now jush watch out, Ben,' she said. 'Shimonsh a cheap drunk. Two glasshes of wine and he'sh away.'

I nodded reassuringly. A few minutes later, Simon came over to where I was chatting to the ambassador of somewhere or other, and whispered conspiratorially: 'Hey, Ben, Jay doeshn't handle her alcohol very well, sho we better keep an eye on her tonight, hey?'

I'd already made a pact with myself to keep an eye on both of them. Sensing I needed to get my new hosts to some food, we bid the diplomats goodbye, and headed to a nearby cafe, where Jay immediately ordered three shots of vodka. I was surprised, but confident I could handle it after all my practice.

'We going to do this in one?' Simon asked, picking up his glass.

'Of course,' I said.

I necked mine with all my newfound Polish bluster. Simon did what I usually do – gulped, wheezed, steadied himself on the table, then recovered. Jay took a tiny sip, grimaced, and put the glass back down, never to be touched again.

We had a quick dinner, then headed back to Simon and Jay's house, ready to call it a night. 'Right,' Simon said as he pushed the front door open, 'should have some more shots of vodka and look at photos?'

I was about to agree until I realised he was joking. Jay and Simon wandered off to bed, while I went and packed my bag, refreshingly sober for my second night in a row.

*

I was up early the next morning, said my goodbyes to Simon, and then Jay walked me to the bus stop to get me to the airport (I just had to tell the driver I wanted the miedzynarodowy terminal, not the krajowy).

'Well, I hope we've shown you a different side of Warsaw,' Jay said as the bus pulled up.

I laughed. 'What, like, daylight?'

It was true though, I had seen a different side of Warsaw, with some very different, but equally lovely people. If this is what backpackers are like when they grow up, I thought, then I'm ready to grow up, too.

Cycling Killed the Radio Star

'Oh, the other week I was real wobbly. It was someone's going away drinks, and mate, I haven't dived into the syrup like that in a while. Still, I haven't come a cropper yet.'

Kroket consumption time check: one hour.

I'd been craving krokets. You don't usually hear people rave about Dutch food because, basically, there is no Dutch food. You wouldn't go out for 'Dutch' – not even in the Netherlands. One thing the Dutch do well, however, is greasy snack food. Whether this goes hand in hand with the decriminalisation of marijuana, you decide. But still, if you've got a hankering for a deep-fried snack, Holland's the place to be. Their chips with mayo are amazing, something called a *frikendaal* is also great – but the king of snacks, the ruler of all the Netherlands' greasy goodness, is the kroket.

There's no way to describe a kroket that's going to make it sound appetising. Basically, it's like someone's taken the filling from a meat pie, added a few artificial flavours to it, somehow moulded it into a cylindrical form, battered it and deep-fried it. What you end up with is a steaming hot roll of crispy, gooey goodness.

Having travelled straight from Amsterdam's Schiphol airport, I had about a five-minute window at Sloterdijk train station before my train to The Hague rolled up. I seized my opportunity and ran down to the snack bar underneath the platform. The line at the counter was huge, but fortunately, hungry travellers in the Netherlands have a better option than queuing. Most Dutch snack bars have rows and rows of little windows next to the counter which are filled with easy-to-handle hot snacks like hamburgers and krokets and frikendaals. Rather than actually go through the hassle of speaking to someone to place your order, you just choose a window, put the right amount of money in the slot, open the window, and remove your deep-fried item of choice.

I did exactly that at the kroket window, shoving a euro coin into the slot and removing the tasty treat inside. I ran back up to the platform and dived onto my train to The Hague, just in time. The kroket was everything I'd hoped for – a greasy, steaming, sloppy mess. With a little mustard on top. Perfect. Just as I was finishing it off, my phone tinkled with a message from my first Dutch contact, Eefje. 'What do you feel like eating tonight?' it read.

I texted back: 'Whatever, I'm easy. Just had a kroket so all set.'

'Thank God!' she replied. 'I thought you would want Dutch food. Okay, I will decide.'

*

All I needed was the tiniest suggestion of an invitation to the Netherlands and I was going to lock it in. I love everything about this funny little pancake-flat country in Europe's west. I love the people, the quaint little towns, the canals, the houseboats, the liberal politics, the cheeses, the bicycles, the clogs and the silly hats.

So all I needed to read of Michael's email was the word 'Amsterdam' in the subject line, and I was in. He could have followed on with something about his living in an underground squat with smack addicts, lepers and the Jonas Brothers, but it would have been too late. I was coming. 'Just checking to see if you want to include "Sin" City (Amsterdam) in your budget round-the-world trip,' Michael wrote.

> My partner, Jillian, and I have lived here for *bijna* (nearly) three years and might be able to put a more local perspective on a city that everybody visits once. Like the saying goes though, there is no such thing as a free lunch, or accommodation as the case may be – there is a personal cost to you. I host a breakfast radio/TV show and you would be required to come on and tell your side of the travel story!

The original plan was to head straight to Amsterdam to stay with Michael, then head out to Haarlem for a night to stay with a guy called Campbell, then back to Amsterdam for one last night with a guy called Luke. But, as was the trend with this trip, I ran into some trouble. Luke was first to pull out, citing uni exams and a visit from his brother. Fair enough. But pretty soon my Haarlem excursion was cancelled too when Campbell emailed to tell me that my planned date coincided with his girlfriend's birthday, so he wouldn't be able to accommodate me after all. So I was just left with Michael the radio star.

Then I remembered an email I'd got a few months ago from someone called Eefje in The Hague, who'd even admitted to occasionally leaving comments on my blog (no one admits to that – it's like trying to find someone who actually voted for George W Bush). I'd originally knocked back Eefje's offer because there wasn't really an offer there – she was keen to meet up for a drink and some dinner, but lived in a 'shoebox' and couldn't put me up. That hadn't sounded ideal when I'd had other offers pouring in, but now, faced with the possibility of spending my whole time in the Netherlands in the one neighbourhood, I decided to spend an evening hanging out with a real Dutch girl in *Den Haag*, then crash in a hostel before heading back up to Amsterdam.

That was how I found myself monstering a piping-hot kroket at Sloterdijk train station an hour after I'd arrived in Amsterdam. I shouldn't have been at Sloterdijk – I should have been on a fast train straight to The Hague. However, after having written a blog about how reliable and easy to use Dutch trains are, something had to go wrong. It came in the form of Eefje's text message when I got off the plane: 'Good luck getting here – line is down somewhere and no trains running.' Perfect. I'd finally figured out that I could do a small lap of the country to get to The Hague the other way when Eefje phoned to see how I was getting on.

'Hi Ben, it's Eefje here.'

I paused. 'Oh, hi!'

'I bet you were wondering how to pronounce that weird name, weren't you?'

I had been. 'No, not at all.' (For the record, it's like 'ay-fee-yeah'.)

We worked out a way to meet – I was to take trains to Sloterdijk, Leiden and then The Hague, then walk towards the far end of the platform and look out for a girl with huge curly hair. As it was, I spotted Eefje while the train was still moving down the platform, her brown curls threatening to stage a revolution and take control of the station. Prepared for the traditional Dutch greeting of three kisses on the cheek (which the Dutch usually announce to foreign friends in a high, sing-song voice: 'Three kisses!'), I was surprised when Eefje limited herself to a single peck on the cheek – a hangover, I found, from a few years living in Scotland and New Zealand. She also presented me with a stack of *stroopwafels*, the paper-thin, toffee-filled waffles that are my second favourite Dutch treat.

'How did you know?' I laughed.

'I think I read that you like them on your blog,' Eefje said. 'You've had a kroket, so your food tour of the Netherlands is now complete.'

Eefje led me outside the station and onto a tram into the centre of town. As it was getting late, we'd decided to check out the city and have dinner before I checked into my hostel, which was fine, except it meant I had to lug my backpack around on the walk through the city. The town itself looked much like Amsterdam, only with fewer canals. There were paved streets, tall, thin houses, and bicycles everywhere.

'So are you from The Hague?' I asked Eefje as she led us off the tram.

'No, I've only been here for a year. I'm actually from Zeeland, you know, in the south of the Netherlands?'

'Yeah, sure. I actually used to live in Wemeldinge,' I replied, referring to the town in Zeeland where Top Deck's coaches are based, and where the drivers and cooks hang out between tours.

Eefje was amazed. '*You* used to live in Wemeldinge? There are about 20 people in Wemeldinge!'

Eefje and I had more than just our old neighbourhood in common. She was a journalist too, although where I'd been working for a men's mag asking girls about their plans to have pillow fights with their girlfriends, Eefje was working in The Hague for a bridal magazine, asking girls about their plans to get married.

Eefje was kind enough to keep our city tour short, given I was doing it with 17 kilograms on my back, taking me past the houses of parliament, the museum that houses the *Girl With A Pearl Earring* . . . and that was about it. The city was already striking me as the Netherlands' version of Canberra – a small, mostly featureless capital populated by people who wouldn't like to admit to being from there. It did have a lot more charm than Canberra (and a lot less roundabouts), but it was no Amsterdam.

Something The Hague did have in common with Amsterdam, though, was the equally high chance of being mowed down while trying to cross its streets. My 'almost killed' time check was about 20 minutes. It's not just that the traffic is coming from the wrong direction. It's that there's so much to look out for when you're making a crossing. First, there's a bike lane (if you remember to look for it). Then a lane of cars. Navigate that successfully, and there are two lanes of silent-but-deadly trams, then another lane of cars, and another bike lane, before you reach the blessed safety of the opposite pavement. I didn't even make it past the first bike lane in The Hague, timidly stepping out before I heard the single 'ding!' of a bike bell. I dived out of the way just in time, flattening myself on the pavement, much to Eefje's amusement.

Eefje's choice of restaurant, given she'd been freed of the responsibility of feeding me Dutch cuisine, was an Italian place in the middle of The Hague's main square. There, over huge plates of pasta, Eefje explained why she'd left New Zealand a few years ago.

'I just decided, I'm a European,' she said, shovelling in a mouthful of food. 'New Zealand's nice unless you like, you know, culture. Maybe Australia's different, but there's just nothing to do in New Zealand. It really made me miss home.'

'So you just left?'

'Yep. Well, I broke up with my boyfriend, so that sort of did it as well.'

Glancing at my watch, I realised it was already past 10pm, and as my hostel shut its doors at 11pm I was forced to say a hurried goodbye. The hostel was standard fare, walls filled with 'cool' graffiti, bored backpackers hanging around the lounge listening to music from home and watching movies from home, and a blond, strung-out surfer dude on reception. He coolly took the 30 euros for my dorm bed (30 euros!), and pointed me towards my room. 'Here's your sheets,' he said, passing over a plastic-wrapped bundle. 'Bring them down when you check out. There's no one else in your dorm tonight, so you're lucky.'

*

After a breakfast of muesli I checked out, and asked a different blond, strung-out surfer dude how to get tickets for the tram back into town. He looked at me doubtfully.

'Where are you going?'

'Just into the centre of town.'

'Man, I wouldn't bother with a ticket, hey. I never do. Just jump on.'

With a few hours to kill before I took the train to Amsterdam, I headed, on Eefje's advice, straight to the Marinshuis Museum, home of the famous-thanks-to-the-movie painting, *Girl with a Pearl Earring*. There, I did what I usually do in art galleries that feature famous paintings: I spent about 20 minutes wandering around looking at paintings I wasn't really that interested in, convinced I was culturally advanced enough to enjoy all of the works, then gave up and headed straight to *Girl with a Pearl Earring*. Then I left.

I spent some time aimlessly drifting around town after that, called in to Eefje's favourite book store, then headed to the train station to get up to Amsterdam – fortunately, the lines were back to full capacity.

It's only when you jump on a train in the Netherlands that you realise how small the country is. Just like English tourists who can't believe it takes a couple of days to drive from Brisbane to Cairns, so most Australians are surprised that you can travel the length of the Netherlands in a few short hours. The Hague to Amsterdam takes about 45 minutes – a journey studded with the sort of canals, houseboats and little villages that make you want to leap out of the train and just stay put for a few, well, years.

At Amsterdam's Centraal Station, I noticed immediately that everything was different. Having been in Poland and country Czech Republic for the last few weeks, I'd got used to being one of the only tourists in town. Amsterdam's a *little* different. I was lucky to spot a single local along the Damrak that runs off Centraal – tourists were everywhere.

Most of the accommodation is in the area immediately around Centraal and Dam Square, extending over to the famous Red Light District and the Nieuwmarkt. However, I was headed somewhere different, so I bought a tram ticket (no chance of dodging it in Amsterdam), jumped on the No. 2, and headed out to meet Michael, who had told me to get off at the second stop after the Van Gogh Museum.

Waiting for him at the stop, I went through the usual process of guessing how I'd know I'd found the right person. A few minutes later I spotted Michael across the street, although if it wasn't for all the buildings around, I probably would have spotted him from The Hague. Dressed in shorts, a ridiculously bright orange T-shirt and slapping along in thongs, Michael stuck a hand out. 'G'day mate! How are ya? Let's get rid a that bag for ya, eh?'

We crossed the road and headed down a tree- and cafe-lined street. 'This is like the Double Bay of Amsterdam,' Michael said in a broad Australian drawl that he'd brought straight from Cronulla. 'You see the paparazzi hanging out here, taking pictures of movie stars and that. Course, I don't recognise 'em. Could be anyone for all I care. Some pretty nice houses around here too. Course, the bank pays for ours, so there's no problem.'

I took 'the bank' to mean Michael and Jillian had a loan, but I was way off. Jill actually worked for ING, and had been transferred to Amsterdam three years ago from Sydney. Part of the relocation package she'd received was to have her rent in Amsterdam taken care of, which explained why they lived in such a nice area, and in such a nice house.

Their flat was in one of those typically tall, skinny Dutch terrace houses, on a quiet street lined with bikes chained to pretty much anything you could get a chain around. Up a narrow staircase, Michael and Jill's flat occupied the top three floors, with lounge and kitchen on the lower level, two bedrooms and bathrooms on the middle level, and a beautiful wood-decked terrace on the top level. 'Plenty of barbies up here, mate,' Michael said, pointing at a well-used Weber on the deck. 'We get the locals over, show 'em a real Aussie barbie. It's beautiful.'

'You must get to know your neighbours pretty well,' I said, pointing at the rows and rows of flats opposite Michael's, all with large windows that you could basically look straight in to.

Michael laughed. 'Oh yeah, I think we've seen pretty much all of them nude now. One night we got up to watch the rugby from Australia on TV, and two of them were having a bit of intercourse across the way. Provided a bit of extra entertainment for us, I can tell you.'

Fornicating neighbours or not, this was the way to do expat living, I thought, staring out over the Amsterdam rooftops, taking in the breeze. Get yourself a nice job, and get the company to pay your rent. It beats pulling pints in a bar. Jill's company paid the 3500-euros-a-month rent, and had even paid for them to move over in the first place.

Michael and Jill were both in their mid-40s. Michael was a teacher (and only a part-time radio star), so he'd found work at the local international school when Jill had been transferred by ING. They'd both been learning Dutch, although Michael was more proficient than his Zimbabwean-born and Afrikaans-speaking partner.

'The trouble with the Dutch,' Michael told me as we walked back down to the kitchen to grab a drink, 'is that they don't understand bad Dutch. They're just not used to hearing it. I mean us, we're used to hearing English in all sorts of accents. But no one really learns Dutch, so they're not used to hearing it spoken badly. They just switch to English, mate. They laugh at you.

'Everyone here speaks English. Half the bloody TV shows are in English. But look, I'm livin' in their country, I reckon it's polite to at least try to learn the language. Some of our friends here have been here 10 years, and they haven't even bothered. And they're the same ones that complain about people moving to Australia and not learning English!'

Jill, with short blonde hair, dressed casually in jeans and a T-shirt, laughed. 'You wait till you see Michael walking around here,' she said. 'He knows everyone. You'd think he'd been here his whole life.'

I could see how Michael had made plenty of friends though. The area around Cornelis Schuyt Straat had a real village feel to it, and it was hard to believe that the world famous Red Light District could be only a 10-minute bike ride away. Here there were tree-lined streets, small cafes and bars, friendly little grocery stores, the inevitable bike shops, and locals standing outside each one, calling out to Michael as he strolled around.

This was the side of Amsterdam I'd come to see. Everyone knows about the seedy side, but most of the people who actually live in this city wouldn't dream of going there unless it was to show wide-eyed visitors what it was like. Most of the locals don't smoke pot either. It's 'tolerated', but it's mostly the tourists who end up using it. Michael and Jill were no different. They were living the life Dutch. They had Dutch friends, hung out in Dutch bars, and watched Dutch TV.

Michael, however, still had a brilliantly Australian turn of phrase, describing the Van Gogh Museum as being, 'just a driver and a seven iron from here'.

'So it's an easy walk?' I asked.

'Oh yeah,' he replied. 'You just make a left out of here, first right, walk a few blocks, and Bob's ya former prime minister.'

It was a conversational style that you wouldn't think would suit doing radio in a foreign country, but on Thursdays for the last two-and-a-half years Michael had been hosting a community radio station breakfast show. Things kicked off at 7am, taking over from the Surinamese DJs who worked the midnight-to-7am shift. My penance for being Michael's house guest, as per his email, was that I had to co-host a show with him while I was in town – not a huge ask given my enjoyment of talking about myself.

Michael was excited about having me on, which was nice,

but what he hadn't reckoned on was my extremely poor form as a morning person. My mum always tells stories about her having to wake *me* up when I was a baby, rather than the other way around. Still, I was determined to do my best for Michael, so I was up doing my impression of bright-eyed and bushy-tailed by six the next morning.

Outside Michael's place, he unchained a rusty bike for me and started adjusting the seat.

'She's a bit old this one, but I reckon she'll be fine for you,' Michael said, tightening bolts here and there. 'I actually pulled it out of the rubbish dump one day. But it's been goin' fine ever since.'

I was dubious – the bike looked like it'd spent some serious time in a canal – but I jumped on what I'd already silently christened 'Martha', and we started pedalling through the cold Amsterdam morning.

There's no better way to get around the Dutch capital – or anywhere in the Netherlands – than on a bike. For starters, the entire country has all the topographical variance of a stroopwafel. The highest point is Vaalserberg, which tops out at a fairly pathetic 322 metres, but you'd have to ride a long way from Amsterdam to get there. The 'Dam itself has nothing steeper than the small rises you have to climb to get over a canal bridge, so it's made for getting around by pedal power. (You could catch a tram, but I raced one from the city back to Michael's place once, just to see what was faster, and I won with ease.)

There's an amazing feeling of freedom when you throw your leg over a bike in Amsterdam. It's not a big city, and you can pedal just about anywhere in 20 minutes or so. You know you're alive when you're zipping along a cobbled street on a cold morning, and nothing makes you feel like more of a local than dinging your little bell at the moronic tourists who step out onto the bike paths without looking.

There aren't all the rules and regulations you find in Australia for cyclists either. You don't have to wear a helmet if you don't want to – and from what I could tell, no one wants to. And cyclists rule the road. Dutch drivers will always give way to cyclists, even if they technically shouldn't, mainly for fear of hitting one and incurring the wrath of the bike-friendly Dutch government. Every street has a dedicated bike lane on it, and even little traffic lights just for cyclists.

This doesn't, however, mean you won't be killed. In fact, just like if you're on foot, there are a lot of things out there that can kill you on a bike. For starters, there are those damn electric trams, which creep up on you like big, boxy assassins and attempt to silently mow you down. Get one of your tyres wedged in a tram track and you'll not only buckle the wheel, but you'll also be laughed at by any Dutchie that sees it happen. Manage to miss the trams and the tracks though, and there are always those cars ready to take out the inexperienced cyclist. Plus, 50cc mopeds are also allowed in Amsterdam's bike lanes. They're supposed to be limited to 40km/h, but most aren't, meaning the bare-headed occupants can swipe you on their way past at any given moment.

It's all a bit daunting for the first timer, but locals – and Michael – couldn't care less. That first cold morning, Michael screamed through red lights, zipped over tram lines and headed the wrong way down one-way streets.

'You just get used to it after a while, mate,' he yelled as Martha and I careened over a bridge. 'Jill and I ride everywhere. Go out to the pub, and you don't have to worry about a taxi or anything, you just jump on the bikes.'

'You must have a few wobbly rides home then?' I asked, swerving a parked car.

'Yeah, yeah. Oh, the other week I was real wobbly. It was someone's going away drinks and, mate, I haven't dived into the syrup like that in a while. Still, I haven't come a cropper yet, so it's all good.'

Cycling along behind Michael, dodging traffic and preparing

myself for my impending, ugly death, I was still having a ball. Life was good. Here I was in Amsterdam, peddling along cobbled streets, over canals, past huge windmills, with the sun rising into a clear blue sky. If I was going to get knocked off Martha and drown in a canal, I was going to do it a happy man.

*

The radio studio was in Amsterdam's north, in an industrial area that still looked beautiful through my rose-coloured tourist glasses. We headed upstairs and Michael fiddled with dials and cued up songs while I let the other co-hosts – Isabelle, Silvia and Leslie – in the front door. While the show was aimed at Amsterdam's entire expat community, it had a strong Australian bent, with Michael setting up interviews with all of the Australian bands coming through town. He'd had Jimmy Barnes, Eskimo Joe and the Cat Empire in recently, as well as a former astronaut and his local chef from around the corner.

Michael's panellists were just as amateur as he was. Isabelle was the token Dutchie, there just to get some experience and have some fun. Leslie was an arts student from Chicago, hoping to crack it as an actress, and Silvia was a Kiwi obsessed with film, but trying to kick-start a career in radio as well. Throughout the show they fumbled their way through, taking cues from Michael and trying not to talk over each other.

The star attraction that morning, however, was a tired, gravelly voiced journalist from the *Sydney Morning Herald*, who could clearly have used a few more hours in bed. After a quick weather update, Michael introduced me. I moved in to the microphone and tried to talk, but what came out was a throaty growl that sounded like Darren Lockyer after Mad Monday. A few songs and cups of coffee later though, I was warmed up and ready to go. I read out the local sports news, put in my two cents during an argument about celibacy in the Catholic Church, and introduced a few songs.

Basically, I had a blast, and was almost completely awake by the time the show was wrapping up two hours later.

'Yeah mate, it's pretty good fun,' Michael told me later. 'I mean, I had absolutely no experience before I started. Never done anything like it. I'm just a teacher. But this bloke asked me to come down and be on the show one day, and then they just asked me to do it every Thursday. I love it, but it's getting hard, you know? It's the preparation. The actual show is great fun, but you have to put a lot of work into it to make those two hours you're on air a good two hours. I don't know if I can still do that, with teaching five days a week and doing other stuff outside that. I'd like to keep it going as long as I can though.'

Riding home with Michael from the studio, the locals were starting to make their way to work, and I remembered something I'd forgotten about the Dutch: they're enormous. I have no idea why the Dutch are such a gigantic race, but nothing makes you feel more of a shorty than wandering the streets of Amsterdam. I'm about average height back home, which makes me look like a garden gnome in the Netherlands. The average Dutch man is 185cm tall – up there with the tallest in the world. I was at a bar one night and found myself dwarfed by the two girls serving drinks. 'They must be standing on something,' I thought, until the pair of them started walking through the bar to collect glasses, and I realised I'd have to improvise some sort of stepladder arrangement to even be able to talk to them.

Still, none of that really matters when you're flying around on a bike, desperately trying to stay alive. I ran the gauntlet after the radio show as Martha and I made our way over to the Jordaan area, Amsterdam's trendy artsy suburb that Michael announced, 'would probably be where you and the Lawyer would live if you moved over here.'

In my dreams. The Jordaan is perfect, the kind of place I'd happily chuck it all in to move to tomorrow. It's everything that's good about Amsterdam. The streets are mostly too narrow for cars, meaning only cyclists and brave pedestrians can use the cafe- and gallery-lined alleys that make up the area. There are second-hand clothes stores everywhere, and people walking the streets looking like one of those second-hand clothes stores threw up on them. No one seems to care that they look like they got dressed in the dark some time in 1972. Mainly because they still manage to look good.

Locking up Martha (tightly – bike theft is rampant in the 'Dam, according to Michael), I wandered the streets, walking past cool canal-side cafes, a tapas bar, wine bars, art galleries and fashion boutiques. I ate in the sun at the Westermarkt, eating a club sandwich and the best damn apple pie in the world at a place called Winkel.

By the time I jumped back on Michael's rusty old pushy and started heading home, I'd made all sorts of plans to uproot my Australian life and shift it all to the Jordaan. Work, money, rent, the Lawyer's job et cetera would take care of themselves, surely?

It's not like there's anything wrong with the rest of Amsterdam. I could live in any of it, really. The whole place is a fairytale of duck-inhabited canals lined with tall skinny buildings that seem to lean on each other like drunks walking home from the pub, their mushy foundations causing them to sink in places and giving the whole city a slightly wonky *Alice in Wonderland* feel to it. And that's without a smoke.

*

Back at the house, Jill was feeling the effects of some drinking the night before. Not a hangover, but the realisation that she'd bought some artwork she really didn't want. 'My friends are leaving, so they're trying to get rid of all their stuff,' she explained. 'So I'd had a bit to drink, and I decided I liked one of the pictures on their wall. They gave it to me for some ridiculous price. Only problem is, it's too big to get up the stairs.'

Looking around, I realised most of the furniture in Michael

and Jill's house was far too big to fit up the tiny staircase that's the only entry to their flat. Dutch houses are all built like this, but they're also built with an ingenious way of getting around the problem. If you walk the streets, you notice large hooks attached to the top of each building. These are used as pulley systems to winch furniture up into the top flats, usually through the living room windows. Jill was pretty sure they'd need to rig up a rope to get her new painting into the house. Fortunately, they were in luck – the bendy frame could be manoeuvred through the staircase, saving them a fair bit of hassle a few days later.

That night, Jill opted for a night in to ensure she didn't purchase any more paintings, so Michael and I headed out to meet some of his teacher mates at their favourite restaurant. Situated just off Leidsestraat, the main tourist strip running from the Leidseplein to the Damrak, the restaurant should have been packed with tourists, but thanks to poor signage and a complete lack of desire to do anything about it, the place was a strictly local haunt. The comically surly service, too, wouldn't have impressed the tourists, but Michael and his mates loved it. One of the teachers ordered a whisky and coke, to which the waiter replied: 'So you don't like whisky?' Everyone at the table had a chuckle. Sitting outside, we then asked to be moved in. The same guy flicked his hand in our direction: 'No, you're outside now.'

'Is there a vegetarian menu?' I asked sarcastically, having realised this was a fiercely meat-lovers' restaurant.

'Sure,' the waiter said, pointing down the street. 'It's in that restaurant down there.'

Again, you couldn't exactly call what we were eating 'Dutch' fare. It was just huge chunks of meat cooked on the bone and served on cutting boards. But that's what's great about Holland – you can eat whatever you want, and not feel guilty about ignoring the national cuisine, because there isn't one.

'Do you miss anything about Australia?' I asked Michael as he tore into what looked like an entire lamb.

'Yeah, for sure mate, plenty of stuff. I mean, this is all great, but I'm an Australian at heart, you know? I've been missing taking the old surf ski out at Cronulla lately, just going for a bit of a paddle. Even just a normal Friday night, it'd be nice to be able to leave work, and then be standing on the deck at the yachties, drinking beers with 100 mates within half an hour or so.'

'So you reckon you'll move back to Cronulla eventually?'

'I dunno mate, probably not actually. I reckon we've got a year left in us here, then we'll look at heading back. But after being here though, I don't know if Cronulla would be right. Need a bit more culture. So we're thinking maybe somewhere in the Eastern Suburbs. It's still closer to Cronulla than here.'

From the restaurant, we headed to a going away party for a few of Michael's fellow teachers at a local bar. Several beers later, we jumped back on the bikes and pedalled home.

'See, that's a typical Amsterdam evening,' Michael said as we dodged killer trams in our wobbly, half-cut way. 'You have some dinner with a few friends, then just drop in to a local bar for a few drinks. There are so many bars like that. We try to go to a different one each time, and they're always good. Lots of character, good people. Then you get a bit tipsy, jump on your bike, and ride home. Too easy.'

*

The next morning, once Michael and Jill had headed off to work, I went in search of breakfast. Sitting outside a cafe called Van Dam (which, obviously, I picked because of the name) I ate a toasted sandwich oozing with Gruyere cheese on top of thick slices of ham, sipped a cappuccino served with a miniature stroopwafel, read a copy of the English *Guardian* newspaper, and watched the world go by.

It made me feel much better about what I had planned for the afternoon: a trip to tourist town. I'd come to be a local, but there are certain things in Amsterdam that have to be seen, regardless of how many times you've seen it before. And since Michael hadn't officially given me any advice on what to do, I could only go with what I knew.

Grabbing Martha, I headed to the Leidseplein, a square lined with touristy bars, a Bulldog 'coffee shop', and populated with all manner of buskers and travellers. (For the uninitiated, there are two types of cafeteria-style bars in the Netherlands – in a 'cafe' you'll get coffee; in a 'coffee shop' you'll get stoned.) From the Leidseplein, I pushed the bike down Leidsestraat leading into the city and Dam Square.

The streets started to get narrow and windy around the square, meaning I was soon lost, riding about aimlessly on Martha. It had got to the point where I was going to give up and actually consult a map, when I saw it, like a shining beacon to the unstoned man: Aratxos. A 'coffee shop'.

Why was I going there? Because, like in Paris where I'd failed to avoid the Eiffel Tower despite my mission to bypass the tourist traps, I decided I just couldn't come to Amsterdam and not partake in the number one tourist activity: smoking pot.

I've smoked pot in Amsterdam before. Although officially we had to tell our Top Deck passengers that drugs are bad, most of them were usually keen for a smoke anyway, and they'd want the crew to steer them in the direction of somewhere 'safe'. You have to be careful with Dutch weed. Some of it is nice and mild. Some, though, is super strong, for experts only. Many's been the passenger determined to try pot for the first time in Amsterdam who's wound up vomiting into the nearest canal.

As I didn't want to turn up back at Michael and Jill's place in that sort of state, I was a bit hesitant about what to buy. Going into the coffee shop, I headed to the counter piled with Tupperware boxes filled with stinking greenery, and asked the bald English guy behind the counter what he had. 'I have everything, mun,' he said in a faux Jamaican accent, spreading his arms to indicate the filled boxes. 'I am a greengrocer.'

I settled on a single pre-rolled joint, for 3 euros, which was supposed to give me a 'mild body high'.

'Can I buy a lighter too?' I asked.

'Mun,' the greengrocer replied through pierced lips, 'I will let you borrow one. Here. If you try to run away with it . . .' He shrugged. 'I will not chase you.'

I sat down and lit up, sucking back the noxious fumes and immediately almost coughing up a lung. Across the room, three girls were sharing a joint of their own, giggling to themselves through a haze of smoke. Another English guy stood at my table, rolling one up. After a few puffs of mine though, I realised there was a problem. Smoking by yourself is a bit like drinking by yourself – it's either not much fun, or you've got a problem. I wasn't having much fun. For starters, there was no break from the joint – no one to pass it to so you can take a few lungfuls of sweet, sweet oxygen. Then you find that, while things do seem just that little bit funnier, you've got no one to share the joke with. Or tell you jokes. In fact, I was pretty bored. Disappointed, I stubbed out the joint, tossed it in the bin, handed the lighter back to the 'greengrocer', who was now chatting up a pair of Canadian girls, and headed out into the light of the street.

From there, there's only one thing to do when you're mildly stoned in central Amsterdam: walk the Red Light District. Again, it was a place I knew well from my Top Deck days. This time, however, I noticed a change. I'd heard the city was trying to clean up its famously dodgy district, but I had no idea how far along they'd come. The most obvious signs were the windows. Sure, plenty of them were still guarded by lingerie-clad women, but plenty had changed as well. The mayor's idea had been to boot the prostitutes out and turn the windows into art galleries and fashion boutiques, which I thought would ruin the place, but actually fit it quite nicely. I wasn't even offered cocaine – although it *was* two in the afternoon.

Jumping back on the bike, I started cycling towards Michael

and Jill's place, when my fear of the last couple of days was realised. Old Martha was a trusty steed, but she'd been showing signs of wear and tear. Aside from all the rust, she'd been rattling away like a Warsaw tram every time I went over a cobbled street, which, in Amsterdam, was a lot. Finally, Martha could take no more. Whatever was holding the rear mud guard in place suddenly broke, letting the guard slip down and wedge itself under the tyre. This would have been a minor problem had I been stationary at the time. However, I was whipping along at mad, semi-stoned full pelt, so the wedged guard locked up the wheel, sending me skidding across the street towards oncoming trams/cars/pedestrians/other cyclists. It was all I could do to stay upright, before I came to a very inglorious halt a few centimetres from the tram tracks, much to the disappointment of the 10,000 or so tourists who'd been watching my struggle.

I managed to rig the mud guard back on with some wire, MacGyver style, mentally checked off another of my nine lives, and continued on to the Vondelpark, a beautiful city park just near Michael and Jill's place filled that afternoon with Dutchies relaxing in the sun. I'd come to the park ostensibly to enjoy a leisurely pedal around. I'd also come, however, to see if amorous locals were making use of one of the city's more peculiar rules. See, there are plenty of things you can't do in the Vondel Park: you can't litter, you can't let your dog off its leash, and you can't make too much noise. It is, however, perfectly legal for you and your partner to strip off all of your orange clothes, step out of your clogs, and have sex right there on the grass.

No one I talked to had ever seen anyone making use of this odd quirk in the city laws but, still, I wanted to check it out for myself. As suspected, I didn't catch any gigantic Dutch couples playing the beast with two backs on the manicured lawns. I did, however, see a complete absence of litter, and all dogs on leashes.

The sex rule is one of the little quirks of Dutch life you find out about after living there for three years. Michael and Jill also thought it was hilarious that married couples in Holland make a big deal out of their 12-and-a-half-year anniversaries. 'Most men can't even remember the normal date,' Jill said. 'How are they supposed to remember a half-year date?'

And then there's Christmas, which the Dutch always celebrate with a 'secret Santa'-style round of gift-giving.

'But here's the difficult thing,' Jill told me. 'When you give your person their present, you also have to write a little poem about that person. It's actually very funny. We've started doing it now, although our families were a bit freaked out about it at first.'

For our final night together, Michael, Jill and I made the most of not having to eat Dutch food and went for tapas at a little place just a short bike ride from their house.

'I had a bit of an incident on the bike today, Michael,' I admitted.

'Ah, did you, mate? You didn't come a cropper did you?'

'No, just missed out. I think old Martha's days are numbered though.'

'Maybe, mate, maybe . . . Hang on, who's Martha?'

The restaurant, like everything else I'd experienced with Michael and Jill so far in Amsterdam, was excellent. The food was great, the atmosphere was relaxed, and the people were friendly.

'How are you ever going to leave this behind?' I asked my two hosts.

'Dunno, mate,' Michael said, shaking his head. 'I mean, it's just such a liveable city. The rent's not that cheap, but, you know, we don't have to worry about that, do we? But the people are great, the food is good, the bars are friendly, the beer's good, you can ride anywhere you want to go on your bike. It's the life, mate, for sure.'

'You can even have sex in the park,' I said.

'Yep, yep. As long as your dog's on a leash.'

The Dull Life

'They had a Eurovision theme last time – you should have seen some of the outfits.'

Alison didn't like that – me nicknaming it 'the Dull'. It was innocent enough. The place is called East Dulwich, so if I was going to shorten it, in the way Australians do with everything, I'd call it 'the Dull'.

I'd just met Alison at the train station, and we were walking down the high street back to her flat.

'So how long have you been living in "the Dull"?' I asked.

She cocked an eyebrow at me. 'Why do you call it "the Dull"?'

'I dunno, just a shortening of Dulwich, I guess. Dulwich – the Dull.'

'Oh. Right. It's just that a lot of people kind of do expect it to be very dull around here.'

'Really?' I laughed. 'Sorry about that. Let's just go with East Dulwich then, hey?'

Truth is, I had no idea where East Dulwich even was. A quick google confirmed that it had no Walkabout, no Slug and

Lettuce, no local AFL team, no listings on Gumtree . . . it didn't even have a Tube line. My ignorance was excusable, however, because Australians don't usually stray too far off the beaten track in London. It's a huge city, but most of us tend to congregate in Fulham, Earls Court, Shepherds Bush and Putney. A few crazy ones live in Wimbledon. But that's it. It's a rite of passage for Australians to take their 'big trip' to the mother country for a year or two, but we like to stick close to each other when we get there.

Unlike Africa, I knew the invitations would pour in from London. Of the 400 people who ended up emailing me, 43 of them lived in Great Britain's capital. There was Matt from Putney, Ayesha from Putney, Liz from Fulham, Santiago from Earls Court, Karen from Camden Town . . . Okay fine, there was one from Camden Town. But the rest of the invitations pretty much reflected the spread of Australians around Great Britain. On top of the 43 Londoners, I had one invitation from Birmingham, two from Manchester, three from Edinburgh, and, incredibly, one from Elgin, the tiny Scottish town I lived in for six months when I worked a gap year job on a strawberry farm.

As a writer going out to visit readers of an Australian travel blog, I could hardly avoid London. But I could avoid the usual clichéd Australian spots, and Alison's offer sounded perfect.

> I'm sure you have thousands of offers in London, but I thought I would add ours (my Welsh flatmate and me) to it. You'd be welcome to crash with us in East Dulwich (SE22) if you fancied checking out the pubs of south-east London.

Finding my overland train from Paddington, I stared out the window as we headed towards Alison's hood, passing by the Millwall FC ground – a football club not exactly known for its good-natured fans and pleasant surroundings. I was starting to wonder what I was getting myself into. Was I going to be staying on a council estate? Was PC Hollis from *The Bill* going to have to come out from Sun Hill to save me? A few minutes later, though, we were out of the bad lands, and into the Dull.

Alison was 32, with a bright, smiling face framed by short dark hair. She'd been in London three years, and had almost completely lost any hint of Aussie accent.

'So how did you come to end up here?' I asked as I lugged my pack down the street, a nice little place with a village-type atmosphere, filled with the usual array of pubs and curry houses, and not a single football hooligan.

'A friend of mine recommended it actually. I was in Putney, but I had to move. It's the most at home I've felt since I moved to London. It's not on the Tube line, but that just means you get less expats living out here, which is nice.'

We traipsed past a park and an old church, down a small suburban street with rows of little cottages, and eventually found Alison's flat – a bizarrely built two-bedder with each room of the house on a slightly different level. You'd walk up a flight of stairs and enter the house in the living room, then, if you turned left, you could step down a few stairs to get to the kitchen. If you turned right though, you'd step up a few stairs to the bathroom, then up a few more stairs to Alison's flatmate Ang's room, and, a few more stairs and a winding hallway later, you finally got to Alison's room. I was going to be based in the lounge room, on a blow-up mattress on the floor.

'So I've had to catch up on a few of your blogs lately,' Alison said, pouring out two glasses of rose in the kitchen. 'I felt so bad – I've been really busy at work for the last few weeks. Usually I sit down on a Thursday and read it, but I've been so busy that I've missed the last few. So the other day I had a bit of a catch-up.'

'You really didn't have to – some of the people I've stayed with have only ever read one post.'

'Really? No, I really do love it; I've just been so busy!'

Alison worked as an events coordinator, although in her words, 'not the exciting kind'. She organised doctors' conventions. When doctors or medical people wanted to get together somewhere to discuss stuff, it was Alison's job to make it all happen. It's one of those jobs which, I guess, someone has to do. And in her spare time?

'I'm into quilting,' she confessed as I spluttered a little of my wine.

'Quilting?' I was confused. Was this some sort of bizarre S&M practice she was going to spring on me in the middle of the night?

'Yeah, I make quilts. Like that one over there,' she said, pointing to a sheet of finely stitched cloth hanging from a bookcase. 'That's for a competition in Australia. Mum and Dad own a quilting shop at home, so they send me most of the supplies I need.'

'No kidding. You know, I don't think I've ever met a quilter before.'

'Really? Well, we're around.'

'So what's the plan for tonight?'

'I'd been trying to figure out what we were going to do with you, because it's a Saturday night in London, so there are plenty of choices. We tossed a few things up, but in the end I got us tickets to this night called Secret Cinema. I went a few weeks ago, and it was great. Everyone gets really dressed up, really into the theme, and it's a fun night out. They had a Eurovision theme last time – you should have seen some of the outfits.'

A Eurovision theme night sounded more frightening to me than a spot of late-night quilting, but I didn't mention that. I'd actually known about the Secret Cinema for a few days now, because Alison had had to warn me about the theme to give me time to prepare. All the invitation had said was 'wear bright colours', so I'd stopped off at a second-hand store in the Jordaan a few days ago and picked up a sweet neon yellow shirt to wear.

'Yeah, that shirt should do fine,' Alison laughed as she saw me pull the retina-burning masterpiece out of my backpack.

I donned my shirt, Alison slapped on some garish make-up, clipped a purple feather fascinator into her hair, and we set off into the night. We jumped on a bus, ignored the inevitable stares, and headed for the Coronet Theatre in Elephant and Castle, where we found a long queue of 20-somethings dressed as if Elton John had exploded somewhere nearby. They were being entertained during their wait by actors in Jamaican dress charging down the street selling fake watermelons, smoking fake joints, or preaching from a fake Bible. It was a carnival atmosphere obviously created to disguise the fact that we all had to wait in line for an hour to get in.

'You know,' Alison said as we shuffled along in the queue, adjusting her fascinator and brushing away the offers of watermelon, 'I've been coming up with a list of reasons why I can't leave London, and this is definitely one of them. You just can't get this sort of thing in Australia. There are others, too.'

'Like?'

'London public transport, which is far better than at home. Oh, and Zara. You know the clothes shop? Until Sydney gets a Zara, I refuse to go back.'

I laughed. 'My girlfriend's obsessed with Zara too. What's with that place?'

'It's just brilliant, the clothes are great.'

'Better quilting shops in Australia though.'

'Ha ha, well, my parents' shop anyway.'

The line was still moving forward slowly, although we were now being treated to a full Jamaican reggae band dancing down the street. The challenge at a Secret Cinema event is guessing which film is going to be screened. You know the theme when you book the tickets, you just don't know the film. It's usually a cult film, or something pertinent to some event that's happening around the world. At the Eurovision theme night, they'd shown a doco on kids entering the junior Eurovision, which had gone down a storm. Tonight's . . . I was struggling. Something to do with Bob Marley? Usain Bolt? I'd exhausted my knowledge of Jamaica already.

Inside, there were no more clues – just a bar on one level, and the theatre on another, where a Jamaican guy (or at least a black guy with dreads and an accent) was revving up the crowd by screaming, 'Are you feeling the vibe-a?' He was followed by gospel singers, who warbled away for a good half-hour before the lights finally went down and everyone held their breath as the film began. The screen flickered into life and, at the sight of a beaten-up old bus rounding a corner, a small cheer went up from one section of the crowd. Alison looked at me and shrugged. I had no idea what it was either. Eventually, the title came up: *The Harder They Come*. Another cheer from the crowd. Alison looked at me and shrugged. I still had no idea what it was either.

As we found out later, thanks to the mighty powers of Google, *The Harder They Come* is a cult Jamaican film from the early 70s that 'put Jamaica on the map'. It also had a soundtrack that put reggae on the, um, musical map. Still, cult it may have been, but it didn't impress many of the cinema goers, who were now walking out. That's the risk you take with a secret event like this – there's every chance you won't like the surprise. We managed to last about half an hour of not being able to understand what the hell anyone was saying through the really bad sound system before Alison whispered, 'Should we just go?'

'Yep, let's do it.'

So we waved down a bus and made our way back to 'the Dull' for some dinner. It was 10pm, and both the pubs on the high street seemed pretty busy, but there was only one restaurant still open, and even there we had to talk the chef into letting us in for one last dinner sitting. I was starting to get the impression my nickname might have been on the money.

*

What's with the hand towels? Sometimes my hosts would just give me a single bath towel to use during my stay – others would present me with a neatly folded tower of towels on top of my bed. Not just a bath towel, but a hand towel and a face washer on top.

The hand towels confused me. Do I take them with me every time I need to go to the toilet, so I can dry my hands on it? And does that mean I have to keep it on my person at all times, maybe stuffed in a pocket somewhere?

Alison had started throwing towels of varying sizes at me the moment I'd walked in the door, but I'd managed to talk her out of the face washer, leaving me with just a small mountain of bathing accessories. I had a shower that next morning, nervously ignoring my hand towel, before we headed up the high street to the Bishop, a pub that apparently did the best coffee in south-east London.

Coffee's a big thing for Australians. I've written some interesting blogs about hard-hitting topics (all right fine, I haven't), but still, one of the most popular I've written was about where in the world you can get the best coffee. The general consensus was: anywhere but Britain. British coffee is crap. They might know their way around a cup of tea, but most coffee in Britain tastes like watery mud. The few caffeinated havens in the city are well known to most Australians – there's even a cafe in the upmarket suburb of Richmond that advertises out the front: 'We have Australian baristas'. Pretty weird for a country that's about a two-hour flight from Italy.

'What do you think of British food?' Alison asked me as we made our way to the pub.

'Ah . . . Fairly average really. Unless you're getting a curry.'

'True. Want to hear my favourite story about English food?' I nodded. 'Okay. So this year marks the 50th anniversary of the first ever Italian restaurant in Britain. They've only had Italian restaurants here for 50 years. So anyway, they released a book this year to mark the anniversary, called *The Spaghetti Tree*, because of this April Fools' joke the BBC played on the whole country in the 60s.

'They filmed this fake documentary about Italian people harvesting "spaghetti trees" over in Italy. They were just normal trees, but the producers had, like, hung all these strands of spaghetti from the branches. Anyway, the Brits totally bought it, and there were all these people calling up the BBC wanting to know about how they could grow their own spaghetti trees. So funny. That says a lot about the British attitude to foreign foods to me.'

Handing me a menu as we walked in she said, 'Have a cappuccino, trust me. And the eggs Benedict. Where should we sit?'

I looked around. 'Can we get in the sun somewhere?'

In Australia, I try to stay out of the sun as much as possible. I've got ridiculously white skin, almost translucent, which means that spending anything longer than about half an hour in the sun leaves me looking like one of those pensioners in Florida. Then I peel, and a few days later I'm back to my original whiteness. In the northern hemisphere though, minus the gaping hole in the ozone layer, things are different. For starters, the sun's not nearly as strong. And you can't just rely on the sun being out all the time. In fact, you can pretty much rely on its not being out. Which means that as soon as you see a tiny ray poking through the clouds, you get this weird urge to get yourself under it *now*.

It had happened to me in no time – I'd been in England two days. I looked out the window that morning and thought: Must. Get. In. Sun.

So Alison duly got us a table in the sun, where we whiled away most of the afternoon drinking good coffee, before switching to beers when the British Grand Prix started on TV.

'You don't find many Aussies around here,' said Alison, proudly surveying her local.

'Um, I think that couple over there is Australian,' I said, pointing to a far table. Alison listened in for a second.

'Oh. They are too.'

'And those guys over there?' I said, tilting my head at the couple next to us. 'I think they are too.'

'Hmm . . . they are too. Well, there you go, there are a few Australians here.'

Alison said this with a smile, but I could see there was a slight resentment at her Australian-free haven being invaded by more colonials. Australians are funny like that – we love to travel, but as soon as you find another Aussie, it's like your experience has been spoiled by having to share it with someone doing the same thing.

Our afternoon in the pub over, we made our way back to Alison's funny little flat.

'I don't really have much planned tonight,' she confessed. 'I was just going to cook something up in the kitchen, maybe watch some TV. Is that going to be okay?'

I could think of nothing better. So we went to an actual supermarket, bought actual food, cooked it in an actual kitchen, and then watched some actual TV. *Top Gear* was on. Nice.

*

I said goodbye to Alison the next morning; her going to organise doctors' conferences, and me free to roam the city. Well, not completely free. I had two very English sporting events to experience in the 24 hours before I headed to Brazil. The first was a day at the All England Lawn Tennis Club in SW19. The second was a State of Origin match at an Aussie pub.

Joining me on this cultural extravaganza was an old mate of mine from Australia, a guy who, confusingly, was also called Ben. First up was Wimbledon. It was day two of the famous tournament, a day when the great British hope, Andy Murray, would be playing, and our own 'little' Lleyton Hewitt was also taking the court. We didn't have tickets, of course, because that would require careful planning and organisation, so our aim was to turn up on the day, and get ourselves some general admission tickets at the gate.

The first clue that we were in a bit of trouble when we arrived at Southlands station at 11am was the sign: an arrow pointing towards something called 'The Queue'. You know that when a queue has graduated to capital letters and inverted commas, it's a pretty serious piece of lining-up apparatus. Directed down a small road, we arrived to a horrifying sight: rows upon rows, lines upon lines, thousands upon thousands, of tennis fans. And all were quietly indulging in that great English passion: standing in line. Wandering past thousands of people standing, sipping drinks, or lying in the grass sunbathing, we finally found what we thought was the end of the queue, and were each handed a small card and a little book by someone official-looking.

'There's yer queue card, don't lose that,' the girl said.

We both looked confused. 'Queue card?'

'Yep, hold on to that so you can go out of line if you want to, and get back in the queue. See, there's the number you are at the bottom there.'

I looked down, and laughed. I was officially number 12,102 in line. I couldn't believe it. Making up the rows and rows of patiently waiting people were 12,101 other tennis fans, hoping to get in for the afternoon. None seemed particularly agitated. Or even grumpy. You had to wonder: in what other country could this system possibly work? No one appeared to be cutting in line. There were no lane ropes or markers to keep people in place – they'd just obediently formed their own snaking queue, and were sticking to it. Some were even flicking through the incredible 40-page booklet we'd just been given: *A Guide to Queuing for the Championships*.

Ben and I took a quick look through it, picking out such gems as, 'You are in the queue if you join it at the end and remain in it until you have acquired a ticket at the turnstiles' and, 'If you have to leave the queue, you should negotiate your position with those around you'.

A few entries gave us the impression we might be in line for a while. One said: 'All pizza/takeaway orders must be arranged for delivery at the Wimbledon Park Road gate'. Another advised: 'Overnight queuers should use tents which accommodate a maximum of two persons'.

'Any idea what time we're likely to get in?' other Ben asked the queuing attendant.

'Hmm . . .' She looked around the field. 'Probably not for another five hours or so.'

'Five hours?!'

'Yeah, sorry guys, it's a really busy day today. Andy Murray's on, plus Lleyton Hewitt is pretty popular over here too.'

'Popular?' Ben spluttered. 'I'm Australian, and I hope he dies in a comet accident!'

This was met with a confused look, and then a shrug. 'Sorry guys.'

We considered our options. We could stand in a field for five hours and probably only see one match – maybe two. Or, we could not pass go, and head directly to a local pub.

Fifteen minutes later, Ben and I were sitting on a rooftop terrace at a pub in Wimbledon proper, watching the tennis on a big screen and sipping Pimm's and lemonade. Close enough, we decided.

*

I don't actually care that much about the State of Origin. I know it's sacrilegious for an east coaster to say that, but I don't really like rugby league, and I don't really like rugby league supporters, so I tend to take a passing interest only. Hell, I'm so casually involved that I even changed which team I support in my 20s. I'd grown up in Queensland as a NSW supporter, mainly due to the influence of my dyed-in-the-wool Blue dad, and the fact that I disliked most of the people playing for and supporting the Maroons. After moving to Sydney though, I discovered New South Welshmen were much the same as the Maroons supporters I'd hated in high school, and that it was a lot easier to support Queensland when you weren't surrounded by Queenslanders.

In London, it doesn't really matter. There are probably about

20 million people in the city who couldn't care less, and then there are the Australians, who all somehow seem to get out of whatever it is they're supposed to be doing during the day, and make it down to either a Walkabout or Slug and Lettuce to drink early-morning pints and yell at the TV.

The day after the Wimbledon debacle, Ben and I had decided to go watch the footy in the heartland: Fulham. We wanted Australiana, and we knew where to find it. We'd been told of an Australian theme pub on Fulham high street which was going to be showing the game, and, keen to avoid the Walkabout cliche (in favour of a slightly different cliche), we headed in for the 11am kick-off. Half an hour before the game, and the place was heaving with board-shorted blokes and their surprisingly enthusiastic girlfriends. The Slug was the perfect setting, all faux wooden walls groaning under the weight of tacky Aussie memorabilia like 'Last dunny for 200km' signs, and cheap Foster's from the tap.

We grabbed a few pints and settled in to watch the match, and soon realised that for most Aussies this is pretty much quintessential London life. You come over, work hard during the day, collect your pounds, and piss them up the wall at the Sluggo or the Walkabout at night. And from what I could tell from the hordes cheering their teams on from the other side of the world, they were having a ball doing it.

I was too. But I had a plane to catch.

Getting a Brazilian

'Don't worry mate, I'm not a big black cab driver.'

I can get along with most people most of the time. It's a product, I think, of a childhood spent trying to ensure people of all different ages and backgrounds didn't want to beat me up. I wasn't always 100 per cent successful in that endeavour, but it has meant I've grown up with the ability to make friends – on a superficial level at least – with most of the people I meet.

In Sao Paulo, however, I was having a problem. The people I was meeting weren't speaking my language. Not in a 'they don't get me' kind of way – they literally could not speak my language.

As I've said before, I'm pretty crap with languages, and I'm not one of those people who expects that everyone in other countries should be able to speak English, so don't take this as a slight against my new Brazilian friends. It's just hard to make conversation when your only common words are 'yes', 'no', and *'feijoada'*. Although you'd be surprised how long you can keep up an exchange with just that trio.

I'd touched down in Sao Paulo in mid-afternoon, but, as my

contact Adriana wouldn't be home from work until 8pm, I'd decided to kill four hours or so in the airport. I had the feeling Sao Paulo wasn't the sort of place you'd want to roam around for a few hours in the dark with your every possession strapped to your back. Fortunately, at the airport I was able to indulge in every Brazilian's obsession: football.

I'd always wondered if Brazilians would be as obsessed with football as everyone made them out to be. You just never really know until you get there. And I knew literally as soon as I got there. By the time my flight touched down in Sao Paulo, the Brazilian team had taken the field in the Confederations Cup semi-final against South Africa. I could tell this, because everyone in the airport was watching the game. Everyone. The passengers, the customs officials, the baggage guys – all had downed tools and were watching the TV screens that were dotted around the arrivals hall. As I waited patiently in the customs line, hoping for the ball to go out for long enough for someone to turn around and do something with my passport, the entire airport erupted in a huge roar, people hugging and cheering. Brazil 1, South Africa 0. Now, if someone could just stamp my passport.

It's not hard to persuade someone to come to Brazil. I had to tick off at least one country in South America, so it might as well be the land of sun, sand and string bikinis. I was prepared to go to any city, just as long as it contained the words 'Rio', 'de' and 'Janeiro'. I waited patiently for weeks. I had offers from Valparaiso in Chile, from Buenos Aires in Argentina, and from Bogota in Colombia. And two from Brazil – one in Sao Paulo, and the other in Belo Horizonte. Neither city had a beach. Nor, I had to assume, any string bikinis. Just, in the former case, the chance to get shot for no reason. Still, I was tempted by Adriana's email.

Hey Ben, you're welcome on my couch for a day or two when you come to Sao Paulo, Brazil's coolest city. I've got two cats, so I hope you're not allergic. I'm a 28-year-old translator/travel writer from Brazil who reads your blog every now and then. I'd love to show you around.

Staying in Brazil with an actual Brazilian? That was hard to turn down. And then there was a late invitation from a guy called Nick – but we'll get to him later.

First up was Sao Paulo, a city I was hoping to see if I ever made it out of the customs line. Eventually, Brazil won the football, the airport went nuts, everyone got back to doing what they were supposed to be doing, and I went down to the bus stop. Adriana had given me instructions on which bus to catch and where to get off, but I'd been hoping to call her from the airport to make sure she was going to be home. For some reason though, I couldn't get through. I seemed to have another 'wrong' phone number. It was now dark, and I didn't really fancy being stranded on the streets on my first night in Sao Paulo, so I just had to hope she lived where she said she lived.

I managed to find the right bus, and get off at the right place, and was soon standing outside the metal grille barring the way into what I hoped was Adriana's house. I pressed the intercom. Nothing. I tried it again. Nothing. I pulled out my phone, and tried to call her. I got a few weird noises, and what I'm pretty sure are the Portuguese words for 'this number doesn't exist, someone's taking the piss out of you'. Or something like that.

As I stood there on the street, waiting for someone to knife me and run off with my inflatable neck pillow, two guys wandered up to the iron grille and stared at me for a second. Uh oh.

'Adriana?' one of them said in a thick accent. I nodded, and he broke into a grin. 'Adriana!'

The other guy nodded at me. 'You go to see Adriana?'

'Yep.'

'Okay, we take you in. He does not speak any English,' he added, jabbing a thumb at his grinning mate, who I would later find out was William, Adriana's boyfriend. They unlocked the grille and we made it into the foyer, walked up some stairs and into a flat, where Adriana was patiently waiting. Obviously I'd buggered up the intercom somehow.

'Ben! You made it! I was so worried about you,' she gushed, giving me a hug. Adriana was quite tall and slim, with frameless spectacles and slightly curly hair. 'Okay, welcome to my house. You've met William and Joao. These are my cats, Piccolino and Puma. You'll see a lot of them.'

The cats! Of course. I'd been warned about the cats. I don't mind cats, I'm not allergic to them or anything – I'm just not a huge fan, so I was just going to have to put up with Piccolino and Puma. Adriana's flat looked nice enough, and, from what I could tell in the darkness outside, it was in a nice enough neighbourhood. Adriana gave me a quick tour of the flat – there was one small bedroom, a bathroom, a small kitchen, and the living room, which featured my bed: the couch. There was also a huge photo of Uluru on one wall, as well as a framed photo of Adriana kissing a dolphin, with a Coffs Harbour logo in the bottom corner.

For my first night in town, Adriana had planned to take me to a *churrascaria*, a traditional Brazilian barbecue joint that serves meat in an all-you-can-eat way. Joining us for the night were William and Joao, plus Vanessa and Claudia, two more of Adriana's friends. On the way over there in Claudia's little hatchback, William tried to strike up a conversation, which is no mean feat when you have no common language. He'd babble at me in Portuguese, then one of the others (all of whom spoke pretty good English), would translate.

William: '*El epode dancar o samba?*'

Adriana: 'He wants to know if you can samba dance.'

Me: 'Er . . . I can try.'

William: '*Eu vou ensina-lo esta noite. Diga a ele para ficar como e ele vai ficar bem.*'

Adriana: 'He says he will teach you tomorrow night. You stick with him.'

Me: 'He has no idea what he's getting himself into . . .'

William: '*Sera que ele o apoio de uma equipe brasileira?*'

Adriana: 'He asks if you support a Brazilian football team.'

Me: 'Not yet.'

William: '*Diga a ele que ele tem para apoiar Sao Paulo.*'

Adriana: 'He says you can support Sao Paulo FC now. That's his team.'

This continued when we arrived in the restaurant, with a grinning William telling me, through the help of his translators, to just order whatever he ordered, and I'd be fine. As it was, I did need help. I'd been to a churrascaria in Sydney before, so I thought I knew what to expect – a few pots of salads on the table, and waiters who would come around with a few different cuts of meat on giant skewers, and slice off bits if I decided I wanted some. And this churrascaria was just like that, only super-sized.

Rather than have a few salads on the table, there was an entire salad bar about the size of a football field, with everything from pasta dishes and casseroles to vegetables and cold salads. We went over there first and filled up our plates, before returning to the table and waiting for the meat to come around. I had no idea what most of it was, but it tasted amazing, and there was an amazing amount of it. Being an inexperienced churrascarano (a made-up word), I got a bit excited and made the classic rookie error: saying '*sim*' to every single piece of meat presented to me. It all looked so *good*. I took steak, I took another type of steak, I took chorizo sausage, I took chicken hearts, I took pork with crackling. Pretty soon I had a giant pile of meat on my plate that I was never going to be able to work my way through.

Around me, the conversation was flowing. Trouble is, it was flowing in Portuguese. Every now and then I picked up the word '*gringo*', so I knew they were talking about me, but that was it. This was a new experience. So far I'd mostly stayed with Australians, or at least those who counted English as their first language. Now I was surrounded by proper Brazilians, who knew all the local haunts and great places to go, but who also had the frustrating habit of speaking their own language. Every now and then Adriana would turn to me and explain what was going on, but most of the time I just sat quietly, trying to work out how I was going to ingest the entire cow now arranged in little bits on my plate.

To be honest, I wasn't that worried about not being able to participate in the conversation. By that stage I'd been awake for about 30 hours, and it was all I could do to keep my eyes open and my jaw working on all that meat. Three-quarters of the way through my plate though, I gave up, and put my knife and fork down.

'Already?' Adriana said, shaking her head. 'That's terrible! We are all still eating. Not a good effort at all.'

William was unperturbed by my culinary wussiness. He jabbed me with his finger, raising his chin questioningly: 'Feijoada?'

I looked to Adriana, confused. 'Oh,' she said, 'he wants to know if you have tried feijoada yet.'

'Ah, no,' I said. 'I don't even know what feijoada is.'

Adriana fired something off in Portuguese to William, who immediately turned to me, a concerned look on his face: 'Feijoada?'

I put my palms out, shaking my head. '*Non.*'

William just grinning, clapping a hand on my back reassuringly: 'Feijoada.'

I turned to Adriana again. 'Don't worry,' she smiled, 'he will make sure you try feijoada before you leave.'

I still didn't know what feijoada was, but that night, I didn't care. I was stuffed. Pretty soon the bill arrived, and I got my first experience of Brazilians' obsession with bill splitting. Don't get me wrong, I've split the bill with people plenty of times in Australia. But there, it's a roundabout thing: the total is $128, you've got four people, so you say, well, that's about $35 each, with a tip. But that's not how it works in Brazil.

Once the bill arrived, Vanessa whipped out her phone and started punching numbers in. 'Okay, you had a meal and a beer,' she said, tapping away, 'so that's . . . 32 reais for you.' She went around the table like that, everyone carefully peeling off bills and paying the exact right amount. This would happen every night we went out, to the point where Adriana once even asked if we could all order on separate bills to make things easier. Some restaurants would even give each diner a card with a number on it, so we could just order for ourselves. It seemed a little stingy to me, but if that's the local custom, I'll go with it.

*

'You do like football, don't you?' Adriana asked the next morning as she dried her hair. I nodded, trying to shovel cats off my doona. 'Okay, good. I thought I should check. I have to go to work today, but my friend Paolo is going to take you to a football museum. I think he speaks a bit of English, so you two should have fun.'

A 'bit' of English? This was going to be interesting. Before Paolo turned up, I decided to check some emails on Adriana's laptop, and was immediately surrounded by cats again. They seemed intent on sitting on top of whatever it was I was taking an interest in at any given time. I managed to work them off the keyboard and onto my lap, and I sat there like an evil dictator, patting a couple of cats while I fired off important communiques like Facebook status updates and funny photos.

Paolo turned up about an hour late (a Brazilian custom, I later found out), and we hit the street, headed for the football museum at Pacaembu, one of Sao Paulo's more central football stadiums. We chatted while we walked, and I soon found out that while Paolo had a lot to say, it was going to take him a long time to say it, because his English was pretty rusty.

'So,' he'd say. 'You . . . aah . . . you have, aah, seen . . . football before?'

'Yeah yeah, plenty of Australians play football.'

'Like, aah . . . like, proper football? Aah . . . Soccer?'

'Yep, proper football. It's popular in Australia.'

'Ah, okay. And . . . aah . . . You, aah . . . You . . . know Brazil-ian . . . how you say? Aah . . . Players?'

'Brazilian players? Like Kaka, Robinho, Ronaldinho?'

'Ah, yes. Good. I, aah . . . My team . . . is Santos.'

'Oh. William told me I support Sao Paulo.'

Paolo looked horrified. 'No, no, no. Sao Paulo aah . . . not good. Santos. Pele, he, aah . . . he play for Santos.'

Sao Paulo actually has four major teams – Sao Paulo FC, Santos, Palmeiras and Corinthians. All of Adriana's friends seemed to support a different club, including the girls. They all, however, were united in their hatred of the Argentineans.

This was the first time I'd really had the chance to look at Sao Paulo, and it certainly wasn't visually spectacular. It was gritty, hard, with graffiti-splashed old buildings and cracked pavements. Down near Pacaembu there were a few nice houses, but they were surrounded by electric fences and CCTV cameras. Nothing had happened so far, but I was still expecting to get robbed at any minute. It had also started raining lightly, which didn't help matters. Paolo looked up.

'Sao Paulo is . . . aah . . . how you call this?'

'This sort of rain?' I said. 'Drizzle.'

'Ah, yes. Sao Paulo . . . aah . . . is called . . . "The City of Drizzle".'

'Really? Nice.'

'Yes. It is aah . . . always drizzle here.'

They should really put that on the tourism brochures, I thought. Sao Paulo is actually known as the business centre of Brazil, a massive, sprawling city of 11 million. Flying over it the afternoon before, the city had just seemed to stretch on and on, an incredible urban sprawl from horizon to horizon. The state itself has more people in it than Australia does. While Brazilians have a reputation for being laid-back, beachy types, Paulistas are seen as the uptight bunch, the rat-racers who are always in a hurry.

It's a place most tourists give a wide berth, but I figured I had an invitation from a real Brazilian, so I couldn't really turn it down. There had to be more to this city than urban sprawl and violent crime. Right?

For starters, there's the football museum, an ode to the passion of every Brazilian. Housed under the stands at Pacaembu stadium, it's full of memorabilia, video highlights and trivia about the game. Unfortunately, most of it is in Portuguese, leaving us monolingual morons a little underwhelmed. Paolo was doing his best to translate though, which was probably doing more harm than good. I'd just begun to roughly figure things out for myself when Paolo would start up.

'This . . . aah . . . You knooooow . . . rules of football?'

'Yeah, I play at home.'

'Oh. Good! Okay. This, aah . . . he, aah . . . he say about, ummm . . . referees.'

I nodded. We'd actually come to my favourite part of the museum. Bugger the displays dedicated to Pele's dribbling skills, or Garrincha's shooting ability. This one was dedicated to the referees who, Paolo told me, were commonly referred to by Brazilian fans as 'son of a bitch'. The museum's idea? They'd interviewed some of the referees' mums – or, the 'bitches'. It was a pretty funny idea, and I'm sure it would have been even more interesting if I could understand a word the 'bitches' were saying. Still, they seemed pretty good humoured about the whole thing, so that's nice.

*

If there's one thing Brazilians seem to love almost as much as football, it's dancing. Now, football, I can do. I've been playing it since I could walk. Dancing, however, is another story. You'd think that foot coordination would cross all boundaries, but you'd be wrong.

That night, Adriana and her friends were going to be treated to the full hopelessness of my dancing ability. First though, there was some respite, in the form of dinner. I'd headed with Adriana, William, Paolo, his girlfriend Gabi and their friend Regina to a tapas-style restaurant, where Adriana plonked herself down and proceeded to order for the whole table. 'And just so you know,' she said, closing her menu, 'the foreigners always pay the bill. Ha ha!'

Funny, I thought. This foreigner's going to be getting out his calculator, don't worry. Before the waiter ran off, I managed to get in an order of my own: one caipirinha. This is the classic Brazilian cocktail, a sweet mix of fruit, sugar, ice, and *cachaca* – which is kind of like rum. I was having a regular lime caipirinha, the norm in these parts.

'Watch out,' Paolo said. 'They are . . . aah . . . strong.'

'He'll be okay,' Adriana jumped in. 'Australians, they drink so much. They just drink all the time, it's crazy.'

I laughed. Adriana had lived in Sydney for two years, so she knew a bit about Australia. It was still interesting to hear a foreigner's take on my home country. I asked around the table about what people knew about Australia.

'Um, kangaroos,' Gabi said.

'And beaches, surfing,' Paolo added.

'That's it?'

They all looked at each other. 'Yes.'

Most Brazilians, I was to find, don't know a great deal about anything outside of Brazil. It's a huge country with hundreds of exotic cultures, so there's probably not much room on the news for anything else. And Brazilians don't seem to travel very much. Most of Adriana's friends hadn't even been to Rio, let alone overseas. So it was no wonder they didn't know much about Australia past kangaroos and beaches.

I was also surprised to find that Australians aren't really thought of as the knockabout larrikins that the rest of the world seems to think we are. Instead, Brazilians (or at least Adriana's friends) see us as being another version of the British – all cold personalities, stiff upper lips, and rampant alcoholism. Even Adriana, who'd spent two years abroad, felt the same way.

'I'm so happy I came back to Brazil,' she said. 'You know, Australians . . . they're not very welcoming. I had fun, but I'm so glad to be in Sao Paulo. You miss the warmth of Brazilians, the friendliness.'

I had to admit, Adriana's friends had been pretty good hosts so far. While their tendency to refer to me as 'the gringo' even though they all clearly knew my name was annoying, they were all overly friendly and accommodating, and genuinely seemed to want me to have fun in their country.

'So,' said Gabi, 'what are your impressions of Sao Paulo so far?'

I thought for a second. 'Well, in Australia, everyone thinks of Sao Paulo as being this very dangerous place, somewhere you just wouldn't want to go because you'll get mugged, but I don't think it's like that, you know?'

Gabi and Regina exchanged glances. 'Well, it is really,' Gabi said.

'It is?'

'Yes. Most of us, our friends, have been robbed at least a few times.'

'I was robbed last week,' Adriana added.

'What, like, you had your pockets picked?'

'No, they pulled a knife on me! On my street. I was just walking home from work and two guys mugged me. Took my phone and my wallet.'

Gabi jumped in. 'Yeah, and a friend of ours, last week he was driving in his car – it's a nice car – and he stopped by the side of the road to buy some flowers for his wife. When he stopped, a guy on a motorbike stopped right behind him, pulled out a gun and fired twice into the car, and took his wallet. Our friend had a bullet lodged in his back.' She paused to let that sink in. 'This . . . This is a dangerous place.'

Adriana and her friends were actually a little obsessed with security – probably understandable when you've been robbed at knife-point on your own street. Every time we got on the Metro someone would make sure I had my bag on my front, while another would check to see if I had a wallet sticking out of a pocket somewhere.

As I sat there contemplating what it feels like to have a bullet lodged in your back when you were just stepping out to buy the missus some flowers, my caipirinha arrived. As Paolo has warned me, it was strong, but thanks to all the fruit and sugar, it was damn easy to drink. I'd knocked two off and was ordering another by the time some more of Adriana's friends joined us – two Brazilian girls, Ladys and Anna, and a huge English bloke called Ollie. I smiled. Sweet, another gringo.

'Can you dance, mate?' Ollie asked in the cab on the way to the club the girls had decided we were going to.

'God, no,' I said. 'You?'

'Ha ha! Nope. It's okay, mate, we'll just give it a bash and see what happens.'

I was dubious. I don't really dance at the best of times. It's all part of my policy of trying to avoid doing things I'm blatantly not good at. Now, here I was in Latin America, hitting a club with people who definitely could dance. It was in their blood. I was in serious trouble.

William was grinning like a madman by the time we paid our 10 reais (about $5), and headed into the club, babbling something in Portuguese that included the words 'samba' and 'salsa'. I cringed. Fortunately, we wandered in and found a whole lot of people sitting at tables, and absolutely no one dancing.

Ollie and I headed straight to the bar for a few fortifying caipirinhas, while the Brazilians sat at a table and studiously avoided drinking. We chatted for a few minutes, before something amazing happened. A muscly, tattooed, bald bloke in a skin-tight sleeveless shirt – making him look like a lycra sack filled with rockmelons – grabbed a microphone, and stepped up on stage. He called out something in Portuguese, and everyone, to a man and woman, jumped up and headed for the dance floor. There, they formed orderly lines across the floor, and broke into perfectly choreographed dance moves, all led by the sack of rockmelons on the stage.

What the hell? I thought this stuff only happened in crappy American college films. You know, the dorky guy takes the dance floor, and all of a sudden he busts a few moves out, and everyone around him breaks into the same steps? This was the kind of stuff that was happening now, except the dorky guy (me) was definitely not busting a few moves out. At the girls' urging I had taken the dance floor, and was soon desperately trying to follow the moves our leader was taking everyone through, hampered by my complete lack of co-ordination, and the fact all of the instructions were coming in Portuguese.

Suddenly, I felt a couple of hands clutching my hips. It was Adriana's friend Anna, a tall, slightly batty and undeniably attractive Brazilian girl. 'Your body has three parts,' she yelled into my ear. 'Up here,' she touched my shoulders, 'here,' her hands moved to my hips, 'and here,' she pointed at my legs. 'These are all separate. Move them differently! You gringos, it's like you are a board.'

I looked around. Sure enough, all of the non-gringos were gyrating around the dance floor, their hips seemingly separated from the rest of their bodies as they swayed to the Latin grooves. Me, I was struggling. As Captain Rockmelons called out some new moves, I tried desperately – but unsuccessfully – to make my hips go in a different direction to the rest of my body, succeeding only in crashing into a few of my fellow dancers, and looking like someone trying to use an invisible hula hoop. Anna just laughed, casually swishing around me with style. I was relieved to see Ollie making a similar fool of himself, laughing as he crashed his way back to the bar, where I promptly joined him.

Once our instructor had had his fun, a live band started up, playing samba, salsa, and all sorts of Latin-American musical styles I couldn't identify. Unfortunately, the Brazilians hadn't given up on me yet. Regina stalked over, grabbed my hand and led me to the dance floor. 'I TEACH YOU,' she yelled into my ear. And I'll give her her due, she really did try. But if the mark of a bad dancer is stepping on their partner's toes, then I went one better, not only stomping all over Regina's feet, but treading on three or four other couples who must have wondered what the hell was going on.

But I stuck it out, and eventually left the dance floor when we all got kicked out at 3am. I had to grudgingly admit, I'd actually enjoyed myself, and the Brazilians were all nice enough to tell me that I wasn't a *really* bad dancer.

They lied for me. I was touched.

*

William and I stared at each other in silence. I picked up a piece of toast and bit into it thoughtfully. William did the same.

'Bom?' he asked.

'Bom,' I replied.

We went back to munching our toast. It was the morning after the night before, and William and I had a slight problem. With Adriana having gone to work, we were left in the house on our own. I didn't speak Portuguese (except for 'bom', which means 'good'), and he didn't speak a word of English.

We'd realised our dilemma early on, when William launched into a stream of Portuguese when I woke up. I'd looked up at him, scraped a cat off my chest, and shrugged my shoulders. He went through a pantomime of . . . something. I shrugged my shoulders again. He smiled, and put his finger in the air, like he'd had an idea. He grabbed the phone, chatted to someone for a while, then passed it over to me: 'Vanessa.'

'Hello?'

'Hi Ben, it's Vanessa. William said he's going out to the shops to get breakfast, and wants to know what you want.'

'Ha! Tell him I really don't mind.'

I passed the phone back to William, who listened for a second, then hung up and headed out the door, muttering something in Portuguese. Ten minutes later, he was back. He cooked up some scrambled eggs for us, and that's how we found ourselves staring at each other over our toast, repeating our only common word at each other intermittently for conversation.

William raised an eyebrow and grinned. 'Feijoada?'

I nodded. 'Feijoada.'

William then put his finger in the air again, and grabbed the phone. He dialled, and chatted away for a few minutes. Then he looked over at me, frowning with concentration. He covered the mouthpiece for a second, and said: 'Feel.'

I nodded, slightly confused. He listened again, then said: 'At.'

'Mmm hmm.'

William listened again, then put the phone to the side: 'Home.'

Okay. He grinned, pleased with himself, trying out the whole phrase together: 'Feel. At. Home. Feel at home. Feel at home?'

I nodded again, smiling.

'Feel at home!'

I realised William had just called someone – probably poor old Vanessa again – to learn how to tell me to feel at home. I was starting to see what Adriana was saying about the warmth of Brazilians.

After breakfast, William pulled out his laptop, and logged on to YouTube to show me (I think) the different dance styles I should learn while I was in Brazil. Samba seemed to be his favourite, and we watched a few instructional videos, William dancing about the lounge room and trying to get me up to join him. Next, he moved to videos of Carnivale in Sao Paulo. Then, as I looked on, a little confused about what I was supposed to be looking at, William had another one of his little bolts from the blue. Grinning, he opened a new web browser, and clicked through to the Google translator page. He clicked 'from Portuguese' and 'to English', and started typing.

He punched in '*Ola!*', hit the translate button, and spun the screen around to face me. We waited a few seconds.

It flashed up: 'Hello!' I looked up from the screen. William was grinning at me, waving.

I laughed. 'Hello, mate,' I said, waving back.

He typed something else in. We waited a few seconds, until it translated: 'I think this is a good system.'

There followed a conversation fuelled entirely by Google – William told me about all the Brazilian foods I should try (number one of which, unsurprisingly, was feijoada, which turned out to be a big hearty stew of rice, beans and pork), and I told him about my lack of dancing experience. There were only a few hiccups, like when Google translated William's sentence to, 'I like ride a suitcase' (unless that's what he actually meant), but all in all, we had a good, if strange chat. By the time William typed in, 'We have to go now', we'd been chatting away on his laptop for about an hour.

We spent the afternoon with Vanessa, Gabi and Paolo, who wasn't able to do much talking this time, as the girls were both fluent in English and pretty much took care of all the chatter. They took me on a mini walking tour of the city, despite the fact it was cold and drizzling again, past the old church in the middle of the city, and down to the Mercado Municipal, an area filled with street stalls and guys with huge speaker stacks playing Michael Jackson songs (he'd died about a fortnight ago). We also went inside the main food market to taste two Paulista specialties: *pastels*, and mortadella sandwiches.

The pastels were basically deep-fried pastries filled with salted cod or prawns – tasty, if a little bland. The mortadella sandwiches were something else though. We're not just talking a slice or two of processed meat here – we're talking a gigantic hunk of it, almost too much to get your mouth around in one bite. Cover that with oozing processed cheese and a soft bun, and you've got every Paulista's favourite treat. It's a heart attack in a sandwich, and it tastes great.

That night at dinner, Vanessa proudly told Adriana that I'd managed to ask for some food in Portuguese at the market.

'Really?' Adriana looked at me, amazed. 'What did you say?'

'Just, "one more please",' I said.

'You said this? In Portuguese?' Adriana looked at the others for confirmation.

I nodded. 'Sure. *Mais uma por favor*, right?'

'Wow,' she said, shaking her head in amazement, like someone watching a monkey put different shaped blocks into the right holes.

That night, much to William's joy, I finally got to try feijoada. It's supposed to be a strictly lunchtime food, but I'd run out of time, and really wanted to try it. It arrived in a steaming bowl, all rice and beans and spices and fatty pork. I took a small mouthful, and chewed it for a while as William watched. I finally put my fork down and smiled, giving William a big thumbs-up. He grinned widely, rattling off something in Portuguese as he put a triumphant arm around my shoulders.

Adriana was concerned. 'Are you sure you like it?' she asked. 'It's not too exotic for you?'

'It's beans and freakin' rice,' I wanted to say. 'It's not exactly boiled sheep nuts, is it?'

I didn't say that, of course, because you generally don't go insulting people who have let you stay at their house for free for three nights. Instead I just gritted my teeth and said, 'No no, it's really nice.'

*

'Don't worry mate, I'm not a big black cab driver.'

It was Nick, on the phone. I'd been expecting to see a white Australian guy waiting for me at Ilheus Airport in Bahia. Instead,

Getting a Brazilian

I'd found a tall Brazilian carrying a placard with my name on it. Shaking my hand, the guy told me to wait while he brought the car around. A few minutes later he pulled up in a new, air-conditioned sedan, and we were off towards what I assumed was the resort Nick worked at. I wasn't actually sure what was going on until Nick phoned the chauffeur and he passed the phone back to me.

'It was just easier this way mate,' the voice on the other end of the phone said in a broad Aussie drawl. 'I'll see you here in half an hour or so.'

Fair enough, I thought, reclining on the nice seats, enjoying the air-conditioning and the soft Brazilian music the driver had put on, and thinking about the luxury eco-resort waiting for me at the other end. Bye bye drizzle and misery of Sao Paulo, hello paradise.

Nick sounded like a character to me. His original email, sent a few weeks after I'd finished planning the trip, and completely devoid of punctuation, had me hooked:

> gday benny, been a reader of yours for ages now. i even screwed a girl in your office years ago . . . well, not in your office, you know what I mean, she works for The Age. Ok. Im an Aussie, I have lived mainly outside of Australia since 96, Im nearly 33, have a brazilian Mrs, with a Brazilian, and i fucking own this city! My Mrs and I have decided to move back to Brazil (Bahia), I hated Rio, stayed there 6 weeks til the smell of piss (not my own) got to me. Her family has a resort in Bahia, 5 stars and 14 bungalows, pool on the beach, yadda yadda yadda. Ive never been there but we are moving in April, maybe March, No matter where we are, you can come and crash. I got 6 guitars, Im a muso, I drink beer, no fucked up religion or other issues to make it a weird stay, and basically, am 'normal'. the mrs . . . well, she's just brazilian. Nuts. So, if you wanna crash, its all good. And, by the way, if you are into ayahuasca, you can do/try that too, highly recommended. Not your average trip.

It was going to cost me about $600 to fly up to Ilheus for a couple of days, but Nick's place sounded too good to pass up. I could see I'd made the right decision from the minute my chauffeur pulled out of the airport (actually, from the minute I realised I had a chauffeur). Gone were the high-rises and bustle of Sao Paulo. Where the skyscrapers had once stood, I could now see palm trees. Where the pedestrians had hustled down the streets, there were now just locals lounging around the beachfront. The drive up to Nick's hotel was alongside one long beach, hemmed in by small villages filled with barefooted kids. Even the temperature was better: it might have been cold and dreary when I flew out of Sao Paulo, but in Bahia it was about 30 degrees, and the sun was shining. Not bad for a winter's day.

Half an hour later we pulled up at the resort gate, an inconspicuous green sheet of metal with no signage by the side of the road. Nick had a huge smile on his stubbled face, and was wearing the regulation Bahian uniform: thongs, board shorts, and a bright-coloured singlet. He also had arms full of tattoos – a three-quarter sleeve of tigers and snakes on one arm, and a few Aztec-looking designs on the other.

'G'day mate! Come on in,' he said, motioning me out of the car.

We wandered through the gate, and into the jungle. This is what qualifies you as an 'eco-resort', I later found out. You just don't cut any trees down. The bungalows at the resort were all surrounded by tall palm trees and scrub. 'I'll give you the grand tour in a second mate,' Nick said. 'But do you want to get out of those jeans first?'

I looked down at my jeans and closed-in shoes. 'Hell, yeah.' It was the last time I'd see them for four days. Nick hadn't even brought jeans with him when he'd moved to Bahia from Buenos Aires three months ago.

We wound our way through the dense jungle and through a small fence separating the resort from Nick and his partner Jessica's house. It was a two-storey shack, made completely of wood with a thatched roof sheltering a large wooden patio. I brushed past an Australian flag hung from the ceiling at the front of the house on my way up to my room, a big open space on the second floor.

'Now,' Nick said, 'I killed a couple of rats in here the other day, so you should be right now.'

'Just a couple?'

'Yep. Took me a while too. I called one of them Michael Jackson, because he was black and white. They were only small though, not too much to worry about.'

I was sick of rats. But in a house where the walls and ceiling were about 30 centimetres away from joining up with each other, I guess it came with the territory. There was something else to worry about too.

'This is the downstairs bathroom,' Nick said, swinging a door open to a bare room with holes in the walls for windows. 'You're fine to use it, but just keep an eye out for the toilet monster.'

'The toilet monster?'

'Yeah, it's this lizard that usually hangs out here at night. It's fuckin' huge! It just hangs around on the ceiling, staring at you. You get used to it though.'

'Anything else I should know about?'

'Um . . . Nope, I think that's it.'

With my jeans off and boardies on, Nick and I grabbed a couple of beers from the fridge and headed back into the resort, which, being low season, was completely free of guests, meaning we had the place to ourselves for three days. The path took us out of the jungle, past a deckchair-ringed pool, and up to the bar – a large wooden veranda set about 10 metres back from the palm-lined beach. In other words: paradise.

'So, what do you think of the office?' Nick asked, cracking a beer and settling into one of the lounge chairs.

I looked around for a few seconds. 'I'm never leaving.'

We were soon joined by Jessica, Nick's four-months-pregnant

and pretty darn attractive Brazilian girlfriend. The two had been living together in Buenos Aires when Jessica's sister, the owner of the resort, had invited them to move up and take over the day-to-day running of the place. That was three months ago. 'Jessie does most of the work,' Nick confessed, 'and she's good with the clients. I do the odd bit of work, but I mean, they've got staff on here to do all the maintenance, so I don't really have to do much. Am I lazy? Probably. But fuck it, I don't want to bust my arse around here for about $20 a day.'

Nick and Jessica had met over the internet. Nick had just been divorced from an Argentinean girl and was living in Buenos Aires, while Jessica was living in Rio. Jessica didn't speak any English, so the two communicated in Spanish, which Nick was fluent in after eight years in Latin America.

'Yeah mate, it just all took off,' Nick told me, grabbing another beer from the wooden bar. 'You know, Jessie organised a "cyber dinner date", where we got all dressed up and had dinner together over web cam. Looked pretty funny when I was in the internet cafe, I can tell you! Nah, just kidding. So then I moved up to Rio. We'd already decided we were going to give it a go, and it just exploded. But I hated Rio. I was there for a couple of months, and had to get out. I told her I was leaving, going back to BA, and a few weeks later she joined me. That was about a year ago. And now here we are, running an eco-resort, and she's knocked up! Fuckin' crazy, mate.'

Although there were no guests at the resort, there was no shortage of people around, as it was Jessica's brother Rogerio's birthday, and there was a barbecue planned. The staff – who still worked despite the absence of anything to do – were all there, as well as Jessica's sister, Claudia, and a whole bunch of kids. The barbecue was an open fire in the middle of a grass-covered clearing near the bar, where Carlinhos, the gardener, was grilling bits of meat on huge metal skewers.

Nick stuck his head out from the bar and yelled, 'Who wants a caipirinha?'

Several hands went up – two of them belonging to Carlinhos. While Nick mixed the drinks, he told me how he'd once been a bartender and croupier on a Caribbean cruise ship, before getting sick of the life and wanting out.

'The only thing was, I had to get myself fired,' he explained, bashing away at a couple of limes in a cocktail shaker. 'See, we were in the US, and if I quit, I'd have to find my own way home, and I was stone broke. If they fired me though, they couldn't just leave me stranded, so they'd have to pay to get me home. I asked them to fire me, and they wouldn't do it, so then I took it upon myself to *get* fired.

'It was fuckin' funny. We went deep-sea fishing one day, and you're not allowed to bring fish back onto the ship, for quarantine reasons. But I caught these two huge mahi-mahi, so I was like, "Fuck this, I'm bringing 'em back." I was pretty drunk too. So I got caught, blind drunk, trying to drag these two huge fish back onto the ship. That did it. Thing is though, I gave the fish to the officers to eat, so instead of locking me in a room like you're supposed to do when you fire someone, they let me have the run of the ship for the next few days until we got into port. Then I got cuffed by security, led off the boat, and flown home. Fuckin' sweet.'

Nick, a Melbourne boy, had been travelling for 14 years – although he called it 'travelling without moving'. He'd worked in bars mostly in Argentina and Uruguay. He'd done the cruise ships in the Caribbean, worked in a casino in Uruguay, and flitted between bars in Buenos Aires while playing lead guitar in a classic rock covers band. The band broke up about the same time Claudia's offer came so the decision was easy.

'That Australian flag at the house is the only thing I've had with me the whole time, since 1996,' Nick said. 'I've used it as a sarong, worn it as a cape, used it as a towel, hung it in a window. Now it's hanging in the house. It's not going anywhere.'

The caipirinhas made, Nick and I made our way down to the picnic area, grabbed a massive plateful of meat and salads, and sat down at our own little 'English speaking' table to eat. Jessica still didn't speak a word of English, which made communication between the two of us a little difficult. Still, between my crap Spanish and Nick's interpreting, we got by.

With lunch over, the Brazilians all gathered around the TV to watch the final of the Confederations Cup, between Brazil and the USA. Since Nick had no interest in what he called 'wog ball', we decided to go catch some fish. Not by fishing – all this entailed was walking down the beach a few hundred metres to meet the *jungalas* as they landed for the night. Jungalas are the local fishing boats, although 'boat' is a bit of a stretch. They're really just four large logs lashed together, with a wooden mast stuck in the middle, and a small outboard motor balancing at the back.

As Nick and I walked along the sand in the long shadows of the palm trees, passing a few girls in magnificently tiny Brazilian bikinis, we could see the white triangular sails of the jungalas making their way in to shore. 'We'll give 'em a hand to pull the boats in,' Nick said. 'You usually get a better price for the fish if you do that. It's like the old Egyptian method. You have a couple of logs under the boat, and roll it up to shore. Bit of hard work, but it's all good.'

As the boats came in, I could see how flimsy they were. Crewed by three men, who spent the whole day miles out to sea fishing with hand lines, they sat low in the ocean, water seeping up through the gaps in the logs. We waded into the water and helped push the boats onto the logs a boy had rolled out to the shore, and then up the beach, running the logs from the back of the boat to the front as it crept over them. The fishermen, for their part, seemed nonplussed by the two tattooed gringos straining to shift their boat up the sand. They ignored us as we sorted through their catch, picking out seven fish of breeds we could only hazard a guess at. 'We'll have some for breakfast tomorrow,' Nick said, 'then I'll make a *moqueca* for dinner with the rest.'

The fishermen weighed the fish, collected their money (about

$5 per kilo), and we headed back to the resort, where Jessica had made a rice casserole with the leftovers from the barbecue.

'So what about this *ayahuasca* you were talking about in the email?' I said to Nick over dinner. 'My mum was pretty freaked out about that. Probably shouldn't have told her actually.'

'Ha ha, nah, probably not, mate. Anyway, nothing to worry about, I haven't managed to find any up here yet. You know what it is, right? This hallucinogen the Amazonian shamans make from a tree root. I've done it five times now though, and I'm keen for more. I just haven't found any shamans up here. I've never really hallucinated that much from it though. The shamans reckon I might have some sort of "block" because of all the weed I smoke. Jessie's only had it once, and she tripped out. She saw these three huge angels standing around her, and one of them pulled her heart out, passed it around to the other angels, they all kissed it, then stuck it back in her chest. That's wild, man.'

'I'm surprised you could get it in Buenos Aires – I thought it was a real Amazonian thing.'

'It is, but a lot of the shamans have moved to the cities now, and they're still practising, so that's pretty cool. We had some wild times in BA man, good times.'

*

There's a downside to buying your fish fresh off a jungala on a Bahian beach: you have to buy them whole, meaning the gutting and scaling is up to you. The next morning, Nick pulled the fish we'd bought the previous evening out of the fridge, grabbed a couple of knives, and we walked down to the beach to get into the dirty work. It was another incredible day, the sun beating down as Nick slung the fish onto the sand and pulled out the knives. 'Right,' he said. 'You scale, and I'll gut.'

I'm no fisherman – I think I've caught maybe three fish in my entire life, all of which I immediately felt sorry for, seeing them flopping around on the deck – but I kind of know how to scale a fish. So I grabbed a knife, held one of the fish by the tail, and started scraping off the scales with short, sharp flicks of the knife. Nick, meanwhile, was tearing out fistfuls of guts from the other fish, hurling them into the sea.

I was just starting to get a hang of the scaling when disaster struck. On a swift downward movement, the knife slipped across the scales, sending my hand straight into the sharp spines running along the fish's back. I yelled in pain. One of the spines had gone straight into my thumb, lodging itself deep under my thumbnail. It had snapped off too, leaving only a tiny bit of spike hanging out of the end of the nail. In shock, I showed Nick.

'Ooh, that's a painful one,' he said, helpfully. 'Go up and see Jessie, she'll sort you out.'

I set off back to the house, wondering how I was going to explain to Jessica what had happened, given I didn't know the Spanish words for 'There's a bloody fish spike embedded in my thumb'. As it turned out, I didn't need to. Jessica took one look at it, let out a little scream, and ran off in the other direction. Great, I thought. So I went into the bathroom, and rummaged around for a while with my good hand until I found a small pair of pliers. Still unable to locate Jessica, I pinched the spike with the pliers, and wrenched it out from under my thumbnail, reflecting that if this was indeed used as a form of torture by some cultures, then they knew exactly what they were doing.

By the time I'd extracted the spike (and taken a photo of it), Jessica reappeared with some disinfectant and a bandage. We doused my thumb, wrapped it up in a bandage, and I headed back down to the beach. 'Well, mate,' Nick said, surveying the wound, 'that'll be a good story for the book, won't it?'

An hour later, I had my revenge on the fish, eating it with a few fried eggs for breakfast. Nick, meanwhile, was waxing lyrical. 'Hey, did you follow that "greatest job in the world" thing that Queensland Tourism did?' he asked.

'Yeah, some English fella won it, right?'

'I think so. Anyway, what does he have to do? Hang out on an island for six months and get paid $150,000 for it?'

'Yeah, something like that.'

'Yeah, well I was thinking, you take the $150,000 away, and that's pretty much my life right there. I mean, look at this place. I do exactly the same thing as that English prick'll be doing, I just don't get paid for it. You can stick your greatest job up your arse, you know? Some of my family, they can't understand this life. They keep telling me I'll have to rejoin the real world some time. Why? This right here . . . this is what they're spending their lives saving up for so they can do it in their retirement. I'm just doing it now. You know, they're running around the city talking into their blueberries or whatever, getting stressed . . . Screw that.'

Nick *was* living the life. He wasn't really working at the resort, as he'd explained. Instead, he did little jobs around the place when he felt like it, or caught up on his reading about conspiracy theories and the rise of the Illuminati (a la *The Da Vinci Code*). Aside from that, he gutted and scaled the odd fish (which he managed to do without hideously impaling himself), made caipirinhas for the guests (when there were guests there), and that was about it. How does a person afford to do this, you ask? Well, I did too.

'Workers' comp mate,' Nick confided, rolling a sleeve up and pointing to a couple of lumps on his forearm. 'Check that out. They're metal screws. I was doing a bit of construction work on the Gold Coast. Decided I wanted to go back to Australia for a while, so I was working there. Anyway, I was using this masonry drill, which is this huge fuckin' drill, and basically, there was a chance this thing could bite into a bit of metal, and then I'd be fucked.

'So you can guess what happened. It bit, started spinning around and slammed into my arm, absolutely shattered it. It was literally just hanging there, completely shattered. They had to operate on it for six hours to put it all back together. I still don't have full use of it. So I picked up my workers' comp payout, and fucked off. That was about 18 months ago.'

It left Nick with a lumpy arm and a lot of free time – time we were using that day to visit Itacare, a nearby town that Nick said was, 'sorta like Bahia's Byron Bay.' With Jessica in tow, we caught the local bus from outside the resort, and hopped off half an hour later when we got to Itacarezinha, a beach about 15 minutes outside of town. After walking down a dirt road for a few minutes, we arrived at yet another beautiful, white-sand beach. Just behind it was a little restaurant with a few tables scattered under the palm trees, where we took a seat and ordered '*tres cocos*' – three green coconuts with straws sticking out of them, allowing you to suck out the sweet coconut water inside.

Cocos sucked dry, we had a dip in the ocean, where I soaked my throbbing thumb in the sea water and stared at the girls running around in about the smallest pieces of material you could still possibly refer to as a bikini. Then we headed in to Itacare proper. Normally you would do this by public transport, except the hourly bus had flown past just as we made it back to the road, meaning we had three options: wait for the next bus in an hour, pay about $20 for a taxi to come out and get us, or hitchhike. Nick and I, dressed in wet board shorts and thongs, stuck our thumbs out.

Three cars later, a banged-up old ute pulled up, and the driver stuck his head out of the window.

'Itacare?' Nick shouted.

'Sim!'

We piled into the back of the cab and we roared off, giving us a chance to check out our hosts. The driver was a skinny, balding, leathery-skinned guy in a singlet, while the girl in the passenger seat looked about 20 years younger. Glancing down, I noticed a machete lying on the floor at our feet. I nudged Nick, and raised my eyebrows. He nodded, then whispered: 'I think I'll ask these guys if they've got any weed. They've gotta be the type.'

As we pulled into town, Nick piped up in a bizarre American accent he subconsciously seemed to slip into when he was talking to people whose first language wasn't English. 'Hey guys, do you know where we can get some smoke?'

The driver looked around. 'Well . . . I have a little. You want some?'

'Yeah yeah, totally man. Can we buy some?'

'I don't, ah, have enough to sell. But . . . Maybe we smoke now, hey?'

Nick looked at Jessica and I. 'Sure man, let's do it!'

Our driver, whose name turned out to be Edgar, fired the engine up, and we roared towards another beach, this time on the other side of town. There, Edgar rolled a joint, and we picked our way through the palm trees down to the beach, where a few surfers were out enjoying the breaks. We sat on the rocks by the beach and smoked Edgar's joint, staring out at the waves crashing below us. We also got chatting to Edgar (or Eddie as Nick called him), who turned out to be a local fisherman. Not one of the jungala fishermen though. Eddie, apparently, had a whole fleet of trawlers, and seemed to be doing pretty well for himself.

With the joint finished, we headed back to the car, passing a bunch of Brazilian surfers also headed the same way. As we watched, one of the dreadlocked guys threw his board down and shinned up a palm tree, ripping off green coconuts and throwing them down to his friends. There, they cracked the tops of the coconuts against the tree, and upended the fruit, letting the water pour down into their mouths and down their chins, Solo Man–style. 'God, what a cliche,' Nick laughed. 'No imagination, those blokes. I mean come on, Brazilian surfers, picking coconuts, drinking them on the spot? Please.'

Back in the ute, we headed, once again, into town, where Eddie and his girlfriend joined us for lunch. Down in a small bay, near a beach where a bunch of locals were kicking a football around, we found a little cafe, and settled down to eat a '*comida e kilo*' – where you fill your plate from the buffet, have it weighed, and pay a certain amount per kilo.

Itacare did look like a Brazilian version of Byron Bay, with cool hippy restaurants, nice beaches, plenty of hostels and travellers around, and a laid-back atmosphere. While we ate, and shared a Skol beer (which seems like more of an instruction than a name to me), Nick kept peppering Eddie with questions. Eddie, it turned out, wasn't just a pot-smoking fisherman. He was also a biologist, he said. He took that up after he'd finished training horses in Kentucky. He'd also spent two years in the Brazilian army working as a sniper in the Amazon. At this point, he got a bit serious, slowly shaking his head. 'No good memories from those days. No good memories.'

'Did you ever have to shoot anyone?' Nick pressed.

Eddie sighed. 'Two people. But bad memories.'

We figured that if even half of Eddie's stories were true, he was probably the most interesting man alive. He had to get back to his boats before we could find out any more though, so we bid him farewell, and went in search of *acaraje*, the Bahian food I'd been told I had to try. Acaraje is street food, sold by vendors set up on most corners. It's a bean cake that's deep-fried, then sliced in half and filled with bean paste, chilli, and a mix of small prawns pan-fried with their shells still on. Nick, Jessie and I ordered one each and were just biting into the sensational snacks when we heard the roar of an engine and the beep of a horn. We looked around, and there was Eddie, wild-eyed and wavy-haired, hanging out of his ute yelling: 'Acaraje!'

We waved, yelling back, 'Acaraje!' and gave him the thumbs up. Brazilians, apparently, were determined to communicate with me solely through the names of their foods.

That night, Nick dealt with the last of our fish, cooking it up with some curry powder, herbs and coconut milk. 'I thought I was just making a fish curry the first time I made this,' he told me as he stirred the pot. 'But then Jessie tells me I've just made a moqueca, which is this traditional Bahian dish. Okay, fair enough, I'm making moqueca.'

Nick, however, wasn't always on the money. We sat down to eat that night, and Jessie took a few mouthfuls before putting her fork down and shaking her head. 'This is not moqueca.'

*

'Shhh,' Nick said, a finger pressed to his lips as he tiptoed through the jungle. 'You've got to be very quiet.'

I padded along behind him, a bit dubious. We were out 'hunting', sure – but our prey was coconuts. Not the most feared beast in the jungle.

'Mate, it's either you or the coconuts out here,' Nick continued, silently swinging a long pole up into the trees, attempting to knock down the ripe green fruit. It was mid-morning, the perfect time for coconut hunting, apparently. It was kill or be killed. Fortunately, the cocos were in a docile mood and practically jumped out of the tall palms as Nick wielded his stick. They bounced onto the ground, where I, like a faithful hunting hound, scooped them up and brought them back to the house. There, we cut their heads off with a machete, dipped straws into the raw wounds and sucked them dry. Good coco hunting.

Today was a big day for Nick and Jessica – we were heading in to Ilheus for Jessica to have an ultrasound and find out the sex of the baby. Having no car, the three of us caught the local bus in to Ilheus, which, although it only has a population of 220,000, is the big smoke in these parts. While Nick and Jessie went into the clinic I had a quick walk to kill time.

I found a few kids on the pavement practising capoeira, the Brazilian martial art. I watched as the kids, in baggy pants and with six-packs rippling, ducked and weaved around each other, throwing kicks miles from each other's faces as the rest of the troupe looked on, rattling makeshift percussion instruments. Martial art it may be, but it's hardly good self-defence to prance around with your shirt off doing fake fly-kicks a couple of metres away from your attacker.

By the time that little demonstration was over, I spied Nick and Jessie walking hand-in-hand out of the clinic.

'What's the verdict mate?' I asked.

'We're having a girl,' Nick said, not particularly enthusiastically. 'As soon as I heard I thought, "Great, another woman in my life."'

'I bet Jessie's stoked though.'

Nick said something to her in Spanish, then said to me, 'Oh yeah, she's happy.'

Back at the resort that night, Nick and I were on our own, as Jessie had gone to celebrate the news with Claudia, so we grilled some prawns on the barbecue, then toasted the baby girl in the only way we knew how: caipirinhas and pot. By the time Jessica arrived back around 10pm we'd had plenty of both. Jessie didn't look happy, and said something in Spanish to Nick. 'Ha ha! She wants to know how we can drink so much,' Nick laughed. 'I told her it's all practice.'

Jessie rolled her eyes, muttering something in Spanish that included the phrase '*muy fumado*'.

'What's that mean?' I asked Nick.

He giggled. 'Very stoned.'

*

I woke up the next morning to the smell of pancakes cooking. Jessie was awake, whipping up breakfast. The table was already filled with fresh fruit juices, pots of coffee and toast by the time I wandered down the wooden staircase, the tang of salt drifting in off the ocean. I was going to miss this, I thought. In fact, I was going to miss everything about this place. There had been a few people on this trip I'd been genuinely sad to leave, and Nick and

Jessie were definitely two of them. Even Jessie, who I hadn't even been able to communicate with, had been a fantastic companion.

As my taxi pulled up, Nick threw an arm around my shoulders. 'Any time you want to come back man . . . Any time. It's been a pleasure.'

Jessie wrapped me in a big hug, before pulling back and slowly saying, 'I sorry no English.'

I laughed, trying some of my appalling Spanish in return. '*Lo siento no Espanyol y Portuguese,*' I said, really hoping it meant, 'I'm sorry no Spanish and Portuguese.'

It probably doesn't. But, as I'd learned from William back in Sao Paulo, it's nice to try.

Stars and Stripes

'I feel like pretty much everywhere you go, people speak American anyway.'

Brooklyn? Who the hell lives in Brooklyn? When Australians move to New York, they go straight to Manhattan. They never leave Manhattan. It's like the Shepherds Bush of the US. Hell, some New Yorkers don't even leave Manhattan. So when I got an invitation to stay with someone in Brooklyn, I was interested.

To be honest, I'd wanted to go to Manhattan too. Modestly considered by its residents to be the capital of the known universe, I'd wanted to see it for myself, and thought there'd be at least a couple of invitations from such a huge city. However, I figured wrong. I only got one, and that was from a guy I'd met while travelling through Peru a few years back. Fair enough, I thought, that'll do. Trouble was, at the time I was going to be there, Joel wasn't. It was a rather important weekend on the American calendar, and Joel was leaving the confines of Manhattan and buggering off to San Francisco. Fortunately though, there was still Brooklyn.

There was a simple answer, of course, to what my contact,

Andrea, was doing in Brooklyn: she was from Brooklyn. Born and raised, in fact. She'd never been to Australia, and had barely read the blog, so the better question would be: How did I score an invite?

You won't find many friendlier people than Americans. I knew I'd get plenty of invites from the US, purely because people over there are so generous and excited about showing visitors their little corner of the earth. However, things got even more out of hand than I'd expected, thanks to the plug on AOL's homepage. I got a phenomenal number of hits, most of which were from Americans who'd never read the blog before – not that that lack of familiarity stopped the first-time readers from jumping on board and inviting me to stay.

I hadn't taken up Andrea's invitation immediately because she wasn't even the instigator of the offer. She'd emailed me mentioning her friend Kristen, who was obsessed with Australia, and who thought it would be great if I came to stay. Just, not with her. So Andrea had been good enough to put her hand up, and, lacking any better offers, and desperate to get to New York, I decided to give it a shot.

Things started badly. Andrea had given me detailed instructions on how to get to her place from JFK Airport, so you could imagine my surprise when I found myself standing bleary-eyed at baggage claim at La Guardia. Rather than mess with public transport after an overnight flight from Sao Paulo, I hailed a yellow New York cab, which was a thrill in itself. Pulling out from the airport, we skirted the buzzing hub of Manhattan, that strangely recognisable skyline, and got onto the Belt Parkway, bound for the relative suburbia of Brooklyn. It was a beautiful summer day – the sun was out, and birds chirped on streets which could only be American: lined with Jewish delis, stars-and-stripes-toting bank branches and little 'mom-and-pop' corner stores. Pulling up outside Andrea's detached, three-storey brick house in a quiet Brooklyn street, I could see her taking a few bags out of a car in the drive.

'Oh, hey, Ben,' she said, waving casually. She led me through to the side of the house, down some stairs and into a flat underneath the main house.

'How long have you been living here?' I asked.

'My whole life,' Andrea said, plonking herself down at a table in the kitchen. 'I used to be upstairs, where my dad's still living, but once the tenants down here moved out, I decided to move, get a bit more privacy, you know? That was about eight years ago. So anyway, my friend Kristen has just gone out to get bagels and coffee – she'll be back in a second.'

The flat under the house was small – just a kitchen/dining room, a living room with a ridiculously small TV by American standards, and a bedroom. A few of the walls through the flat had been turned into blackboards, on which Andrea had scribbled everything from instructions on feeding the cat to nauseatingly inspirational quotes, like: 'Life shrinks and expands according to your courage.' I was to sleep on an air mattress in the living room, while Andrea would be in her room, and Kristen would be on the couch next to me. We also had to share the place with Tigger, Andrea's quite portly tabby cat.

Kristen soon arrived with breakfast, or, from what I could tell, about 10 breakfasts. As promised, Kristen, also in her late 30s, was armed with bagels. Lots of them. She also had coffee – gigantic buckets of the stuff which no normal person could drink without dissolving into a quivering mess. Kristen shrugged. 'I guess I just asked for large.'

'Okay. Could you pass the milk?'

'Sure,' she said, handing it over.

'Thanks.'

'You're very welcome.'

I smiled to myself. Americans: they're so polite. I found it endearing, those first few times, their politely returning every 'thank you' with a 'you're very welcome'. But after a few days, it began to grate. They just said it so often, killing me with kindness.

The bagels and coffee were excellent. While I was munching on them, Andrea and Kristen outlined their itinerary for me for the next few days: it involved Central Park, pizza, baseball, hot dogs and more pizza. Sounded good to me. I'd arrived on the third of July – which made tomorrow American Independence Day, that flag-waving, fireworks exploding celebration of all things red-white-and-blue. I'd like to say this was all by design, my being in New York for the biggest celebration on the American calendar, but I'd be lying. It was dumb luck, but I was happy to take it.

Our first day was going to be devoted to the girls' highlights of New York, starting with a trip to Central Park Zoo, where there was apparently a new snow leopard enclosure. Jumping on the D Train from Brooklyn (The D Train! So American!), we headed in to Manhattan, got out at Columbus Circle and walked in to Central Park. There, we took in the freak show that is the world's most famous park: from impromptu jazz bands and buskers, to a guy rollerskating in Hammer pants while balancing two drink bottles on his head.

At the zoo, we saw what was *maybe* the paw of a snow leopard, before wandering down to the monkey cage, when Kristen suddenly stopped dead in her tracks, pointing ahead of her.

'It's . . . Um . . . Oh my God.'

Strolling past us in a white Fedora and sunglasses was Aussie actor Hugh Jackman, out taking his daughter to the zoo. Kristen was dumbstruck. 'Oh my God,' she kept muttering to herself, turning to watch Hugh wander past the non-existent snow leopards. She turned to me. 'Wait, you're Australian . . . Have you met him before?'

'Um . . . No. It's a big country you know.'

'I know. I guess I just thought you might have bumped into him or something.'

Still, our little sighting had made Kristen and Andrea's day. 'Oh wow,' Andrea said, pulling out her iPhone, 'I'm so putting this on Facebook right now.'

Kristen smiled. 'Tell everyone the Wolverine exhibit was definitely my favourite.'

From Central Park, we wandered down some imaginatively named street like 34th or 25th or 5307th to Gray's Papaya, a legendary New York hot dog vendor. I know this because, like most of the valuable culinary knowledge I've garnered in my lifetime, Anthony Bourdain told me so. I saw him visit the place on one of the 'I can't be bothered to leave New York so I'll talk about the food here' episodes of his TV show, and decided I wanted to go too. The girls were only too happy to help me out.

Tucked into a street corner just near the park, Gray's Papaya doesn't look like much – just a scungy counter manned by scungy attendants turning frankfurters on a grill. I ordered the 'Recession Special': two hot dogs and a papaya juice for $US4.45. The dogs were simple but sensational, topped with onions, sauerkraut, and a couple of huge squirts of ketchup and mustard. I'd taken photos of mine and monstered them by the time Kristen and Andrea had even joined me at the counter.

I was still trying to work these two out. They were both into their late 30s, both professionals (Andrea, coincidentally, worked for AOL) – you could have pegged them for stereotypical *Sex and the City*–type girls (this was New York, after all). They were super friendly, like most Americans, but I still wasn't completely sure why they'd invited me to stay with them.

Heading back to the subway station, it was a buzz just to be walking through the Manhattan streets. Not because I was in the 'capital of the universe', but because of this bizarre feeling of recognition. You watch enough Hollywood movies, and you could swear you know New York better than most of its residents. I knew the wide avenues, the yellow cabs, and the corner delis. Granted, I also half expected to see a giant green monster come roaring through to trample the whole lot, but you get that.

I was just taking all this in when we stepped off the pavement to cross a road, and a car swerved in front of us. Andrea exploded.

'Hey!' she yelled at the disappearing car. 'My way! This is my way, bitch!' Then she paused and looked around for a second, slightly embarrassed. 'Well, there's some of the Brooklyn coming out in me.'

For dinner that night, the girls explained we were having pizza in Dumbo, which I originally thought was an insult ('We're having pizza, dumbo'), but was actually a description of the neighbourhood we were going to – Down Under the Manhattan Bridge Overpass. New Yorkers are obsessed with giving areas of their city little nicknames. In retrospect, most were probably coined by real estate agents trying to give their area a modern spin. In New York, you can head to Tribeca, Soho, Noho, Fidi, UES, LES, UWS, LWS, Billyburg and Nolita. (That'd be Triangle Below Canal Street, South of Houston Street, North of Houston Street, the Financial District, Upper East Side, Lower East Side, Upper West Side, Lower West Side, Williamsburg and North of Little Italy.)

It was over our Dumbo pizza (which was incredibly good), that I realised just how American my new American friends were. Not only had they been excited about ticking off all of the New York food groups (hot dogs, bagels, pizza), but they also displayed some Americans' spectacular lack of awareness of the outside world.

Andrea turned to me mid-slice. 'So Ben, how many languages do you speak now?'

'Er . . . Actually, only one, which is pretty embarrassing.'

'Really?' Andrea replied. 'That's not so bad. I feel like pretty much everywhere you go, people speak American anyway.'

Hold the phone. American? I was so shocked that I actually let that one slide – I couldn't digest both that and my pizza at the same time. I later found out that attitude wasn't such a rarity in the States though. Talking about their school days, a few people told me about taking 'American' classes rather than English. And I saw a few 'French-American' dictionaries on the bookshelves. Talk about rewriting history.

That aside though, I was having fun. The pizzas, as I said,

were amazingly good. I don't know what it is New Yorkers do to their pizzas that no one else does, but the mix of good cheese, tangy tomato paste and not-thick-but-not-thin base makes for pizza perfection. There was also some lively conversation bouncing around our table. I almost started to cringe when I realised I was at a table with the 'loud Americans' – then I looked around and realised that, hey, the whole restaurant was full of loud Americans. I might as well just join in.

*

I don't really get into Australia Day back home. I mean, I like being Australian and all, but I don't feel like I have to paint Australian flags on my cheeks, and barbecue animals to prove it. I'm also a bit uncomfortable with the whole invasion aspect of it. I happily take the day off work and get drunk, just not for the appropriate reasons.

However, I knew there'd be no such attitudes in the US on the Fourth of July. I don't know that much about Americans, but I know they're patriotic. And from what I could tell from my American friends in Sydney, they celebrate that patriotism in much the same way Australians do: a few flags, a few hunks of grilled meat, and beer. Not coincidentally, that's exactly what Andrea and Kristen had planned for me on my first Independence Day. First though, another shared tradition: a trip to the beach. We jumped in the car and made our way to Rockaway Beach, a patch of sand just off Brooklyn. On the way there, the conversation turned to musical tastes.

'Hey, Ben,' Kristen called to me in the back seat, cranking up a pop song on the radio, 'who's your favourite Jonas brother?'

'Well . . . I'd like to cause them all slow, painful deaths really.'

Kristen and Andrea glanced at each other in the front. 'Not a fan, huh?'

'Ha ha, you could say that. What are you guys into?'

'Well, all sorts of stuff. You know, I feel like it's a bit weird, but I actually like Rage Against the Machine. I disagree with like, all of their politics, but I like their music.'

'You disagree with their politics?'

'Oh God, yeah. I've got a friend who's into all that. You know, super lefty and everything. He's like, a total Democrat,' Kristen said as Andrea groaned theatrically. 'We have some huge arguments about politics sometimes.'

'So you guys didn't vote Obama then?'

'Are you kidding? Hell no! Man's gonna ruin this country.'

I made a mental note not to mention politics again, although I was sorely tempted to when we went past a billboard for American Cellular mobile phones, which had a picture of a smiling black guy talking on a phone, accompanied by the slogan: 'A network you can believe in.'

After our trip to the beach, which was fairly uneventful given the disappointing dearth of Brazilian bikinis, the girls decided it was time for – you guessed it – pizza. 'This is our tradition, Ben,' Andrea said, glancing at me in the rear-view mirror. 'We hit the beach, then we hit L&Bs. You, my friend, are in for a treat.'

L&Bs didn't look anything special from the outside. Just a daggy little place in a daggy area of Brooklyn. But the pizza . . . Oh, the pizza. This one, unlike the Dumbo variety, was Sicilian style, and it was heroin for the tastebuds. In square slices, it didn't have too much cheese, had a thick crust – but not too thick – and oozed a sensational tomato sauce. I could have eaten about 12 slices, except we had a lunch date, and the prospect of even more food.

To kick off the Independence Day celebrations proper, we were heading to Staten Island, where a few of the girls' friends were having a barbecue at their house. There, in a quiet neighbourhood of tree-lined streets and driveways with basketball hoops in them, we ate an amazing array of gourmet fo— oh, fine, we had hot dogs and cheeseburgers. I'd originally asked for just a cheeseburger when Jay, our generously proportioned host, had asked around to see what everyone wanted, but he'd looked so hurt at my measly order that I'd thrown in a hot dog for good measure.

However, the barbecue wasn't the end of the Americanness (or the fast food): we were going to a ball game. There was a minor league game on at the Staten Island stadium, which faced across the harbour towards Manhattan, where we'd be able to see the Independence Day fireworks. We were also there to watch the Staten Island Yankees (the feeder team for the New York Yankees) play the Loowin Spinners (the Boston Red Sox's feeder team). It was an all-American day out, with little kids holding big foam fingers, big dads holding big beers and popcorn, an overly perky announcer and a team of smiling college girls firing T-shirts into the crowd with a mini catapult, and a ridiculous mascot that everyone thought was hilarious.

'Do you know the rules of baseball?' Andrea asked as we took our seats down near the dugouts.

'I think so. Get three batters out, that's the end of the inning, play for nine innings?'

'Pretty much. It's a great game. These guys playing today would want to make it to the majors one day, play for the Yankees, maybe even make it to the World Series. You know we call it the World Series, right, even though it's only open to America and Canada?'

'Yeah, I know. Are there any plans to change that? You know, because Koreans play baseball, Japanese people play baseball, Cubans play baseball . . .'

'Yeah, but we could kick their asses.'

That'd be a 'no' on the name change then. Regardless, being a sports tragic, I was having a ball. Everything happened the way I thought it would. People drank beers and cheered. The huge guy sitting next to me in an NY cap yelled at one of the batsmen: 'Hey DeAngelo! Steal second, make my day!' After the fifth inning, we all stood up for the singing of 'Star Spangled Banner'. At the seventh inning, we all stood up for the singing of 'Take Me Out to the Ball Game'. I realised that the 'seventh inning stretch' wasn't some fancy term for something that happened in the game, but was literally a designated time for everyone in the crowd to get up and stretch. Somewhere around the eighth inning the fireworks started up over Manhattan, but I was too hooked on the game to care. For the record, the Spinners needed at least two runs in the last inning, but couldn't manage it. Victory to the mighty Yankees.

Heading back over the Verrazano-Narrows Bridge, we decided to check out Coney Island, just so I could say I'd done it (and because they have famous hot dogs there).

'Do you like this bridge, Ben?' Kristen asked as we sped across the harbour in the night.

'Ah, yeah, I guess.'

'I love bridges. I feel like I'm obsessed with them. That's why I want to go to Australia actually, because you can climb the Sydney Harbour Bridge. How amazing would that be?'

Coney Island wasn't what I'd been expecting. In the movies it always seems like this fun, family theme park. Instead, that night it was a cesspit, full of wannabe gangsters and their pregnant teenaged molls. Edging through the crowd, we managed to grab a few chilli dogs from Nathan's, the famed hot dog vendor in the area, before walking back to the car, watching as hundreds of cops suddenly came pouring out of the train station and sprinting towards the Ferris wheel.

One of the traffic cops nearby shrugged. 'Some sorta gang disturbance.' Disturbance? People get shot in American 'disturbances'. We hustled back to the car, half expecting to see someone burst out of crowd spraying bullets everywhere.

We ate the chilli dogs back at Andrea's, although she'd just opted for a plain hot dog again. 'I just don't really like fast food,' she said, casually swirling a nacho through her 'cheesy sauce' and scooping it into her mouth. 'So this makes it seem less like fast food.'

*

I felt like I'd had a good taste of New York. I mean, no one had said, 'Hey, I'm walkin' here!' to me, but aside from that, I'd been to Central Park, been to a ball game, been to Coney Island, been to four of the five boroughs, and ingested more calories than any healthy person should in their lifetime.

I was coming back to the States, but for now, it was time for some Canadian action. To get there, I just needed to find my way to Pennsylvania Station in Manhattan. 'It's easy,' Andrea had said, 'you just get out of the subway at 34th street, then walk south one block.'

It reminded me of an old sketch Billy Connolly used to do about spaghetti westerns. Everyone in the States (and in westerns) always seems to know which way north, south, east and west are. In the westerns, a cowboy would pull his horse up and ask for directions. 'Due west,' someone would reply, and cowboy would yell, 'Thanks!' and immediately wheel his horse around and gallop off in a different direction.

Americans, no doubt, would have emerged from 34th street station and turned unerringly south to Penn Station. I, unfortunately, don't have that same sense of direction, so it took me a good quarter of an hour to figure out I needed to look at the sun, see where my shadow was pointing, figure out what time of day it was, and then make an educated guess from there (making adjustments for the seasons of course). You'll be relieved to hear that I made it there eventually.

A Dose of Reality

'If you need to know how to grow hydro or shoot a porno,
I'm your girl.'

My parents always used to say: be careful what you wish for. This was probably around the time I was chucking tantrums and saying I hoped I'd wake up the next day and they wouldn't be there, so I can't blame them. Still, the saying stuck with me, and it was running through my head again that first night in Toronto.

Just like after my marathon stretch of binge drinking in Poland, for the last week or so I'd been fantasising about spending a relaxing night on a couch, watching TV. The accumulated weariness of three months of travelling and hanging out with strangers was starting to catch up with me, and with only a few weeks to go, I could see the fluorescent glow of my TV at the end of the tunnel. I'm not even a big TV watcher, but it's just those little slices of normality you miss. Within a few short weeks I'd be sitting on my own couch, with my own girlfriend. As much as I'd been having fun on this trip, the idea did appeal.

So you'd think I would have been excited to have a trial run on my first night in Canada. But no. As I sat there on the couch, mulling over the possibility of detonating some sort of explosive to stop us from having to watch a minute more of *Canada's Next Top Model*, I realised that I wasn't, in fact, ready for a quiet night in just yet. Unfortunately, by then I didn't have much of a choice.

How Andrea and Kristen would have laughed to see me there that first night, nursing a cup of tea, snuggled up on the couch with my new hosts watching reality TV. See, Canadians and Americans have a thing. Canada lives in the shadow of the US, and it's not always happy with that. Canadians are also convinced Americans think of them as kind of like their backwards cousins, from a cute little outpost up north where not much happens. And in that, it looked to me like their suspicions were absolutely correct. Andrea and Kristen had said as much, which is why it would have cracked them up to see me spending my first exciting night in a new country watching wannabe supermodels bitch about each other.

Americans might diss their northern neighbours, but I've always liked Canada. I'd only been there as a kid, and that was to the west coast, but I've met a lot of Canadians on the road, and come on, put your hand up if you hate Canadians. You can't possibly. They're not brash and loud like Americans. They don't think they rule the world, like Americans. They aren't completely cloistered from the rest of the world, like Americans. There's a reason they all have Canadian flags sewn to their backpacks – they're different to Americans, and they're proud of it.

Lynzie, who I was staying with in Toronto, put it best: 'You guys, you have this thing with New Zealanders, eh? Like, a rivalry. But deep down, you don't really hate New Zealanders. Deep down, we really hate Americans.'

If you're not American, though – or can at least put on a decent accent – Canadians will welcome you like an old friend. Like their southern neighbours, they're incredibly friendly and generous, but they're just a bit more subtle about it. So I thought there'd be a few invitations from Canada, and Toronto especially, since I'd name-dropped it in my blog ('I don't care if you're from Toronto or Tbilisi . . .'). As it turned out, there were three. There was Heather, who was English but whose flatmates listened to the triple j Hottest 100, so she felt Australian. There was Andrew (yes, my third Andrew), who had taken a trip to Toronto after a spell working in Whistler and had never left, and there was Alexander, who sounded nice enough, but kept beginning his emails with the very formal 'Dear Ben', so, in the name of fun and weird, book-worthy things happening to me, I decided to ditch him in favour of the other two.

Andrew was first up. He'd given me directions to get to his house from the airport – just a bus, a train, and then some walking through his neighbourhood, which wasn't really the cosmopolitan Canadian paradise I'd been picturing. It all looked a bit more rundown than I'd thought it would, with a giant discount store called 'Honest Ed's' on one corner, its walls plastered with slogans like, 'The only thing crooked are our floors!' It all looked pretty American to me – not that I'd mention that to the locals.

I walked through a side gate then around to Andrew's flat, the basement apartment in a detached house. I'd barely rapped on the door when it was swung open by a very tall guy with ginger hair coiffed into a 'faux hawk' style. We shook hands, and he led me into the apartment. I prepared myself for the familiar routine: greet stranger, dump bags, sit on couch, ask a few questions, give a few answers, then sort out what we were going to do for the next few nights. Except with Andrew, things were slightly different. We'd stalled after the initial introductions.

'So,' I said after a pause, 'what are the plans for tonight?'

Andrew looked surprised. 'Huh? Oh, geez. What do you want to do?'

'I dunno,' I said, 'maybe grab some dinner or a beer or something?'

'Oh, yeah, okay. I'll call Lynzie and see what she's up to.'

Lynzie was Andrew's girlfriend, a Canadian girl who, he said, worked as a professional singer, and was the reason he'd never made it out of Toronto since that original holiday.

'Yeah I did the usual thing, working at Whistler,' he said, taking a seat on the couch and flipping the TV on. 'Not many Australians in Whistler I can tell you . . . so after that some mates and I went on this road trip. We bought a van and just drove man, it was awesome. Went all around the States, Vegas, New York, everything. So then we came up to Toronto, I met Lynzie here, and that was it. I'm just working for an insurance company now. It's okay, just something to do really. It pays the bills. I probably wouldn't be here if Lynzie wasn't here.'

I soon found out why Andrew would want to stay in Toronto for Lynzie. At 24, she was four years younger than him, and stunning, with blonde hair, blue eyes, a nose ring and artfully torn clothes. Andrew and I were waiting outside on the pavement when she pulled up in a BMW with Rich, the guitarist in her band. The two had been recording video clips in Rich's bedroom, with the intention of posting them on YouTube to try to raise Lynzie's profile. Another recording of her cover of Kings of Leon's 'Use Somebody' had been viewed 175,000 times, and seemed to have landed her fans around the world.

'Oh my God, I just got this email today,' Lynzie said to Andrew after we'd done our introductions and jumped in the car with them. 'This little girl in Vancouver, she said she's got this old dog, and he's almost dead, and she plays my song to him every day to make him feel better. That is *so sweet*.'

'That is pretty cool,' Andrew said. 'So I was thinking we should go get some dinner somewhere.'

'Okay. Where are we going?'

'I'm thinking Indian,' Andrew said, jerking a thumb at me in the back seat. 'Homes loves the stuff.' (Apparently I was his homeboy already.)

There's plenty of good Indian food in Toronto, because there are plenty of Indians in Toronto. In fact, there's plenty of everyone in Toronto. The city has a Little Italy, a Little Portugal, a Greek Town, a Chinatown, and even a large Tamil population, which spent most of the time I was there blocking off roads to protest against the war in Sri Lanka. We went to a favourite spot of Lynzie's, an Indian restaurant she used to work in before she started making money out of the music game, and ordered the usuals. Once the food had arrived, Lynzie hit me with the tough question.

'So what do you think of our accents?' she asked, pointing a fork at me. 'Do you think we sound different to Americans?'

This was going to be good. 'Um . . .'

'Go on, you can tell us.'

'Well, to be honest, the only reason I know the differences to look out for is from watching *South Park*. You know, the "aboots" and ending every sentence with "eh".'

'We do not say "aboot"!' Lynzie and Rich said simultaneously. 'And you know Terrance and Phillip aren't real, eh?'

'So you do say "eh", then?'

Lynzie laughed. 'Okay, we do do that.'

She was partially right about the 'aboot' thing. Canadians do say 'about' differently to Americans, but it sounds more like 'abote'.

'So what else do I need to know about Canadians?'

'They love two things,' Andrew said, 'organised sport, and smoking pot.'

'Not at the same time I guess?'

'Ha ha, no, not really. But have a look around, you'll see. People have no problem with smoking weed, and everyone seems to be playing sport. There's games of hockey, baseball, soccer, football . . . Always something.'

'Do you play any sport here?'

'Ha! You're gonna laugh at this bro, but I'm actually playing AFL. I'm a Perth boy, it's in the blood.'

'I can't believe there's even a comp here.'

'There is, homes, it's pretty big too. There's like, eight teams. And it's not just all Aussies. You're only allowed eight Australians per team, so there's heaps of Canadians into it too. We play on Saturdays out at this college. There's only one field in the whole city that lets us keep the posts up, so all the games have to be played there one after the other. It's fuckin' awesome. You play an early game, then sit around and drink beers and watch the other games. Good craic.'

We'd finished our dinner early, and I was starting to wonder what Torontonians get up to on school nights. The answer: they go home. We all piled back into the BMW, dropped Rich at his house, and headed back to Andrew and Lynzie's. I still had ideas of Andrew and me going out to a bar somewhere for a cheeky nightcap, but I was wrong.

'Hey, Lynz, it's almost eight o'clock,' Andrew said, throwing his keys on the bench as we arrived back at the flat.

'Really? Sweet.'

Andrew turned to me. 'Lynz loves reality TV. And *Canada's Next Top Model* is on on Tuesday nights.'

This was weird. There I'd been, craving a night in front of the TV. My liver was an engorged mess, I was tired to my bones, and the couch was pretty damn comfy. But I was bored. Is this really what I came to Canada for, I wondered, as some skinny blonde chick complained about the skinny brunette chick. I guess it was up to me – I could have just gone out on my own, checked things out solo. But I didn't know the city, it was getting late, I'd resolved to spend time living as my hosts lived . . . and I really wanted to see if Nina got voted off.

*

I'm over it. I'm done with this.

These were my first thoughts as I woke up the next morning. I'd been on the road almost 90 days now. I'd stayed on 19 strange couches in 14 strange countries, and I'd had enough. I was sick of not being able to spread my clothes around a room like I do at home about three minutes after I've cleaned up. I was sick of making idle chit-chat with strangers I sometimes had nothing in common with. I was sick of smiling ingratiatingly and asking polite questions about my hosts' fascination with bridges of the world, or their passion for sailing. I could care less. I wanted my own bed, my own food, and my own girlfriend.

Fortunately, I didn't have to make much idle chit-chat that day, because Andrew had gone to work at his insurance company, and Lynzie, who only worked at night when her band had gigs, was going off doing whatever it is struggling musicians do during the day. What Lynzie had done, though, was draw me up a mud map of the city, with her recommended highlights endearingly marked out with little pictures.

Closest to the house was Kensington Markets, a small area just around the corner that was the main hippy village of the city (and marked out with little pictures of bongs). Torontonians, I realised, don't mind being pigeonholed. The Little Italys and Portugals of the city are marked on the street signs as such. But there's also the 'Theatre District', where you'll find all the city's theatres, the 'Art and Design District', where all the galleries are housed, and the gay village (marked on Lynzie's map with little love hearts), where all the gays hang out.

Like most hippy-dominated communities, Kensington Market has a fairly strong flavour – and that's a lot like pot. Marijuana laws in the city are pretty relaxed. If you get busted smoking pot in public, Andrew told me, you'd probably just be asked to move on. There's even an annual parade in Toronto dedicated to smoking weed. Whether anyone can be bothered to turn up, I'm not sure. As well as being home to a cafe where you can take in your own ganja and smoke it in the back, Kensington Market also has a shop called 'Roach-A-Rama', a pot-smoking supplies store with the slogan: 'Serving potheads since . . . Ah, I forget.'

There wasn't a lot to do in the village, as it was a bit early for a joint, but it still gave me a chance to appreciate the creativity of

Toronto's beggars, which there were a surprisingly large amount of. Rather than just sit around with their hands out, they were sitting around with their hands out next to scribbled signs that read things like: 'Too ugly to prostitute – spare $$ for weed', and, 'Ninjas are after us – need money for judo lessons'. I still didn't give them any money.

From the markets I headed down Spadina Avenue to Toronto's Chinatown, stepping around large piles of garbage strewn across the streets. What the hell is this, I thought. Canada's supposed to be a clean, green paradise. But every bin in the city was overflowing with garbage, with literally piles of the stuff surrounding the full receptacles.

I later found out this wasn't normal for the city. The garbage collectors, along with a few other council departments who'd gone out in sympathy, were on strike, and had been for the last three weeks. That's three weeks without a single garbage collection. So not only were the street cans brimming, but everyone's houses were also strewn with junk. Canadians, apparently, love a good strike. Maybe it's the French influence, but they've been known to strike for months on end. The garbos even had a strike fund saved up so they got paid while they were walking around in circles chanting catchphrases outside the mayor's office.

When Canadians aren't striking though, they're probably helping out strangers. Throughout my stay in Toronto, I couldn't pull out a map or a guidebook – or even look slightly confused – for more than a few seconds without someone offering to help me. 'Ya need a hand gettin' somewhere?' a smiling Canadian would ask any time I slowed my pace to below a light jog. Canadians, I was starting to realise, are even more ridiculously friendly and polite than I'd thought. And it's not just making visitors feel welcome – they're nice to each other, too. Spend a few minutes on public transport, and you notice the weirdest thing: people *talking* to each other. Not just friends; complete strangers. I lost count of the number of times I overheard people just having a friendly chat on their way to work, getting to know the person they were sitting next to. It always ended with, 'Oh, this is my stop.'

'Well, it's been a pleasure talkin' to you, sir.'

'And you as well. You have a nice day now.'

Crazy bastards. That sort of behaviour would get you shot on the Tube in London.

But back to my wanderings, where I'd decided to go against my better judgement and go up the CN Tower, which is like Toronto's version of Sydney's Centrepoint Tower – a huge and mostly pointless building down by the water on the edge of the city. I'd been trying not to do too many touristy things on this trip, but as it was only 1pm and I'd already covered pretty much everything on Lynzie's map, I figured it would waste some time until Andrew finished work, if nothing else. After paying my 20 bucks and lining up, I was whisked to the top in a lift, where I found a nice view of the city, and about 1000 school kids enjoying it. All up, I spent about an hour in various queues, and 10 minutes at the top, before speeding rapidly back to the bottom.

The last highlight on Lynzie's map was the one marked with love hearts – the gay village. It was nothing too shocking or alternative – just a few trendy cafes flying rainbow flags out the front, and a couple of sidewalk pubs. I pulled up a table at one of those pubs, ordered a pint of beer, and read a Canadian newspaper, which, unlike its American counterparts, actually acknowledged that the rest of the world existed. Once I'd caught up with all of the news, it was time to meet up with Andrew and Lynzie back at the flat.

'So what's happening tonight?'

Andrew had that same worryingly blank look on his face. 'Um . . . I dunno. Maybe have a barbecue or something? We don't really have any beers though.'

'Oh. I can run down to the shop and grab some if you like?'

'Oh yeah, you can do that if you want.'

It wasn't exactly a night of sightseeing and bar hopping, but it would have to do. Following Andrew's directions, I went down to the store that sells beer, which, in Canada, is helpfully called The Beer Store. And that's all it sells. Even if your fancy ranges so far as cider, you'll have to go somewhere else. Fortunately, I just wanted beer. Trouble was, I didn't know what beer. Something local would be good, so when I saw a six-pack of tins called Molson CANADIAN beer, I thought, perfect.

I returned home triumphantly clutching my CANADIAN beer, and Andrew cracked up laughing.

'What are you doing, homes?' he chuckled. 'That's like turning up to a barbecue in Australia with a six-pack of Foster's.'

Fine. He was right though, the beer was pretty bad compared to some of the stuff you can get in Canada. Anyway, it was better than nothing, and it helped wash down the steaks Andrew cooked up on the barbecue in their patio. With the food finished, it was time for . . . more reality TV. Tonight, Lynzie's second favourite show: a whole two hours of *So You Think You Can Dance*. I would rather have auditioned for a show called *So You Think You Can Scoop Your Own Eyeballs Out And Eat Them* than spend two hours on the couch listening to moronic Americans scream things at each other in between silly dance routines, but as I was still going with my 'when in Rome' modus operandi, I gritted my teeth, and let the mind-numbing reality wash over me.

*

For someone trying to avoid doing touristy things, I was failing miserably. Backing up from my trip up the CN Tower the day before, I was about to do the most touristy thing it's possible for someone to do in Ontario: go to Niagara Falls. After saying goodbye to Lynzie (Andrew had already disappeared back to the insurance company), I dumped my bags in a locker at the bus station, and jumped on a bus headed for the falls. There, I joined pretty much every tourist in Canada for a look at the famous landmark.

From Niagara, you could throw a rock and hit the US (which I'm sure plenty of Canadians I'd met would like to do). The falls separate the two countries, so as you don a silly blue poncho and take a ride under the falls on the *Maid of the Mist* boat, you can see hordes of American tourists in silly yellow ponchos doing exactly the same thing on the other side.

The town itself is a weird place, full of huge hotels, casinos and amusement park rides. In other words, a great place to waste a lot of money. Being pretty short on that particular commodity, I took my token photos of the white water, and got straight back on the bus to Toronto, where I was due to meet up with my next host, Heather.

Heather sounded like fun in her email:

> Me and my friends have read your latest travel blog, and because we're all travel masochists and love surrounding ourselves with people who're travelling to make ourselves jealous, we want you to come stay with us. We live in the arts and design district on Queen West, the funky part of town, and we're into all kinds of shiz. We'd love to show you the sights, sounds, and, yes, even the smells of our adopted city . . .

Picking up my pack, I caught a tram out to that 'funky part of town', which I saw immediately that I was going to like. Aside from the mountains of rubbish still piled up next to all the bins, there were art galleries, record stores, clothes shops and cafes everywhere. I swung off the tram, and there were Heather and her flatmate Tom waiting on the corner.

'House is that way,' Heather said by way of introduction, pointing behind her. 'But we're headed to the liquor store first. That cool?'

'Sure.'

This was more like it. Screw TV – that could wait. Heather was from Yorkshire, and she'd met Tom, who was from Swindon, on the flight over to Canada. They were on an organised working overseas program, spending a year in Canada doing whatever jobs they could find.

'So where's the third flatmate?' I asked as we walked towards yet another Beer Store.

Heather and Tom glanced at each other.

'Well,' Heather said, 'that was Tom's fiancee Lou. But, ah, they broke up last week, and she's moved home to Australia.'

'Oh shit, sorry, Tom.'

'That's orright mate, no worries,' Tom grinned. 'It was my idea actually, so, you know, gotta live with that.'

Tom was a big man – massive, actually. He must have been a good head and shoulders above me, and, although I'm no colossus, that still made him pretty big. He had an almost goofy air about him, with three-quarter pants and huge feet jammed into very English sandals. Heather, on the other hand, was a small indie chick, with dark hair, black stockings, and a cute polka dot dress revealing what I later found out was a Jean-Paul Sartre quote tattooed down the top of her spine.

Their flat was on a residential street in said funky part of town. Toronto's good like that – it's set out in a massive grid, and it seems like all of the shops and restaurants are on one set of parallel streets, and all of the houses are on the streets perpendicular to those. So while Tom and Heather had the busy Queen Street West and Bathurst Street to either side of them, their flat was in a quiet area in the middle, a five-minute walk away. The flat itself looked much like most of the places I lived in when I was a student – mismatched furniture, books and CDs everywhere, and old food sitting around in the kitchen. In other words, the kind of place I felt at home in straight away.

The kitchen and lounge room were on the bottom floor, along with a TV, some pretty professional-looking DJ equipment, and 'The List', a blackboard filled with place names and boxes next to them.

'That's our Toronto list,' Heather explained. 'It's all the places we want to go to, like cafes and bars and attractions and stuff, before our year is up. Two people in the house have to have done it before we can cross it off. I think we'll probably do one tonight, actually.'

The bedrooms were on the top level of the house, along with a huge wooden deck. 'This . . . this is the place,' Heather said, sliding open the door to the deck. 'We've had a few parties out here this summer. Not much fun in winter when it's minus a million fucking degrees, but in summer it doesn't get much better.'

Back downstairs, Tom cracked three beers (not CANADI-ANS), and passed them around. 'So what'd you do with your other people here?' he asked me.

'Ah, not that much.'

'Really?'

'Yeah, I've actually spent the last two nights on the couch watching reality TV.'

Heather laughed. 'Watching TV? Were you bored?'

'Out of my mind.'

'Well, they're fucking geniuses!'

'How so?'

'Well, I bet everyone's been taking you out and doing fun things, right?' I nodded. 'So they've taken the opposite approach, and just been really boring. Which means they're definitely going to get in your book! Tom, you and I are going to have to do something pretty crazy now.'

Tom chuckled while fiddling with the DJ equipment, which, he explained, was his. He worked in IT by day, but had been doing some amateur DJing by night. Heather, on the other hand, had just quit her job at a smoothie bar to work for a boutique publisher as an editor.

'It's one of those "only in Toronto" places,' she explained. 'We specialise in books on porn and growing hydroponic weed. Most of it gets sold in Holland I think. So yeah, if you need to know how to grow hydro or shoot a porno, I'm your girl.'

'You serious?'

'Oh, yeah. They want Vadim, this guy I'm kind of seeing, to pose for an S&M shoot for one of their books. I told them he'd be too hairy.'

'Nice. So what are we doing tonight? Not posing for S&M shoots or anything?'

'No, we're going to take you to this cool place called Sneaky Dee's,' Heather said, draining the last of her beer. 'They serve wicked Mexican food, and plenty of vegetarian stuff. We're vegetarians,' she added, pointing at Tom.

'Any particular reason?'

'Ah, you know, the usual. Cruelty to animals, meat has steroids in it, and loads too much oestrogen, gives guys man boobs, blah blah blah . . . I could go on, but you get the idea.'

She was right, I got the idea. I've hung around enough vegetarians to know that it's not a good idea to get them on a roll.

Still, I was happy with the choice of Sneaky Dee's – I may not love vegetarian food, but Mexican I can certainly do. And, like in the Netherlands, there was no chance of missing out on 'traditional' Canadian cuisine, because there isn't any. About the only culinary phenomenon Canadians are known for is their love of chain restaurants. Other than that, throw in bacon and maple syrup, and you've got the place covered.

On the walk to Sneaky Dee's, I did learn another Canadian quirk – their pedestrian crossings. They don't work like ours. Rather than just walk across, you have to signal to drivers where you're intending to go. So you approach the crossing, press a button which makes the light above the road start flashing, then you stand there and point in the direction you're going to walk. It makes you feel a bit like a hunting beagle, standing at attention and pointing your paw at where the scent's coming from. And it's kind of fun.

I soon got my first taste of Torontonian nightlife, and decided this was a scene I could get used to. The big bar was packed with rowdy Canadians tucking into burritos, drinking 'pitchers' of beer, and generally having a good time. No one was dressed up, the bar was dingy, and there was zero pretension – just a bunch of friendly people having a good time. We ordered a pitcher and some burritos for ourselves, and grabbed a table.

'So how's the IT business?' I asked Tom.

'Oh yeah, it's all right. Bit different to the last place I worked, anyway.'

'Where was that?'

Tom grinned. 'Iraq.'

Heather shook her head. 'Bullshit.'

'Seriously, I was working for a company over there for 18 months.'

'Seriously?' Heather said, perplexed. 'How come I never knew this?'

'I dunno, guess I just didn't tell you. It was pretty amazing. I was just doing computer stuff, just near Basra. We'd work three weeks on, then two weeks off.'

'Bet that was nice having your holidays in Iraq.'

'No, no, they'd fly us to Dubai for two weeks. Then every six months they'd fly us anywhere in the world for a holiday. I had some pretty wicked trips.'

Heather shook her head. 'Tom, you're fucking mad.'

After dinner, we walked to a little bar called Squirly's, mainly so we could get a drink, but also so that Heather and Tom could cross it off 'The List' back at the flat.

'So will we see this boyfriend of yours tonight, Heather?' I asked over a rum and coke.

'Well, he's not really my boyfriend . . .'

Tom laughed, nudging her shoulder. 'Oh, come on.'

'All right fine, he kind of is. He's a, um, special boy. You'll see. He's Ukrainian, but he's been here for ages. He just smokes a lot of pot and rides his BMX. I think that's about it.' She turned to Tom. 'You know he got arrested the other day? Some guy caught him trying to steal some sushi from a restaurant, and he made a citizen's arrest! And then, how's this, Vadim starts chatting to the guy who's arrested him while they're waiting for the cops, charms the pants off the guy, and he ends up letting him go! And now they're mates. That's pretty much the sort of guy Vadim is.'

I did get to meet Vadim that night, although he was in no fit state to chat. He sat on the couch for a while, red-eyed in his Birkenstocks and rolled-up jeans, giggling to himself, before he and Heather headed up to bed. At least he didn't try to steal any food, I guess.

*

I slept on the futon in the lounge room that night, and lay awake for a while thinking about how much my approach to this whole caper had changed in the last few months. Those first few stays at strangers' houses, I'd been legitimately scared. Of what, I couldn't remember. There'd been nervousness when I'd first met people, a kind of thrill of expectation before I got to see their house, and this weird fear of sexual tension with the girls that never existed in the first place.

By now, I couldn't give a toss. All those jagged edges had been buffed off by pure repetition. I'd somewhat dangerously come to the conclusion that everyone who contacted me was just going to be a genuinely nice person who wanted me to come and stay, and I had nothing to worry about. So now I'd just say hi, run through my standard list of questions to break the ice, throw my bag wherever there was room to throw my bag, sleep wherever they told me to sleep, and just go with the flow. What had once seemed a dangerous and edgy proposition had become amazingly normal.

So I had a good sleep on the futon that night, barely pausing to open an eye as Tom prepared for his day of fixing computers, and Heather her day of hardcore porn and hydroponic weed. I eventually dragged myself off the futon about 11am, and struggled down to the local cafe to eat some of the awesome hot cinnamon rolls Heather and Tom had told me about.

I had a pretty sedate day of sightseeing planned out. I was going to go for a walk down Queen Street West, check out the galleries, record stores and clothes shops, then head to a fresh food market over the other side of the city, and then, if the mood so took me, sit down and have a beer somewhere. Out on Queen Street though, I made the rookie error of pulling out the guidebook Heather had given me to check out where I was.

'Need a hand getting somewhere?'

I looked around. A girl, a pair of cherries tattooed on each shoulder, waited expectantly for her chance to do her Canadian duty and help a stranger.

'Ah, I'm just trying to get to St Lawrence market, which I think is down this street,' I said, pointing ahead of me.

'Uh huh, that's abote it,' the girl smiled. 'It's great there, you'll enjoy it.'

With that, she waved, and went on her merry way. ('Yeah,' Heather said when I told her about this later, 'and Torontonians are supposed to be the least friendly people in Canada. I mean, what the hell are the other ones like?')

I did get to the market, and I did enjoy it, but it was soon time to head back to the flat to meet up with Heather and Tom for more drinks and dinner. Two nights out in a row! I was getting back into the old routine. I'd just managed to work out how to play my iPod on Tom's DJ equipment when the pair burst through the door, giggling away.

'Hey, Benny boy,' Heather said. 'Thought you might want to check this out – it's the last book I worked on.'

She flicked a paperback across the coffee table, and I had a look at the title: *How to Be Kinky*. I leafed through it. Heather chuckled as I flicked past the chapter on spanking, straight to the hardcore S&M. There were gimps in full leather, guys with ball gags in their mouths, dominatrixes wielding whips and chains. And all with thoughtful explanations written down the side.

I'd like to pretend that I was really shocked by this, but I'm not that prudish. I mean, I used to work at *FHM*, and although we never strayed into that sort of territory, there was a time over a few weeks when our magazine shared a printer with what were known as the 'P mags' – *Picture* and *People*. You'd go to print out your harmless page of girls in bikinis, pick something off the print pile, then look down and realise you were carrying a spread-eagled 'home girl' back to your desk. That was a disturbing few weeks, I can tell you.

'And this is what they want Vadim to pose for?' I asked, still flipping through the book.

Heather nodded. 'I don't think he's going to do it though.'

'So what's the book you're working on now?'

'Oh, just one on hydroponics. Pretty tame after that one, but I know how to grow some good weed, I can tell you!'

As nice as it would have been to sit around the house sampling Heather's new skill, that wasn't very touristy, so we decided instead to hit the town. Heather and Tom wanted to take me to their favourite restaurant, a vegetarian place called Fresh just around the corner from their house. There, we feasted on vegetables and rice, surrounded by Tom and Heather's fellow vego Torontonians, who were all giving off the weird shiny glow of those who don't eat meat.

'It's a pretty alternative city, isn't it?' I commented, looking around.

'Yeah,' Heather nodded, scooping brown rice into her mouth. 'And they love getting naked here. Love it. All the hippy protests seem to involve some sort of nudity. I actually got invited to a nude party the other weekend. I was going to go too, but the guy who invited me was gay, so I was kind of afraid it might be a gay thing and a nude girl wouldn't really be appreciated.'

After the restaurant we went to a tiki bar, where we ordered a 'volcano', a cocktail designed for four people to drink out of a giant flaming volcano-shaped glass, and naturally, things got out of hand quickly. Hearing our accents and seeing our impressive flaming drink, a few local girls came over to chat, and big, goofy-looking Tom was in his element.

'He seems to be doing okay for someone who split up with his fiancee a few weeks ago,' I said to Heather, dipping my straw into our fiery beverage.

She nodded. 'He's loving it. His trick is he goes to bars, then "accidentally" bumps into girls, then puts on his plummiest accent and goes, "Oh gosh, I'm awfully sorry." Works every time, the Canadian girls lap it up.'

*

Next morning, I had none of the trouble getting to the airport that I'd had in New York trying to find my way south to Penn Station. I'd only had time to say goodbye to Tom and Heather and walk down the road to the nearest bus stop before a complete stranger approached me.

'You need any help with directions there, sir?'

And the Emmy Goes to . . .

'You know, you guys are going to have to put some pants on when vacation's over.'

'Nirvana used to play over there,' James said, pointing at a shabby little bar on a corner. 'I think Soundgarden did too.'

I nodded, or I did as best you can with your nose pressed to the window of a van.

'That's where Modest Mouse are from,' he added a few minutes later, pointing to a street sign as we flashed past on the highway. 'And Death Cab For Cutie are from a town about 10 minutes from here. I think Eddie Vedder might live around here too . . .'

I'd always loved the idea of Seattle. This cold, dreary place where scraggly-haired dudes in cardigans sat around morosely writing music that would change the world. A place at once home to three of the biggest worldwide corporations in existence, and a thriving music scene that stood against all that those companies represented. I'd wasted hours of teen angst listening to grunge and wishing I was in Seattle, holed up in some dive bar watching history unfold. Now, I was there, right in the middle of it. I could see where those bands grew up, where they played, where they drank and shot hard drugs into themselves and worked their misery and rejection into musical form. I could go to the nearest record store and look up the bands in the 'local' section, and find Jimi Hendrix, Pearl Jam, Mudhoney, Nirvana . . .

Oh, and James, my host, worked for a microbrewery, so it was all coming up roses.

'I'm living in Seattle and I know my girlfriend and I could put you up for a couple of days if you want,' James wrote.

> I work for a micro-brewery and also a micro-distillery and have worked for a winery in the last two years as well so there will be plenty of stuff to drink. I have a pretty flexible schedule so it's easy for me to show you around if you want. I have pretty good connections to a lot of the 60 micro-breweries in Washington State and a lot of them are here in Seattle, and most brew some pretty damn good beer. Anyway man we'd be happy to show you what living in Seattle is like for a few days.

Hell. Yes. If there's one thing I like more than miserable rock 'n' roll, it's drinking beer while I'm listening to it. I flew from Toronto to James's city, and was waiting out on the pavement at Sea-Tac airport when I got a text from him: 'I'll be turning up in a white Northern Lights Brewery van.' Right, I figured, that should be easy enough to recognise.

A few minutes later a white mini-van pulled up with a huge 'Northern Lights' sticker across the side, and a smiling guy sitting up the front. 'Have you got anywhere pressing to be?' James asked as I threw my backpack into the back of the van next to a few wooden pallets and an old TV.

'I guess not,' I said.

'Good, because I gotta go down to Tacoma to pick up a keg, then we've gotta drop it down at a bar in town. They're putting on a trivia night tonight that we're sponsoring, so I suppose we should make sure they've got some of our beer. Hope that's cool, man!'

I laughed. 'Yeah, that's fine, as long as I get to taste some beer.'

'Sure, man, sure.'

James seemed friendly, with an easy way about him, chatting away in his broad Australian accent.

'How long have you been in the States?' I asked.

'Since I was seven, man!'

'Really? But you've got such a broad accent.'

'Yeah, I know. I dunno why. Just always had it. My brother's two years younger than me, and he sounds dead-set American. You should see me try to explain to everyone that I'm pretty much American too. They don't buy it.'

'How come you guys moved over here?'

'Oh, my mom's American. So her and my dad decided they wanted to move back to the States when I was a kid. I think they settled on Washington because they liked the politics here, pretty liberal, you know? I mean, it is not okay to be a Republican here.'

James sounded as Aussie as Dave Hughes most of the time, but he'd say 'mom' instead of mum, talk about 'college buddies' and his Us sounded liked double Os. So he'd say 'prodoocer' instead of producer.

'Man, it's a nightmare,' James said when I remarked on his accent. 'Americans are fascinated by it, they keep getting me to repeat things I say. Then I go for holidays in Australia, where you think no one would care, and they all want to hear me say things too, because I've got a funny accent to them as well. It's a pain in the arse, man.'

I chuckled as we cruised down the freeway to Tacoma, an industrial town by the coast that was home to the warehouse which stocked kegs of Northern Lights beer. The brewery itself was in Spokane, a city a few hours' drive away, which meant James's boss was also a few hours' drive away. James was a sales rep, and was free to roam Seattle trying to drum up business for the brewery. 'Pretty much means I'm free to show you around,' he said. At one point James's phone rang, and he chatted to the guy on the other end for a few minutes before hanging up and grinning at me. 'Dude wants to stock our beer at his pub. So that's, like, my week's work done.'

After rolling the keg into the van at Tacoma, we headed back up the freeway to Seattle, past rolling hills of tall pines with the snow-capped Cascade Mountains in the distance. You had to wonder why anyone living here would be miserable enough to write good music.

'You know this is where Starbucks started?' James asked. 'Yep, but I never go there. There's some really great coffee here, but that ain't it. What else? Oh, so Boeing is based here as well. Pretty much everyone here works for Boeing or Microsoft. We'll actually go near Bill Gates's house in a second. It's like, mostly underground. But yeah, it's kind of funny, because the grunge thing has died down a fair bit in the last few years, so you know those people going to do their nine-to-five at Microsoft are the same ones who were rocking out to Nirvana a few years ago. They dress all alternative during the weekends, then put on their suits on Monday. I guess you have to grow up eventually.'

James's local radio station certainly hadn't. As we chugged our way through Seattle's outer suburbs, beautiful places set around Lake Washington, or one of the city's harbour inlets, James was listening to a station called The End, which seemed to be my dream radio station, pumping out plenty of 'nouveau Seattle' like Fleet Foxes and Modest Mouse, but also what must rate as Seattle's 'golden oldies': Alice In Chains, Nirvana, Screaming Trees, Soundgarden and Mudhoney. It's not a bad musical history for a city of 600,000.

But as much as Washingtonians love their music, their coffee and their crash-prone computer software, it all pales into insignificance next to their love for beer. American beer gets a bad rap, and for good reason most of the time. The generic stuff, the

Buds and Millers and Coorses, is complete crap. As the Monty Python gag goes, they're 'like making love in a canoe' – fucking close to water. But no one in Seattle drinks that stuff, as I was about to find out. Most bars have 10 or more beers on tap, and none of them are the big three. They're local.

Northern Lights is one of 71 breweries in Washington state. Town fairs almost always have brewing competitions, and the winners get to make up a large batch of their brew at a local brewery. James and I visited Big Al's Brewery a few days later, and found a couple of gumbooted guys out the back who'd called in sick from work for the week so they could brew a few hundred litres of their winning recipe. 'We take our beer pretty serious here,' one of the moustachioed brewers said, leaning over to stir something in a big metal tank.

And it's not just the men who are into it. James and I pulled up outside the bar in the suburb of Madison Park, jumped out and rolled the keg inside. The place was heaving with punters getting ready for trivia night, so James and I grabbed a couple of pints of Northern Lights pale ale and sat at a bench. We'd been there about five minutes before a girl plonked herself next to us.

'So,' she said, looking at the emblem on James's shirt, 'you guys from Northern Lights, huh?'

'I am,' James said.

'Cool. So tell me, why should I try a pint of Northern Lights?'

I can't recall exactly what James said in reply – something about double dry hopping and chill filtering – but it obviously did the job, as the girl got a pint from the bar, and came back to our bench.

'Yeah,' she said, taking a deep slug, 'this is not bad. Not as hoppy as the Pyramid pale. I like it. Good flavour. I'll have to write this up in my beer journal.'

I raised an eyebrow. 'Beer journal?'

'Yeah, I just kinda write down tasting notes for all the beers I try.'

'Like for a blog, on the net?'

'No, just for myself. I like my beer, man. You,' she added, tipping her glass at James, 'have the best job in the world.'

We slipped out before the trivia began, and made our way through the city, the famous Space Needle in the background, across the harbour to West Seattle, where James's apartment was.

'Are you allergic to cats?' James asked.

'No, I'm good. Don't tell me you're a mad cat man?'

'Ha ha, no, they're Kiri's, my girlfriend. Don't worry, she's not a mad cat woman either. We just ended up with these things somehow. They're okay.'

The apartment was pretty regulation for the Western world, with the addition of a few cats. I was sleeping on the lounge room floor, James explained, on one of those three-quarter blow-up mattresses I imagine you take with you when you're climbing one of the snow-capped mountains out in the distance, and don't want to have to carry too much. It wasn't luxury, but I could deal with it. James reappeared a few seconds later in a singlet, those dinky little shorts professional runners wear, and running shoes.

'I'm just going out for a jog, mate,' he said, lacing up the runners. 'You want to come too?'

'That depends . . . Are you very fit?'

'Well, the college I went to, I was there on a sports scholarship as a middle distance runner, so, pretty fit I guess.'

'I see. Were those *Entourage* DVDs I saw next to the TV?'

'Yep.'

'Cool, see you in an hour or so.'

James grinned. 'No worries, help yourself to the beer in the fridge too – there's some new Northern Lights stuff in there you should try.'

With that, he dashed out the door, and I dashed to the fridge, popped the lid off a bottle of stout, and did exactly what I'd been threatening to do, sitting down on the couch and watching Vince and Co tearing up Hollywood. About two episodes later, the front door opened, and there, rather than a sweaty James, was a non-sweaty, good-looking blonde girl.

'Oh, hey,' she said. 'Ben, right? I'm Kiri.'

The two of us chatted for a while until James arrived back, puffing and sweating from his run, which was not a bad effort after the pint of beer we'd had at the pub. Once he'd had a shower we headed into the main part of West Seattle for burgers and fries at a 'tap house' – sort of like a bar that had even more beers on tap than a normal Seattle bar. This one had about 20 to choose from, so we each picked one at random, and settled back to wait for our food.

'So do you think James's accent is funny?' Kiri asked me.

'Yeah, it is a bit. You must like it though.'

'I don't even notice it. All my friends are always like, "Oh, you must love his cute accent," but I'm like, I don't even notice it anymore.'

I was having that problem too. I'd just completely forget James wasn't really Australian, and start babbling on about footy grand finals or cricket scores, and I'd just get blank looks in return. I had to keep reminding myself that he had no idea what I was on about. He'd visited his old home in Torquay a few years back, but other than that, he was about as Australian as Disneyland.

'You like the coffee here?' Kiri asked, immediately swinging the conversation to Washingtonians' other obsession.

'I haven't really tried any yet,' I admitted.

'Oh, you'll have to get James to take you down to my old work. I used to work at this little bakery and cafe which is about a block from the world headquarters of Starbucks. It was so funny, all the Starbucks employees used to come to my cafe for their coffee. Even they know better.'

*

There's just no feeling that quite compares to waking up with a cat on your head. Kiri had done her best. She'd shut the cats in her room overnight, but sometime around the wee hours they'd obviously figured out how to negotiate their way out, and had decided to reclaim their lounge room territory by planting themselves on my bonce.

I managed to shift them into a position where I could at least breathe without getting fur balls, and tried to get some more sleep. As compact and convenient as James's little mattress might have been, it sure as hell wasn't comfortable – particularly not with its feline adornments. So I was only too happy to get up when Kiri went to work and James headed out to pretend he was working while actually driving me around the city.

We kicked the morning off at a little cafe just down the road, drinking perfect coffee that arrived in cups of almost dainty proportions compared to your average American serving.

'Kind of ironic, isn't it?' James said, sipping his little cappuccino. 'Seattle is so famous for Starbucks, but no one goes to Starbucks. Your little place down the road will always do better coffee than Starbucks. No one drinks coffee out of those huge fuckin' cups either, or orders stupid things like caramel mocha frappuccinos. Just good old espresso here.'

That day we'd planned to see one of Seattle's other institutions, one James had never been to either – the Boeing factory. It was my chance to fully embrace my travel nerdiness, to indulge an extremely geeky fascination with planes. When I was a kid I used to collect models of planes, and while I'd had that passion beaten out of me by selected bullies at school, I was still fascinated by things that fly.

The factory is about an hour outside the city and there we embraced our shared nerdiness, joining the groups of mostly male retirees (we were the youngest there by about 30 years) on a tour of the Boeing hangar, which, floor area wise, is the biggest building in the world. We watched the new 787s being put together, oohed and aahed at a cross-section of a 747, and gazed into the sky as a 777 did test flights. It was all highly uncool, and *awesome*.

'Right,' James said as we walked back to the van, 777s roaring above our heads. 'You ready for another coffee?'

'Of course.'

'Excellent. Have I got a treat for you.'

He didn't add to that mysterious statement, so we jumped back in the van and were heading through one of the smaller towns outside Seattle when James apparently found what he was looking for. 'Yep,' he nodded, 'that'll be the place.'

'That little shack with all the construction workers in front of it?'

It really was a little shack too, just a tiny one-person-sized hut in the middle of a car park with a 'Cowgirls' sign on the top. We got out of the van and lined up behind the tradies, and it was only when we got to the window that I realised that this wasn't any old espresso stand.

'Hey there boys, what can I get you?' asked the blonde girl manning the espresso machine.

I paused. 'Um . . .'

It's kind of hard to decide what to order when your barista is only wearing a stars-and-stripes string bikini and high heels. 'Well,' she said again, sticking a hip out and twirling a paper cup in her hand, 'what'll it be?'

'Um . . .'

'Just two cappuccinos,' James said, saving me from further embarrassment.

'Hey, now where's that accent from?' the girl asked, flicking her hair over her bare shoulder as she started pressing buttons on the machine.

James sighed. 'Australia.'

'Oh my God, I love Australians. That is such a cute accent. Hey, do you guys want a photo? I had these shots done a few weeks ago,' she added, passing out a glossy photo of her in lingerie and cowboy boots. 'You guys have that one for free.'

'Um . . .'

A few minutes later we had our coffees and were back in the van. 'Okay,' I said to James, 'what the hell was that?'

He chuckled. 'That's a coffee girl. It's a Seattle thing. You see those little huts, you know they've got hot girls in there. They don't always wear bikinis either. They have, like, theme days. I've never been given a photo though. You must have turned on the charm, man.'

'What, by standing there and stuttering?'

'Yep, I guess so,' he laughed.

'So you probably don't take Kiri to those then?'

'Not really man. That's only, like, the second time I've been to one actually. But yeah, I dunno if I told you this, but Kiri's family are pretty religious.'

'Aah . . . No.'

'Yeah, they're Mormons. Well, actually her dad is, but her mom isn't. They got divorced, so her mom moved out to Washington to get away from all that stuff. But Kiri's still pretty tight with her dad's side of the family.'

From the coffee shop, we made a detour down to Lake Washington so I could check out one of the more morbid relics of the 90s grunge scene – the house where Kurt Cobain shot himself. It's not like it's signposted or anything, but with a quick googling on James's iPhone we got the address, and immediately recognised the facade from the thousands of photos that have been published since that day in 1994.

The house hasn't been turned into a memorial though – it's just a normal place with normal owners, who are probably pretty sick of the ratty-looking kids hanging out on what's been dubbed 'Kurt's bench', a wooden bench in the park next door where it's not difficult to imagine Kurt once sat and wrote songs, even though he probably would have been mobbed by the ratty kids if he ever set foot outside his front gate. It's a proxy grave really, since Kurt was cremated and some of his ashes tipped into the Wishkah River.

'People don't hang out here much anymore,' James said as I

tried to take a few photos of the house without looking too dodgy. 'On the anniversary there's always a bunch of flowers here and stuff, but the rest of the time it's pretty quiet. It's not like they ever let people go through the house or anything.'

Seattle still seems pretty obsessed with its fallen idol though. As we jumped back in the van and headed into the city centre, 'Smells Like Teen Spirit' was even playing on the radio. We were in the city to see Pike Place, the market where big men in waterproof overalls famously throw fish to each other. I'd seen this on a few travel shows, with fish after fish sailing through the air as the seafood shop restacked its displays. However, if we were hoping to see whole schools of fish making their maiden flight at the one time, we were disappointed. Instead, we found hundreds of tourists crowded around a display shelf of crushed ice, with one guy standing guard, chatting and posing for photos. Every now and then he'd scream out something, the guys in the back room would scream out something, he'd pick up a beaten-up old salmon that was clearly the designated 'throwing fish', fling it to the guys in the back, who'd then fling it back, everyone would take photos, and everything would go back to normal. Half an hour later, the whole routine would be repeated for a whole new group of tourists.

One throw was enough for James and me before we headed over to the felafel stand to get some lunch, resisting the temptation to go to the world's first Starbucks just down the road. At the felafel stand, I could hear a guy making his order.

'Y'all got any beers?' he asked.

The woman behind the counter snorted. 'Not allowed man. I mean, you can see naked people riding past here on pushbikes, but God forbid you have an open can of beer.'

I asked James what was going on. 'Oh, they have pretty restrictive alcohol laws here. It's a really liberal state, but some of the laws are really strict. So you can't have open alcohol containers in public. And there's all these laws for the strip clubs too, like you can get a lap dance, but the girls aren't allowed to touch you in any way. Doesn't sound like a great lap dance to me.'

'What about the naked people on bikes?'

'That's this annual thing they have, it's like the world naked bike ride or something like that. It started here. Everyone gets nude and rides their bike around the city. So you can ride your bike with no clothes on, just as long as you're not drinking.'

'Still sounds pretty uncomfortable.'

'Yeah, totally.'

*

I don't think I was the best house guest for James and Kiri. I got along great with James, and didn't see Kiri often enough to find out if we liked each other or not. But I wasn't really on my game. With four nights to go until I flew home to my girlfriend, my family, my friends and my life, I think my mind might have been elsewhere. I should have been wandering the streets humming Pearl Jam songs to myself, drinking great beer and even better coffee, making the most of the fact that, inexplicably, it hadn't rained the whole time I'd been there.

But instead I'd mentally checked out. I'd watched *Entourage* DVDs rather than go out and explore. I think I referred to James as 'Andrew' a couple of times. I'd stayed with that many Andrews (and an Andrea), it just came naturally. I completely forgot which stories I'd told James, and which I'd told the other people I'd stayed with. I would launch cautiously into a tale about, say, carrying goats in Africa, watching for recognition in James's face in case I was boring him with it for a second or third time. He was always nice enough to feign interest though.

As a parting gift to me (not that they owed me anything – more the other way around), James and Kiri took me to Palace Kitchen, one of Seattle's better restaurants, for dinner on my last night in town. There, we drank more good beer, ate sensational food (I almost sent my plate back when I realised nothing on it had been deep-fried), and chatted about, well, beer. The next day, James was going to have to get back to the gruelling task of driving his van around the city trying to persuade pubs to stock Northern Lights' brews. Someone had to do it, I guess.

*

I wasn't even going to write about LA. This book should have finished a few paragraphs ago. I'd decided that since I'd been such a crap house guest at James's place, I wouldn't even try to be on my book-writing game in LA. I wouldn't carry a little notebook around, scribbling down interesting things as they happened. I'd just relax, put my pen away, put on a brave face for my last host, get through two nights, then get on that plane and head home.

At least, that was the plan. Things started going wrong at LAX. Cath had said she'd pick me up from the airport, which was handy, since I'd been told public transport didn't really exist in LA.

Cath's invitation had worked out well. You pretty much have to go to LA if you're hoping to get home to Sydney, so it was a bonus to have someone to crash with. I wasn't really interested in the city itself – it was just somewhere I had to go.

The invitation hadn't even been particularly enticing – or at least no more than the hundreds of others I'd had to turn down from other places. 'Hi Ben,' she'd written. 'I am from Melbourne and now live in LA. If you find yourself here and in need of a couch, you are most welcome to crash at my house.'

Um . . . Okay. I wasn't sure what to expect from that.

Cath met me at the baggage carousel. She was slim, tall, and probably in her 40s. She led me out to her car, and that's when I got my first inkling that this stay might be a little better than what I'd been hoping for. Cath drove one of those fancy 4WDs with leather seats and more computer gadgetry in the console than Bill Gates probably has in his office. The engine roared to life, we pulled out onto a huge LA freeway, and Cath started chatting to me about my stay.

'Now,' she said, 'you'll probably find a few children in your part of the house. It's holidays, so they're just sitting around in their underpants playing computer games. They're nice enough though.'

I nodded. 'Your part of the house' – sounded promising to me.

'So where do you guys live?' I asked.

'We're over in Studio City, where, like, Universal and a few of the TV studios are. It just makes it easier for Gary – that's my husband – to get to work.'

Wait a minute, what? Gary goes to work in the studios? This was getting better.

'What does he do?' I asked.

'He's a TV writer. You know, he does sitcoms and stuff.'

'Yeah? Any I would have heard of?'

'Probably. You know *Becker*?'

'Yeah.'

'Well, he worked on that for the whole run. Then he did *Cybill*, *The Drew Carey Show*, *Murphy Brown* . . . And he's working on a new one at the moment that just got picked up, with the wife from *Everybody Loves Raymond* and the janitor from *Scrubs*. It looks really good.'

Goddamn it. There was no way I was going to be able to leave these people out. The notebook would have to come out again.

'Are you in the industry as well?'

'Me? No! I'm a teacher. At a local private school. We've actually had a few movie people go to school there though. Have you heard of Jake Gyllenhaal? He's a nice kid. And Maggie, his sister, she's lovely too. Who else . . . Oh, Green Day were recording down here last year, so their bass player, Mike, sent his kid to our school. Mike's the nicest guy.'

'Do you run into many celebrities just around the neighbourhood in Studio City?'

'Not that much really. Actually, I ran into the janitor from *Scrubs* at the bank the other day. I heard him talking and I was like, "I know that voice." I said hello to him, you know, told him my husband was working on his new show. He didn't seem to know much about it actually.'

'That's still pretty cool though.'

Listening to Cath, I realised she was like James in reverse. Whereas he was basically American but spoke with an Australian accent, Cath had lived the majority of her life in Australia, but spoke with an American accent. She'd moved over to the States when she was in her 20s, after having met Gary at a mutual friend's wedding. She'd been a school teacher in Australia, so she just kept teaching when she got to the States.

An hour after leaving the airport, we finally pulled into Studio City, and wound up a small hill to Cath and Gary's house, which, even from the back, looked huge. Cath parked in the garage next to a BMW, and led me in the back door, down a few steps and into a huge open living room with a couple of couches, tables and walls of windows.

'Now, you're just up here,' she said, leading me down a hallway, past a couple of kids who were, as predicted, sitting on a couch playing Xbox in their boxer shorts, up a winding set of stairs and into my bedroom on its own level. 'That's Henry and Joe downstairs,' Cath added. 'You can try saying hello to them, but I don't like your chances.'

She was right. When I eventually wandered back downstairs, I said hi to the kids, who were 12 and 14. They glanced up, mumbled, 'Hey,' and went back to mashing their control pads. A bit different to the kids back in the Thai village. Cath also introduced me to the pets. There was Sammy, the dog. ('You're not Jewish are you?' Cath asked. 'We think Sammy might be anti-Semitic.') Then there was Earl, a cat which seemed to be all skin and bones. ('We think he's got some sort of disease,' Cath said. 'Either that or he's got designs on becoming a supermodel.')

Cath then gave me the grand tour of the house, past Gary's office, into the huge lounge room, through the kitchen, and down a set of stairs with a roll of film drawn on the wall, and into a darkened room. 'This,' she said, flicking on the light, 'is Gary's pride and joy – the theatre.'

It was a room about the size of a small bedroom, with two tiers of plush leather couches facing a giant projector screen. 'Gary likes to have movie days for the kids in here,' Cath said. 'He's trying to get them to watch all the classics – you know, *Casablanca*, *Citizen Kane*, those sorta things. So every Sunday they make popcorn and come in here and watch a film together.'

By the time we got back out to the living room, Gary had arrived, dressed in jeans and an old shirt, and with large round glasses on. I was pretty excited. A few hours ago I'd been planning to just slog my way through these last few days and get home. Now I was face to face with a Hollywood screenwriter. I'd never really harboured dreams of cracking the TV writing market, but at that moment I was wishing I just 'happened' to have a blockbuster screenplay in my backpack to pass on to Gary.

He seemed a pretty unassuming guy, and after the greetings we went out to the patio to drink a few beers and chat. First though, Gary had to make a call to a friend whose script he'd just been reading. Lighting up a fat cigar, he slipped a Bluetooth earpiece on and dialled, and was soon flipping through the script giving someone on the other end a few pointers.

Eventually he finished up, slipped the earpiece off, took another puff on the cigar, and turned to me. 'Now, Ben, my wife tells me she invited you to stay at my house, but she's never met you before. Is that true?'

'Ah . . . Yes.'

'Now why would she do a thing like that?'

'I don't know. She's a friendly Aussie?'

'A friendly Aussie. Okay, I'll let you have that. So I take it you met the two lumps on the couch?'

I nodded. Gary eased the sliding door open and stuck his head through, yelling, 'Hey, you guys know you're going to have to put some pants on when vacation's over!'

Henry and Joe nodded, still mashing their control pads.

Cath slipped through the door and slid it closed. Gary sighed, taking a puff on his cigar. 'You know, Ben,' he said, 'one of my greatest regrets is not having better kids.'

'Oh come on,' Cath laughed. 'They were cute when they were first born.'

'No they weren't, they were all red and slimy.'

'Hmm, that's true.'

I smiled. 'So what's it like being a Hollywood writer? Do you work long hours?'

'You know, it's not too bad. It's kind of a nine-to-five thing really. Except when it's your script coming up. See, we have a team of writers, and they all take turns writing a script for one episode. So that's your episode. Then in the week it's going to air, we all get together and tear it apart, see if the jokes work, make it better.'

'That must be rough having people go through your work and pick it apart.'

'Ah, you just get used to it. We get kids come in, the hot shots straight out of college, and they don't like it. We get a few egos around the place. But they soon learn.'

'Are any of the actors you've worked with a real pain in the arse?'

'Ah yeah,' Gary nodded, looking at Cath, 'now he's going for the dirt. You know somethin', Ben? All actors are a pain in the arse to work with. I heard someone the other day trying to describe someone with a blank look on his face, and he says to me, "You know that look actors get when you start talking about yourself for a second?"'

'Right, they're not interested.'

'Not at all. But you know, some are better than others.'

Cath explained that that night, while the kids would remain on the couch playing *Grand Theft Auto*, the three of us were going to a birthday party for one of Gary's writer friends over in Hollywood. A soiree with writers at a Hollywood bar? Gee my life had become tough in the last few hours.

'How are we going to explain Ben?' Gary asked Cath as we were getting ready to go.

She shrugged. 'I don't know, just pretend we don't know him?'

'Yeah, but . . . We don't.'

Cath chuckled to herself. I was beginning to see why Gary was a successful sitcom writer. The three of us got back into the 4WD and headed through Laurel Canyon, with Gary and Cath arguing light-heartedly in the front seat. At one point Gary turned to me in the back. 'See, Ben, you should be taking all this in so you know how to approach your marriage.'

'Sure,' I said. 'If by "approach" you mean "avoid".'

Cath hit Gary on the leg. 'See? Ben's all right.'

And so the three of us sped into Hollywood, where we soon found the bar. Gary flipped the valet a few bucks and we walked inside, joining a crowd of artfully shabby-looking people nursing beers. They were a friendly bunch, all coming over to chat to Gary about their new 'projects'.

'So buddy,' one of them said to me, 'I assume you're in the dirty business as well?'

'No . . . I'm just Gary's house guest.'

'Oh! Well, nice to meet ya anyway.'

I met people who'd worked on *Cheers*, people who'd worked on *Friends*, people who'd worked on *Scrubs*. All in all, it made my little book project seem pretty inadequate.

*

'So how did Gary woo you?' I asked Cath as we pulled onto the freeway. Gary had gone into the studio to work, so, with the kids having become physically one with the couch, Cath and I were spending the day doing some LA sightseeing. She laughed.

'Well, it wasn't too hard for him.'

'Oh yeah?'

'No. We met at this wedding over here, but I had to go back to Australia. This was in the days before email and everything, so we kept in touch, but not that much. Anyway, one day I get this phone call. It's Gary, saying he's been nominated for a Golden Globe, and do I want to fly over and be his date for the ceremony. I'm like, "Oh yeah, I think I should be able to do that."'

'As you do.'

'So I came over, we went to the ceremony, and Gary won the award, so then we get invited to the swish afterparty. Oh my God, it was amazing. Gary had to go to the bathroom at one point, so I'm holding his Golden Globe, and all these people are congratulating me because they thought I'd won it. Then I saw Nicole Kidman, and I'm thinking, okay, Aussie connection, I'll go over and say hello to her. So we're talking away, and all of a sudden she's like, "Oh, have you met my husband Tom?" Tom. Cruise. God it was so surreal. I'm lining up for the toilets and out walks Uma Thurman. So yeah, the rest of Gary and me is history I guess.'

Gary had won an Emmy, too, although Cath didn't want to make a big deal of it. I tried to think of something else to talk about instead of banging on about her husband all the time as we did our little tour, walking up to the Hollywood sign before cruising Sunset Strip, taking a detour down Melrose, and eating fantastic Mexican food in Santa Monica.

By mid-afternoon it was time to head home, as we had an appointment. Gary was bringing a few of his fellow writers over to show them the pilot of his new show, *The Middle*, in the home theatre. We'd been invited to watch, too.

By the time we got home they were already in the theatre, patiently waiting to press play.

'Ben, this is Joe and Jim, a couple of writer buddies of mine,'

Gary said, pointing at the two guys on the big leather couches. They were both dressed all in black, with nervous smiles below dishevelled hair.

'Hey, Ben, what's up,' Joe said, getting up to shake my hand.

'Hey,' I said. 'So do you guys work on the show as well?'

Joe laughed. 'No no, we're just friends of Gary's. We go to the same coffee house to write, so we just know each other from there. We're working on our own sitcom, but,' he shrugged, 'not much is happening at the moment.'

'These guys are pretty talented,' Gary said, 'they just haven't got their break yet, so I'm giving them a little hand every now and then.'

'So are most LA coffee shops filled with out-of-work writers?' I asked.

'Hey man, we've got jobs,' Jim mumbled, running a hand through his hair. 'I'm writing for Disney at the moment, you know, doing cartoons and stuff. What about you?'

I explained how I'd come to wind up in Gary's home theatre. Jim looked impressed. 'Damn it man, that's awesome,' he said, sighing. 'Look at you, out there living the dream, doing what you want to do, that's great. I'm stuck in this damn dead-end job . . .' He sighed again.

With the introductions over, Gary dimmed the lights in the theatre, and I realised I was starting to get worried. What if the show wasn't very funny? I was sitting there on the same couch as the writer. I don't even like American sitcoms at the best of times – I find *Two and a Half Men* about as funny as testicular cancer. I knew I'd have to politely laugh at some point – but when? What if it was appalling?

'So Ben,' Gary said. 'I should explain, this is a single-camera show. You can have single-camera or multi-camera shows. Multi-camera shows are the ones like *Entourage* or *30 Rock* that don't have a studio audience. You don't want to write for one of those, they're a nightmare. Single-camera shows are the ones like *Friends* that have a studio audience. So at least you'll know when to laugh on this one . . .'

I nodded. How'd he figure that out? Gary hit play, and we all settled back to watch. The opening credits started rolling, and I couldn't help myself – I started feeling sleepy, my eyes slowly closing of their own accord. It was dark in there, and warm, and I was tired to my bones, worn out from months of hard travelling and alcohol abuse.

In the last three-and-a-half months I'd stayed on five couches, three futons, three foam mattresses, three blow-up mattresses and eight beds in 11 bedrooms, 10 lounge rooms and one kitchen – in 14 countries. I'd also met 22 amazing, crazy, annoying, funny, eccentric, generous people I would never have had the chance to meet without a travel blog and the appropriate amount of desperation. And now, here I was hanging out with a Golden Globe-winning writer and his Hollywood buddies in a mansion in LA, watching his new sitcom in a darkened home theatre. It was pretty incredible. But still, I wasn't upset about the fact I'd be leaving in a few hours' time.

See, my next house, my next couch, and my next bed were my favourites: my own.

Epilogue

I owe, of course, a huge debt of gratitude to the 400 or so people who so kindly invited me into their homes with little more than a vague idea of who I was and what I was going to attempt to steal when I arrived. This book would never have been possible without them.

My biggest thanks, though, goes to the 22 brave souls who actually had to go through with their end of the bargain. I'm sure some had second thoughts, even after I'd arrived, but they were all unfailingly nice about the dodgy backpacker taking up all of their couch space for a few nights. I'm glad none of them turned out to be axe murderers – as I'm sure they are of me.

This would also have been a far more stressful experience without the undying patience and support of the Lawyer, who was so easygoing about her boyfriend announcing he wanted to go travelling by himself for four months, and then gave me the best gift of all on my return: still being there. After spending a solid week lying on my own couch catching up on a few months' worth of *Simpsons* reruns, the two of us have started planning a trip together. We're going to Laos for a while. And we won't be staying on couches.

A huge vote of thanks, too, to readers of The Backpacker blog. Thanks for the laughs, the occasional abuse, and the support. It means a lot.

Some of the people reading my blog got the wrong idea about this trip. It was never about being a freeloader, of shamelessly abusing my position at the newspaper to score a cheap holiday. In fact, it wasn't even really about travel.

This trip was supposed to be about meeting people, people I would never normally have got the chance to mix with. It was about hearing their stories, seeing how they lived. And, to a person, they were incredible. Funny, interesting, and helpful. And just when I didn't think people could get any more generous or welcoming, they'd flip me the keys to their house, sight unseen, or invite me along to a family function, or just smile and point me in the direction of their washing machine.

It made me realise that I was wrong in my original assertion stolen from Cracked. The worldwide web might be a big, anonymous place, but if you're prepared to take a chance or two, and get out there and explore that world, it's pretty easy to turn your electronic friends into real friends. I realised that the internet – or at least my small corner of it – is actually full of interesting, amazing people. It's not full of dickheads at all.

Well, mostly.

To check out photos from the trip or get in touch with the author, head to www.bengroundwater.com.